N 59

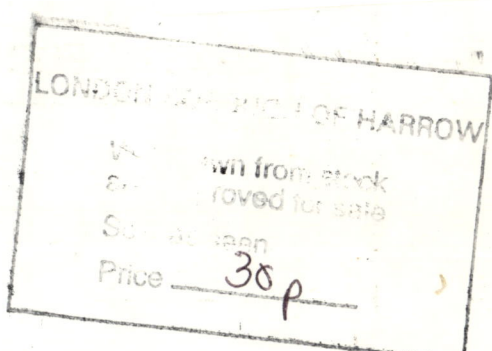
**LOWLANDS
SIXTH FORM COLLEGE**

Organic Chemistry Through Experiment

Organic Chemistry Through Experiment

BY

H. S. FINLAY, B.Sc.

Advisory Teacher and Deputy Warden,
The South London Science Centre, London, S.E.5.
Former Head of the Science Department, The Beaufoy School, London, S.E.11

AND

D. J. WADDINGTON, B.Sc., A.R.C.S., D.I.C., Ph.D.

Professor of Chemical Education, University of York.

MILLS & BOON LTD.
15–16 BROOK'S MEWS
LONDON W1A 1DR

© H. S. FINLAY
D. J. WADDINGTON, 1965

Second edition, 1966
Reprinted 1967
Third edition, 1969
Reprinted 1973
Fourth edition, 1977
Reprinted 1980

© New material in this edition,
H. S. Finlay and D. J. Waddington, 1977

ISBN. 0 263 06293 7

Organic formulae composed by Wright's Symbolset method

TYPESET BY REPRODUCTION DRAWINGS LTD., SUTTON, SURREY.
MADE AND PRINTED IN GREAT BRITAIN BY
THOMSON LITHO LTD, EAST KILBRIDE, SCOTLAND.

Contents

List of Plates

Colour Plate

Acknowledgments

We wish to thank Imperial Chemical Industries Ltd., Shell Chemical Company Ltd., Shell International Petroleum Company Ltd., and the Distillers Company Ltd. for their helpful advice.

Our thanks are due to Mr. Michael Brown (Lecturer in the School of Physical Sciences, University of Sussex) for encouraging us to include a chapter on Observation and Deduction experiments, following the pattern of his book *Practical Inorganic and Organic Problems* (Longmans). We are indebted to the Secretaries of the Oxford and Cambridge Schools Examination Board for permission to include questions from their 'A' and 'S' level practical examinations.

We wish to acknowledge the generous help of Dr. R. P. C. Pockley (formerly Chemistry Master, Wellington College, now Co-ordinator of Science Programmes for the Australian Broadcasting Commission), Dr. G. Van Praagh (formerly Head of the Science Department, Christ's Hospital, and now Nuffield Research Fellow) and the late Mr. G. A. Lees (formerly Head of the Science Department, Collyer's School, Horsham).

We are most grateful to Mr. J. W. Davis (Head of the Chemistry Department, Borden Grammar School, Sittingbourne) for permission to quote his 'Wet Asbestos Methods of Preparation', to Dr. I. W. Williams (Lecturer in Education, University of Swansea) for permission to quote his experiment to demonstrate gas chromatography, to Mr. D. E. P. Hughes (Head of the Science Department, The Schools, Shrewsbury) for permission to quote his method of construction of a gas chromatograph using a flame ionisation detector, and to Mr. D. A. Stephens (Huddersfield New College) for his method of preparing thin-layer chromatography plates. Permission has also been given by the editor of *The School Science Review*. We are also grateful to Mullards Ltd. for permission to quote in detail from Educational Electronic Experiment No. 8 (Mullard Educational Service, 1964), 'Low Voltage Electrometer'.

We express our sincere appreciation to Mrs. P. Kozary for the great care with which she has drawn the diagrams, to Mr. A. Bennett (Chief Laboratory Superintendent, Wellington College) for many helpful suggestions for small-scale apparatus, and to Miss A. Warriss for her help in developing several of the chromatography experiments.

Our thanks are due to boys in our classes who took part in this experimental teaching with enthusiasm and helpful criticism and to our nameless mentors who have developed many of the experiments.

Preface

The experiments in this book are designed to teach students the important principles and facts of Organic Chemistry, and we hope that, in this way, experimental work can take the place of much of the formal teaching.

Unfortunately, owing to lack of time and money, practical Organic Chemistry for students preparing for pre-University examinations has often been ignored. We have therefore designed and adapted small-scale experiments which involve the use of very simple apparatus (consisting of test-tubes and glass-tubing). This apparatus can be readily assembled by the student.

The experiments are economical in time and materials. Often the preparation and reactions of a member of an homologous series can be studied in one teaching period.

For more formal standard laboratory preparations, we have recommended the use of apparatus with ground-glass joints (pages x and xi).

Some modern technical processes are introduced and are described as small-scale experiments, although exact industrial conditions may not be used. The technical processes include the manufacture of olefins (from oil), acetaldehyde, acetic acid, polymers, detergents, and insecticides. For teachers who find any difficulty in obtaining chemicals or apparatus for these experiments, a list of suppliers providing them is given in Appendix III.

A chapter on the purification of organic substances has a section on chromatographic techniques, including gas-liquid chromatography. A chapter is also devoted to observation and deduction experiments, which we feel should play an important part in developing scientific method in practical work. The authors are conscious that more details of observation are given than is sometimes desirable for abler sets. However, the deductions to be drawn from each chapter probably make up for this.

Thus a course in Organic Chemistry for students taking 'A' level, scholarship examinations and 1st M.B. is given, with the omission only of reactions which cannot readily be performed in the laboratory.

H. S. F.
D. J. W.

September 1964

Preface to the Third Edition

The third major reprinting of this book in barely four years provides an opportunity for adding more experiments. We have chosen these from two aspects. Firstly, we have given some preparations that have been put into recently revised 'A' level syllabuses. Secondly, and we hope just as important, we have added experiments that will help to illustrate points that are often not included in practical texts. These include, for example, an illustration of geometrical isomerism, the preparation of a free radical and the use of lithium aluminium hydride.

Finally, we have extended our chapter on chromatography, particularly in describing several ways of illustrating gas chromatography and introducing thin-layer chromatography.

H. S. F.
D. J. W.

September 1969

Preface to the Fourth Edition

In revising this text for its fourth edition, we have been especially conscious of the changing practices for naming organic compounds. We have followed the recommendations made by the Association for Science Education in their booklet *Chemical Nomenclature, Symbols and Terminology* (1972) and by the Joint Statement to Schools by the G.C.E. Boards (1973). However, we have retained the name 'ether'; the alternative—alkoxyalkanes, aryloxyalkanes and aryloxyarenes as appropriate--is cumbersome. Secondly, we have used trivial names for the important α-amino acids, since these are widely used in Biology and Biochemistry. Both these exceptions are accepted by I.U.P.A.C.

Since the book was first written, there has been considerable progress in teaching students to work in safe conditions. At appropriate points, we do emphasise that special care should be used—for example when working with concentrated mineral acids and with flammable liquids. However, great care must be exercised at all times when handling chemicals. Sensible personal protection involves the wearing of protective clothing including goggles, and the use of fume-cupboards when appropriate. We commend, in particular, that the D.E.S. booklet *Safety in Science Laboratories* (H.M.S.O.) is available and read.

Finally, we wish to thank teachers and students who write to us about the experiments. Some seem surprised that the experiments work! For that we reinforce the thanks we gave in the original Acknowledgement to our own students who unerringly discovered ways in which the experiments could fail and helped us to take evasive action.

H. S. F.
D. J. W.

April 1977

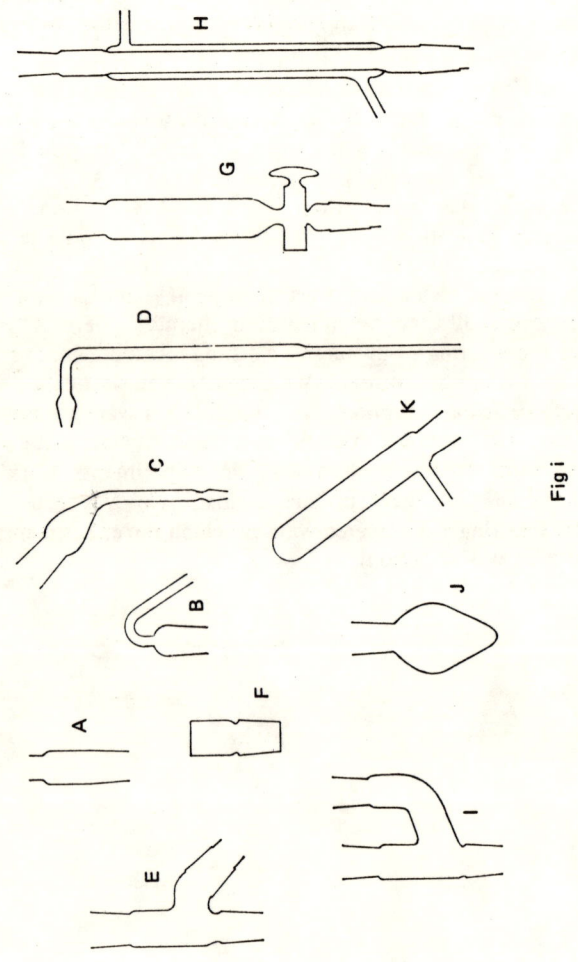

Fig i

Introduction to Apparatus with Ground-glass Joints

The use of apparatus with ground-glass joints is advocated in this book since it leads to a considerable saving in time. For this reason students can concentrate on the reactions, and avoid undue preoccupation with assembling and repairing apparatus.

Sensible precautions must be taken to ensure long life for the apparatus. The joints must be kept clean and the flasks should be heated over a gauze, or in a bath, by means of a small flame, either from a microburner or from an ordinary bunsen burner with the chimney removed.

To co-operate with the authors, Philip Harris, Ltd., Birmingham, have produced a set of apparatus that can be used for all experiments in this book. The same apparatus can also be used for the preparation of many inorganic substances, including gases. The number of pieces has been reduced to a minimum without sacrificing reasonable flexibility.

The apparatus consists of:

A. Adaptor for thermometer, steam lead or air leak;
B and C. Adaptors for collection of gases;
D. Steam lead which can be used also as an air leak;
E. Stillhead;
F. Stopper;
G. Dropping funnel which can be used as a separating funnel;
H. Water condenser which can be used as an air condenser;
I. Flask head;
J. 50 cm^3 pear-shaped flask. A 100 cm^3 round-bottomed flask may be used instead;
K. Receiver with side arm.

Introduction to Apparatus for 'Test-tube' Experiments

'Test-tube' preparations of gases and liquids form an important part of this book, for they are rapid and inexpensive. Each student can carry out the preparation and investigate the properties of the compound.

It is recommended that standard 150 × 16 mm (or 125 × 16 mm) Pyrex test-tubes are used, and that there is an adequate supply of **delivery tubes**. The tubes can be made from 3–4 mm internal diameter soda glass tubing, which can be readily bent in a bunsen flame. Three different tubes are used:

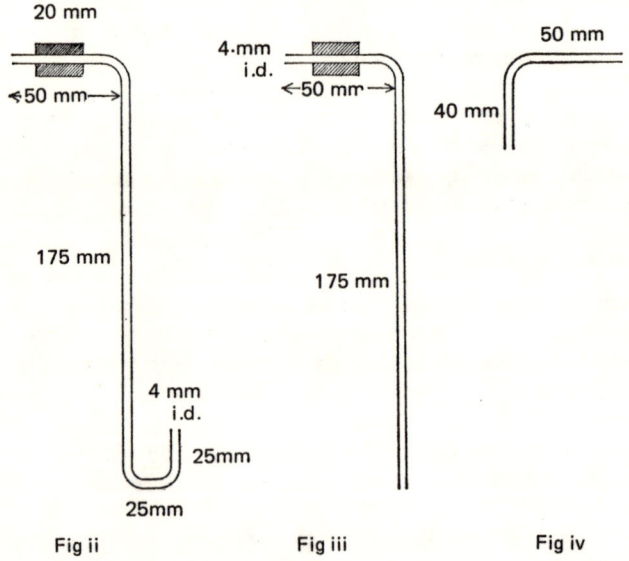

Fig ii   Fig iii   Fig iv

The use of **corks** is satisfactory, particularly if they have been soaked in molten candle wax before they are bored. Rubber bungs, although more expensive, are more robust and last longer, particularly if two holes have been bored in one bung. The disadvantage of rubber bungs is that glass tubing may be difficult to withdraw from them after use, unless they are well soaked in water before easing the glass tube from the bung.

A **dropping pipette** is also frequently used for transferring liquid or gases (Figure v). The pipettes can be made from 5–6 mm internal diameter soda glass tubing, by drawing the tubing apart in a bunsen flame. Cylindrical rubber teats are more expensive than thinner rubber teats but they last longer.

It is useful to calibrate the dropping pipettes, showing 0.5 cm^3 divisions. The tube is inserted in a 10 cm^3 measuring cylinder filled with water. Water is drawn up the tube in 0.5 cm^3 portions. The pipette is marked for each portion with a small dab of paint. The calibration saves much time during experiments.

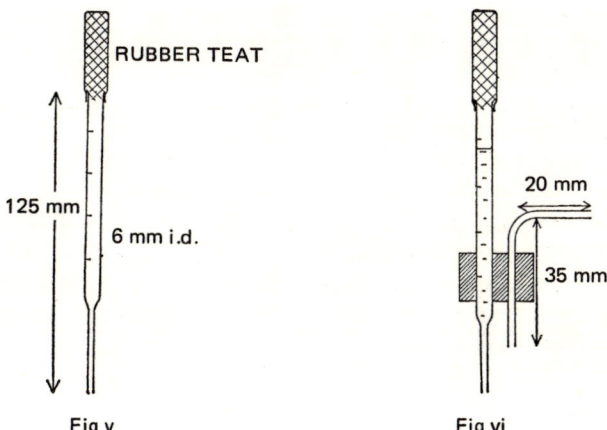

Fig v   Fig vi

A dropping pipette is sometimes used to add a liquid during the preparation of a gas. The dropping pipette is filled with the liquid and then placed in the bung (Figure vi). The end of the dropping pipette should be well below the end of the other glass tube.

It is also useful to calibrate a test-tube in 5 cm^3 divisions. This can be done readily, using a small drop of paint to indicate each 5 cm^3 division.

Introduction to Chemicals used in this Book

A list of reagents used in this book is given in Appendices I and II. Several reagents may not be readily available from some suppliers, and suggested sources are given in Appendix III.

To investigate the properties of an homologous series, we have usually suggested using the simplest member. However, higher members of the homologous series often provide a useful, economical, and rapid way of observing the properties. For example, cyclohexene can be used as an alkene (2.5), phenylethyne as an alkyne (3.3), for, being liquids, they are easier to handle than lower homologues, which are gases.

Whenever possible, different students should study different homologues to illustrate the properties of an homologous series.

Observation and Deduction Experiments

A key to the substances used in Chapter 33 can be obtained from the publishers. They will send the key to the Head of the Science Department or the Head of the Chemistry Department of the school or college on request.

1

ALKANES (Paraffins)

1.1. Test-tube Preparation of Methane

THE 'WET-ROCKSIL' METHOD

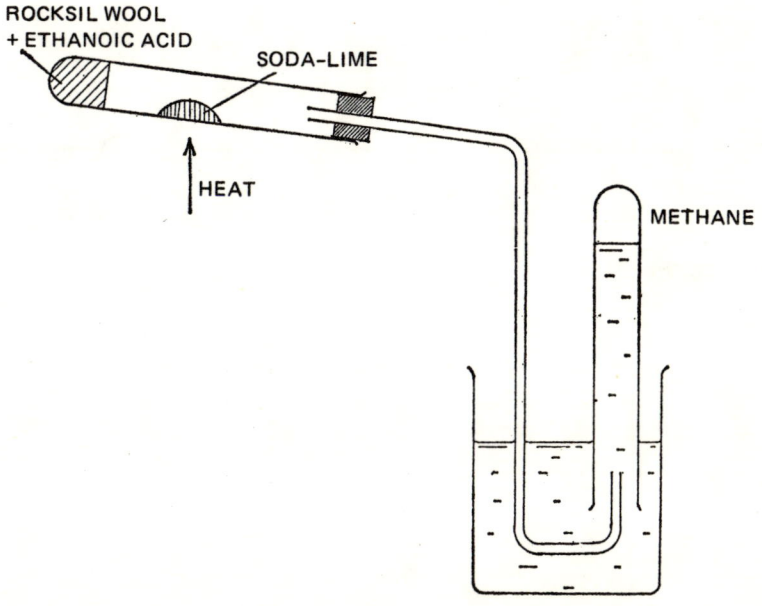

ROCKSIL WOOL
+ ETHANOIC ACID

SODA–LIME

HEAT

METHANE

Fig 1

Pour ethanoic acid into a test-tube to a depth of 2.5 cm. Push Rocksil wool into the liquid with a glass rod until the liquid is soaked up. Set up the test-tube in a clamp and introduce about 1 g of soda-lime half-way along the tube, so that it forms a small heap (Figure 1).

Fit the test-tube with a cork and delivery tube, and heat the soda-lime with a gentle flame (the flame should be just yellow at the tip before placing the bunsen

2

burner under the tube). A few test-tubes of methane can be collected by displacement of water.

$$CH_3COONa + NaOH \longrightarrow CH_4 + Na_2CO_3$$

Alternatively, anhydrous sodium ethanoate and soda-lime can be mixed and heated in a test tube (Figure 20).

1.2. Test-tube Preparation of Ethane

THE 'WET-ROCKSIL' METHOD

(An adaptation of the Wurtz synthesis)

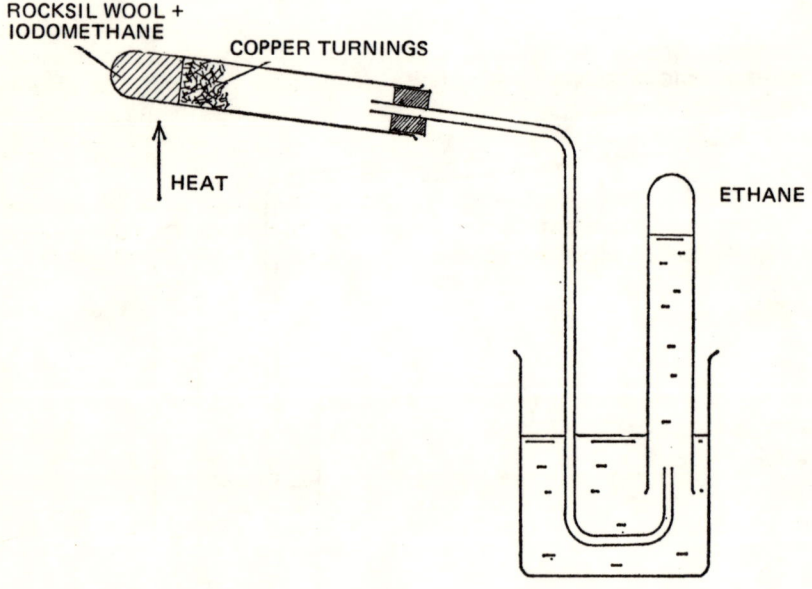

Fig 2

Pour iodomethane into a test-tube to a depth of 2.5 cm. Push Rocksil wool into the liquid with a glass road until the liquid is soaked up.

Set up the test-tube in a clamp and introduce about 5 g of copper turnings so that the solid fills up about 5 cm of the tube (Figure 2). Warm the middle of the tube and collect a few test-tubes of ethane.

$$2CH_3I + 2Cu \longrightarrow C_2H_6 + Cu_2I_2$$

1.3. Test-tube Preparation of Butane

THE 'WET-ROCKSIL' METHOD

(An adaptation of the Wurtz synthesis)

Repeat the experiment in Section 1.2, using iodoethane instead of iodo-methane. Collect several test-tubes of butane.

$$2C_2H_5I + 2Cu \longrightarrow C_4H_{10} + Cu_2I_2$$

1.4. Properties of Methane, Ethane, and Butane

1. Ignite the alkane by applying a lighted splint to the mouth of a test-tube of the gas. Note the colour of the flame.

2. To different test-tubes of the alkane add (a) 5 drops of an alkaline potassium permanganate solution (made by dissolving about 0.1 g of sodium carbonate in 1 cm^3 of 1% potassium permanganate solution); (b) 5 drops of bromine dissolved in tetrachloromethane. Note that there is no reaction, demonstrating that the alkane molecule is saturated (cf. ethene and ethyne in Chapters 2 and 3).

(A slight reaction may take place owing to the presence of small quantities of unsaturated impurities; the impurities could be removed by passing the gas through acidified potassium permanganate solution before collection.)

2

ALKENES (Olefins)

Functional Group $\qquad$ $-C=C-$

2.1. Small-scale Preparation of Ethene (Ethylene)

INTRODUCTION

The preparation involves the use of concentrated sulphuric acid as a dehydrating agent. Ethene, being almost insoluble in water, can be readily collected over water.

Alcohols react with acids to form esters (9.1). The ester formed from ethanol and concentrated sulphuric acid is ethyl hydrogensulphate.

$$C_2H_5OH + H_2SO_4 \rightleftharpoons C_2H_5\overset{+}{O}H_2 + HSO_4^-$$
$$C_2H_5\overset{+}{O}H_2 + HSO_4^- \rightleftharpoons C_2H_5-O-SO_2-OH + H_2O$$

When heated (above about $150°C$), the ester decomposes to form ethene.

An alternative mechanism has been suggested in which the oxonium ion, $C_2H_5\overset{+}{O}H_2$, reacts with the hydrogensulphate ion:

$$HSO_4^-\ CH_2-CH_2-\overset{+}{O}H_2 \longrightarrow H_2SO_4 + CH_2 = CH_2 + H_2O$$
$$\mid$$
$$H$$

(cf. mechanism of the preparation of diethyl ether (6.1)).

REAGENTS

Ethanol (5 cm^3)
Concentrated sulphuric acid (10 cm^3)
Aluminium sulphate, hydrated (1 g)
20% solution of sodium hydroxide (15 cm^3)

EQUATION

$$CH_3CH_2OH \xrightarrow[\text{dehydrating agent}]{\text{Conc. }H_2SO_4\text{ as}} H_2C=CH_2 + H_2O$$

DETAILS

Place 5 cm^3 of ethanol in the flask, then add **slowly** 10 cm^3 of *concentrated* sulphuric acid (Figure 3). Gently shake the flask and cool it under the tap during the addition of the acid. Add 1 g of powdered hydrated aluminium sulphate and connect the flask to a boiling-tube containing 15 cm^3 of 20% sodium hydroxide solution. Aluminium sulphate is added to prevent frothing.

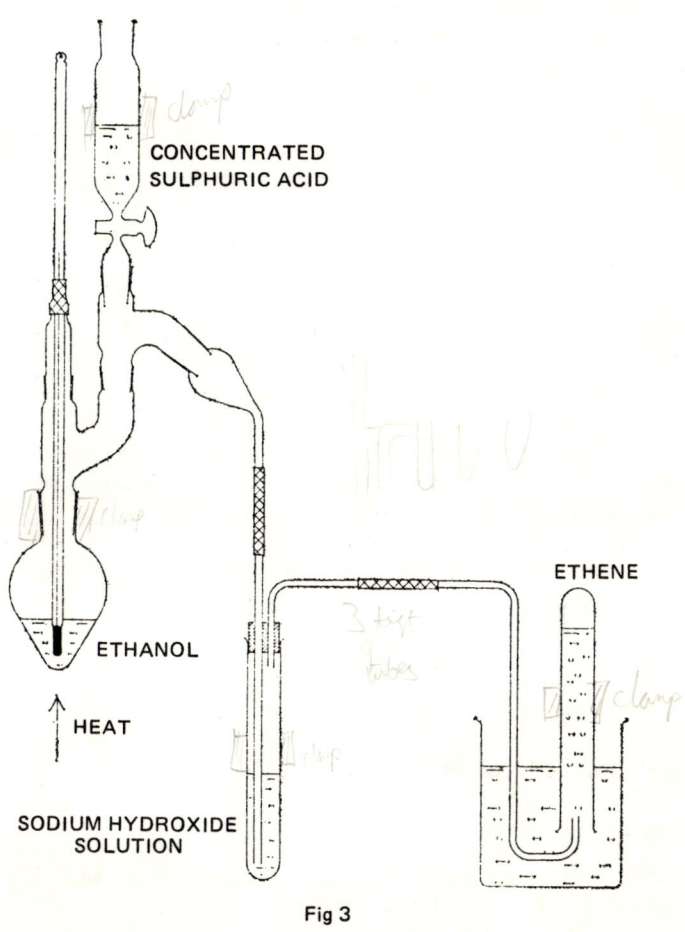

CONCENTRATED
SULPHURIC ACID

ETHENE

ETHANOL

HEAT

SODIUM HYDROXIDE
SOLUTION

Fig 3

The flask should be heated strongly at first but only gently when the evolution of ethene begins. The temperature should not rise above 170° C. Collect the ethene in test-tubes, by displacement of water. Fit the tubes with corks so that the gas may be retained for subsequent testing.

The sodium hydroxide solution removes sulphur dioxide and carbon dioxide, formed as impurities during the reaction.

2.2 Test-tube Preparation of Ethene

THE 'WET-ROCKSIL' METHOD

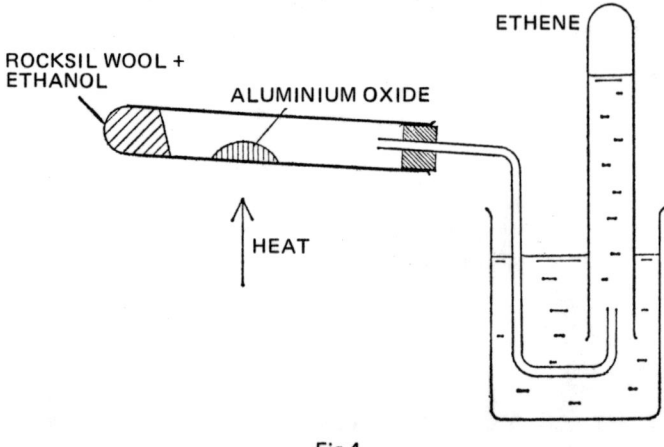

Fig 4

Place ethanol in a test-tube, to a depth of 2.5 cm. Add Rocksil wool until the ethanol has been soaked up. Place about 1 g of aluminium oxide half-way along the tube (Figure 4). Fit a cork and delivery tube to the test-tube and heat the aluminium oxide with a gentle flame. Collect a few test-tubes of ethene by displacement of water.

$$C_2H_5OH \xrightarrow{\text{Al}_2O_3} C_2H_4 + H_2O$$

2.3. Preparation of Cyclohexene

INTRODUCTION

An alternative dehydrating agent is concentrated phosphoric acid. The mechanism of the reaction is similar to that described for ethene.

The dehydration of cyclohexanol is used as the example because the product is a liquid alkene and is easy to handle.

REAGENTS

Cyclohexanol (10 cm^3 ; 10 g)

Concentrated (85%) phosphoric acid (4 cm^3)

Calcium chloride, anhydrous

EQUATION

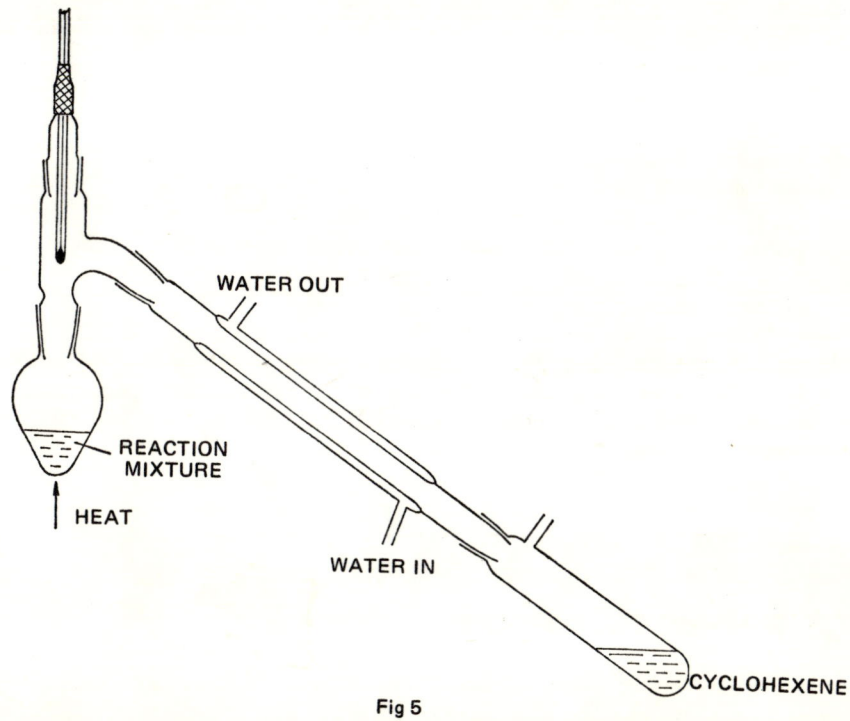

DETAILS

Place 10 cm^3 of cyclohexanol in a flask and add, dropwise, while shaking the flask, 4 cm^3 of concentrated phosphoric acid from a dropping pipette. Assemble the apparatus as shown in Figure 5.

Fig 5

Heat the flask gently and distil very slowly. Pour the distillate into a separating funnel and add 2 cm^3 of a saturated solution of sodium chloride. Shake the funnel and allow the two layers to separate. Run off the lower aqueous layer and then run the top layer (cyclohexene) into a small conical flask.

To the crude alkene, add two or three pieces of anhydrous calcium chloride and stopper the flask. Shake for a few minutes until the liquid is clear.

Decant the alkene into a clean flask and redistil it, collecting the liquid distilling between 81—85° C (Figure 5 and Plate 1).

PHYSICAL CONSTANTS

B.p. 83° C; density at 20° C: 0.81 g cm^{-3}

2.4 Reactions of Ethene

1. Ignite the gas by applying a lighted splint to the mouth of the test-tube. Note that the gas burns with a smoky luminous flame. Pour some lime water into the test-tube. Shake. Note that it turns milky, indicating the presence of carbon dioxide.

2. Add 1 cm^3 of bromine dissolved in tetrachloromethane to a test-tube of ethene. Replace the cork at once, and shake the mixture. The bromine is quickly decolorised as the ethene molecule is unsaturated.

$$H_2C = CH_2 + Br_2 \longrightarrow Br-CH_2-CH_2-Br$$

3. Shake another test-tube of ethene with alkaline potassium permanganate solution (made by dissolving about 0.1 g of anhydrous sodium carbonate in 1 cm^3 of 1% potassium permanganate solution). Shake the contents of the test-tube. A green solution may be first obtained (potassium manganate). Subsequently, a brown precipitate of manganese(IV) oxide is formed. The solution contains ethane−1, 2−diol.

4. Add about 1 cm^3 of acidified potassium permanganate (made up by adding 1 cm^3 of dilute sulphuric acid to 0.5 ml. of 1% potassium permanganate solution). Shake the mixture in a corked test-tube. A colourless solution ethane−1, 2−diol is obtained.

Tests 2 and 3 are used to detect **unsaturation** in an organic compound.

2.5. Reactions of a Liquid Alkene

A convenient liquid alkene to use is cyclohexene. In order to contrast the properties of cyclohexene with those of an alkane repeat experiments 1, 2, and 3 with either a petroleum ether (a mixture of low-boiling alkanes) or hexane.

1. Dissolve a few drops of cyclohexene in 1 cm^3 of tetrachloromethane in a test-tube. Add a solution of bromine in tetrachloromethane dropwise, using a dropping pipette, and shake the tube. The colour of the bromine is quickly removed.

1,2-Dibromocyclohexane

2. To a few drops of cyclohexene in a test-tube, add dropwise, using a dropping pipette, an alkaline solution of potassium permanganate (made by dissolving 0.1 g of anhydrous sodium carbonate in 1 cm^3 of 1% potassium permanganate solution). A green solution may be first obtained (manganate ions). Subsequently, a brown precipitate of manganese(IV) oxide is formed. The mixture contains cyclohexane-1,2-diol.

3. **Preparation of hexanedioic acid (adipic acid) from cyclohexene.** Place 10 cm^3 of concentrated nitric acid in a flask and add dropwise 2 cm^3 of cyclohexene, swirling the contents of the flask after each addition. Set up the apparatus as shown in Figure 10, and heat the mixture under reflux at 100°C for about 20 minutes. Remove the flask from the water-bath and cool in a beaker of ice (or cold water) for 10—15 minutes. Separate the acid by filtration, using a Hirsch funnel. Wash the crystals with cold water and recrystallise from a small quantity of water. Dry the crystals in the oven at 100° C and find the melting-point (Section 31.1).

3

ALKYNES (ACETYLENES)

Functional Group —C≡C—

3.1. Test-tube Preparation of Ethyne (Acetylene)

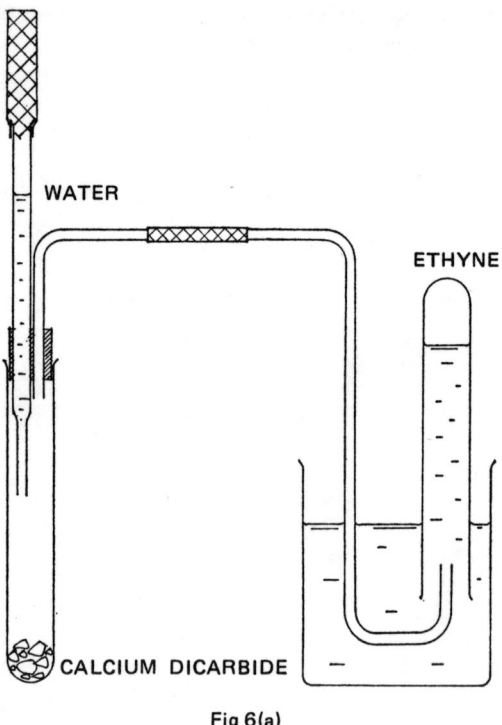

Fig 6(a)

(a) Place 2 or 3 **small** pieces of calcium dicarbide in a test-tube (Figure 6(a)) or flask (Figure 6(b)) and arrange the apparatus for collection of ethyne. Add 2 or 3 drops of water at a time.

$$CaC_2 + 2H_2O \longrightarrow C_2H_2 + Ca(OH)_2$$

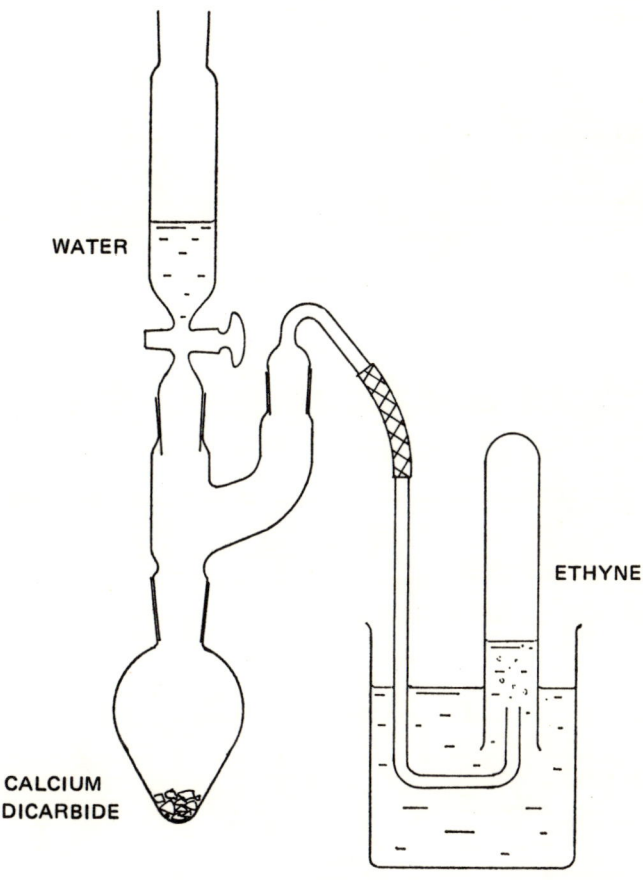

Fig 6(b)

(b) 'Wet-rocksil' method

Prepare some ethyne from 1,2-dibromoethane. Place 1,2-dibromoethane in a test-tube to a depth of 2.5 cm and add Rocksil wool until the liquid is soaked up. Add soda-lime to a depth of 5 cm and set up the apparatus as shown in Figure 2. Warm the soda-lime.

$$Br-CH_2-CH_2-Br + 2NaOH \longrightarrow C_2H_2 + 2NaBr + 2H_2O$$

3.2. Reactions of Ethyne

1. Prepare an ammoniacal solution of copper(I) chloride by dissolving 0.1 g of copper(I) chloride in 1 cm^3 of dilute solution of ammonia.

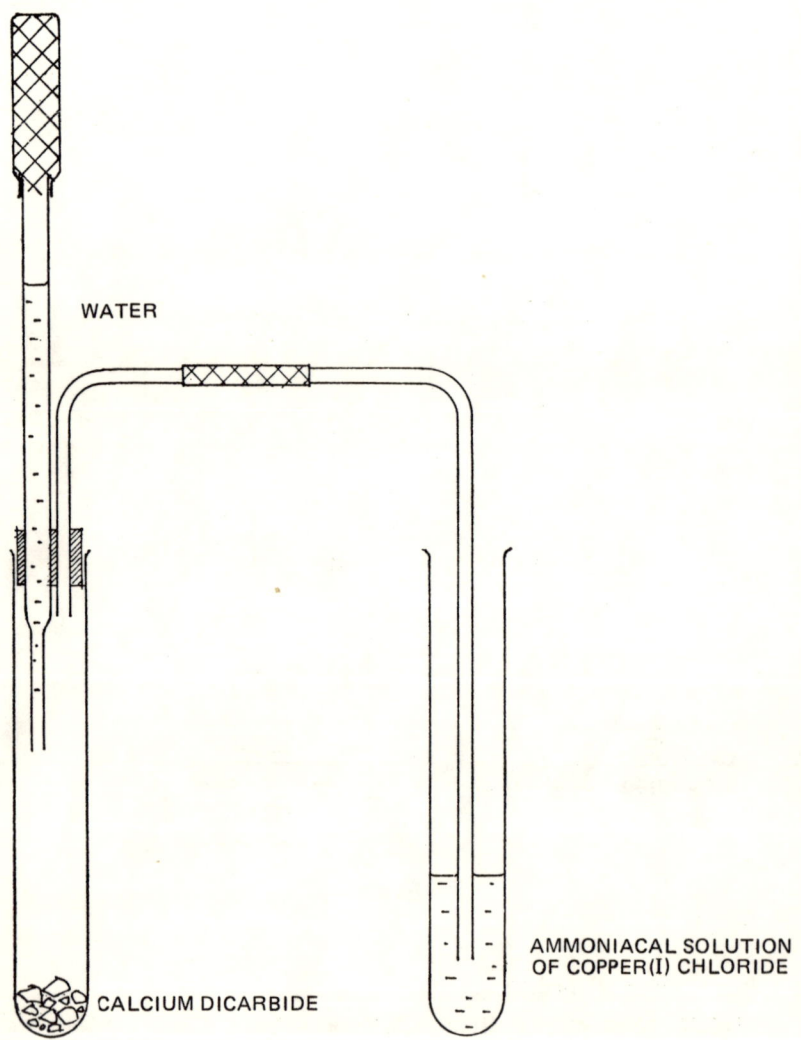

WATER

CALCIUM DICARBIDE

AMMONIACAL SOLUTION
OF COPPER(I) CHLORIDE

Fig 6(c)

Pass ethyne through the solution (Figure 6(c)). A red precipitate of copper(I) dicarbide is formed:

$$C_2H_2 + Cu_2Cl_2 + 2NH_4OH \longrightarrow Cu_2C_2 + 2NH_4Cl + 2H_2O$$

N.B. This reaction is only undergone by alkynes with a terminal hydrogen atom, R—C≡C—H.

When dry, copper (I) dicarbide is explosive. The apparatus must be washed thoroughly after the experiment.

2. Make up an ammoniacal solution of silver nitrate, adding a dilute solution of ammonia to 1 cm^3 of a 5% solution of silver nitrate until the brown precipitate of silver oxide just redissolves. Pass ethyne into the solution (Figure 6(c). A white precipitate of silver dicarbide is formed:

$$C_2H_2 + Ag_2O \longrightarrow Ag_2C_2 + H_2O$$

N.B. This reaction is only undergone by alkynes with a terminal hydrogen atom.

The same precautions must be taken as in Experiment 1.

3. Place about 1 cm of bleaching powder in a test-tube and add 1 cm^3 of concentrated hydrochloric acid. Fit a cork loosely into the test-tube. In a second test-tube, add 2 or 3 drops of water to 1 small lump of calcium dicarbide. Pour chlorine gas into the tube of ethyne. The ethyne ignites and black smoke of carbon is evolved:

$$C_2H_2 + Cl_2 \longrightarrow 2C + 2HCl$$

4. Collect 4 test-tubes of ethyne, and carry out the 4 tests that were applied to ethene (Section 2.4, experiments 1, 2, 3, and 4).

   (a) Ethyne burns with the smoky luminous flame that is characteristic of many unsaturated compounds.

   (b) Bromine in tetrachloromethane is decolorised owing to the formation of **addition products**:

$$H—C≡C—H + Br_2 \longrightarrow Br—CH=CH—Br$$

1, 2-Dibromoethene

$$Br—CH=CH—Br + Br_2 \longrightarrow Br_2CH—CHBr_2$$

1, 1, 2, 2-Tetrabromoethane

Ethyne reacts more slowly with bromine than ethene does; this contrasts with its behaviour with chlorine.

   (c) Alkaline potassium permanganate solution is reduced first to green potassium manganate and finally to brown manganese(IV) oxide.

   (d) Acidified potassium permanganate solution oxidises ethyne to a variety of products, including ethanoic acid. The potassium permanganate is decolorised.

5. Ethanol is manufactured from ethyne (Section 7.2).

3.3. Reactions of a Liquid Alkyne

The reactions of the alkynes are shown by phenylethyne,

$$C_6H_5—C≡C—H,$$

a liquid which is readily available.

1. Add 3 drops of phenylethyne to an ammoniacal solution of copper(I) chloride (Section 3.2, experiment 1). A yellow precipitate of the copper(I) salt is formed.

2. Add 3 drops of phenylethyne to an ammoniacal solution of silver nitrate (Section 3.2, experiment 2). A white precipitate of the silver salt is formed.

3. Phenylethyne, being unsaturated, undergoes the following reactions:

(a) Add 3 drops of phenylethyne to 1 cm³ of bromine dissolved in tetrachloromethane. Bromine is decolorised on shaking.

(b) Add 3 drops of phenylethyne to 1 cm³ of an alkaline solution of potassium permanganate. Potassium permanganate is finally reduced to manganese(IV) oxide.

4. Add 3 drops of phenylethyne to 1 cm³ of acidified potassium permanganate solution. On shaking, potassium permanganate is decolorised. The reaction may need *gentle* warming to decolorise potassium permanganate completely.

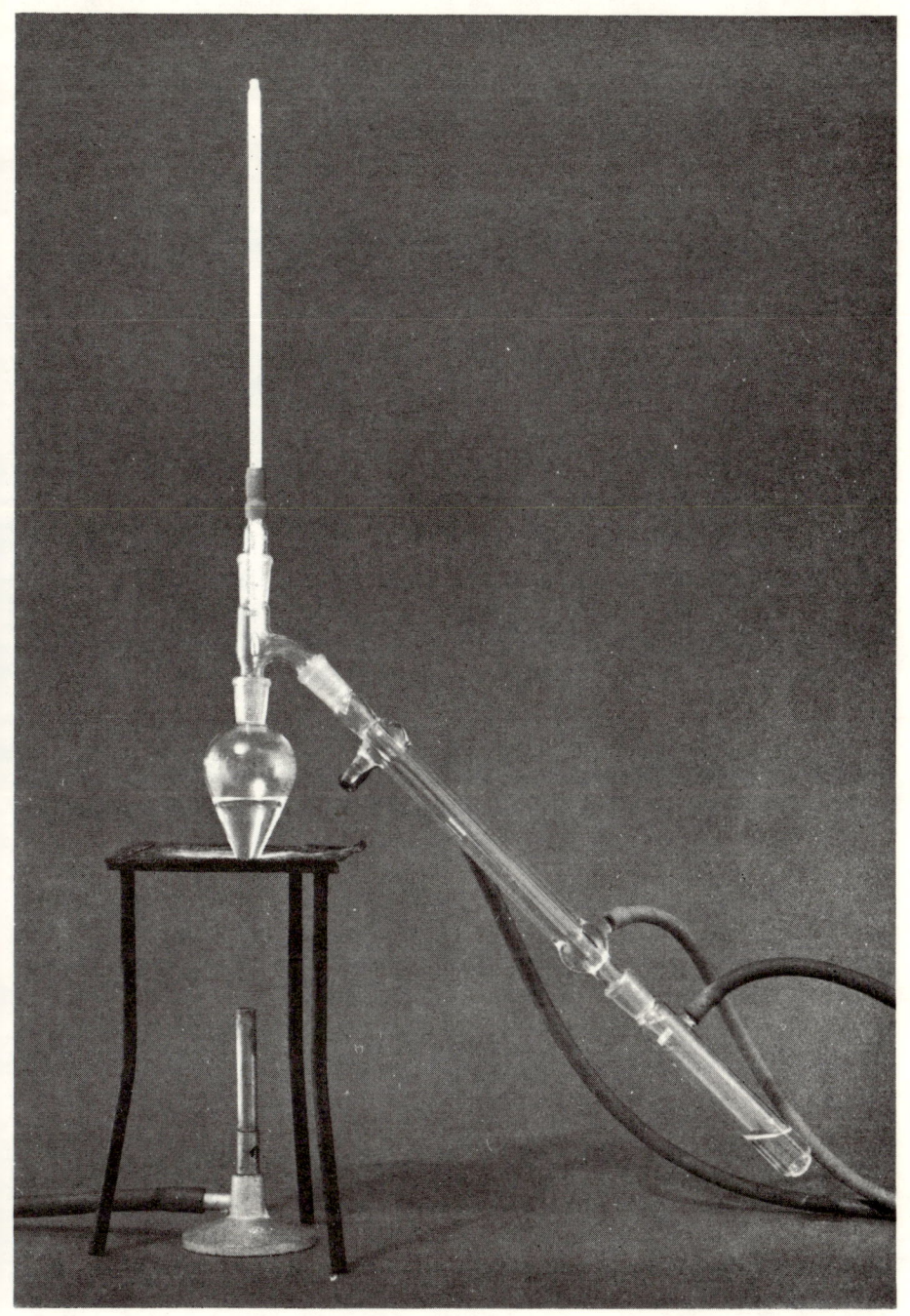

PLATE 1

Distillation of a liquid. Preparations of cyclohexene (Fig. 5 p. 7), 1,2-dibromo-ethane (p. 24), ethanoic anhydride (p. 62), ethanamide (p. 64), ethanonitrile (Fig. 25, p.68), nitrobenzene (p. 102), phenylamine (p. 106) and bromobenzene (p. 118).

4

HALOGEN DERIVATIVES OF ALKANES

ALKYL HALIDES

Functional Group $-X$ ($-F$, $-Cl$, $-Br$, $-I$)

4.1. Small-scale Preparation of Bromoethane (Alternative I)

INTRODUCTION

Phosphorus halides are used frequently in organic chemistry to substitute a halogen atom for a hydroxyl group or to replace the oxygen atom in a carbonyl group by two halogen atoms.

For example:

$$C_2H_5OH + PCl_5 \longrightarrow C_2H_5Cl + POCl_3 + HCl$$

$$CH_3-CO-CH_3 + PCl_5 \longrightarrow CH_3-CCl_2-CH_3 + POCl_3$$

Phosphorus bromides are unstable, and are prepared during the reaction by the interaction of red phosphorus and bromine.

REAGENTS

Ethanol (5 cm^3)
Red phosphorus (1 g)
Bromine (2 cm^3)
10% solution of sodium carbonate
Calcium chloride, anhydrous

EQUATIONS

$$2P + 3Br_2 \rightleftharpoons 2PBr_3$$

$$3C_2H_5OH + PBr_3 \longrightarrow 3C_2H_5Br + H_3PO_3$$

DETAILS

To 5 cm³ of ethanol in the flask, add 1 g of red phosphorus. Shake the mixture, and add 2 cm³ of bromine, drop by drop, from the dropping funnel (Figure 7, Plate 2). The flask should be cooled at first in a cold water-bath. The alcohol vapour is recondensed by the reflux condenser.

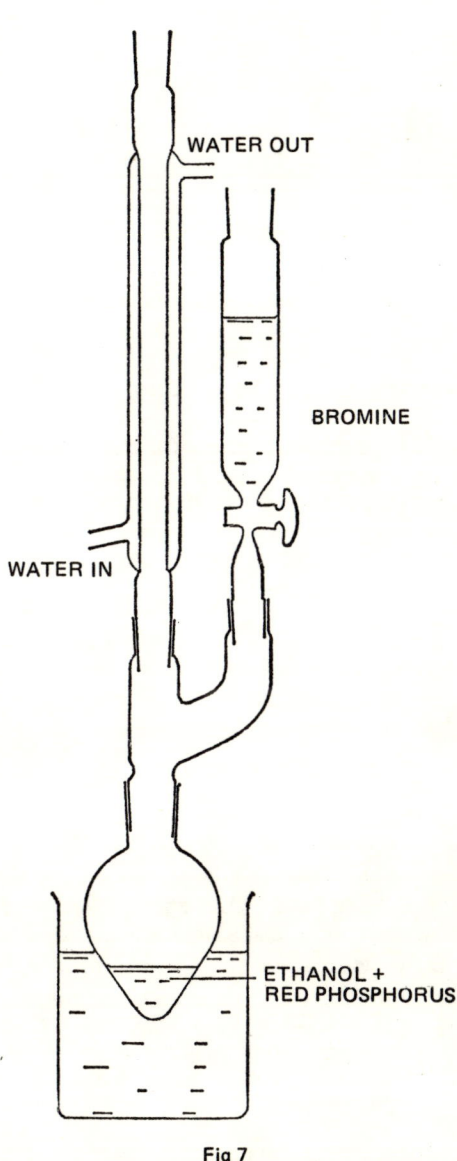

WATER OUT

BROMINE

WATER IN

ETHANOL +
RED PHOSPHORUS

Fig 7

After the bromine has been added, reflux the mixture over a boiling water-bath for about 30 minutes.

Stop the heating, and change the condenser. Distil the mixture from the boiling water-bath and collect the fraction boiling below 70° C, making sure that

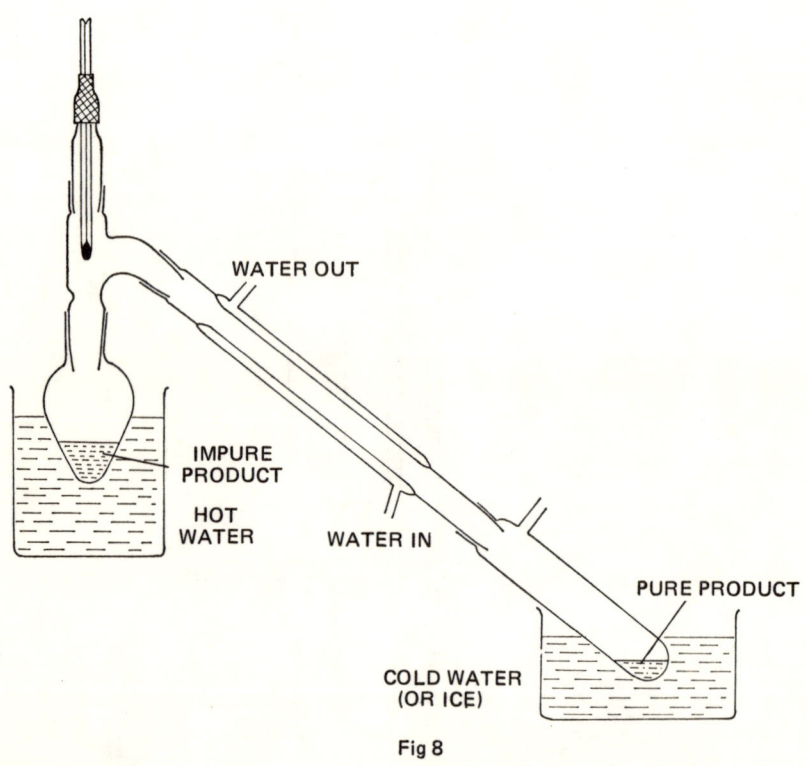

Fig 8

the receiver is immersed in cold water (Figure 8). Heat the flask gently until no more oily drops of bromoethane distil over. Transfer the distillate to the separating funnel. Remove the lower oily layer, discard the aqueous layer, and return the oil to the separating funnel. Add about 3 cm³ of dilute sodium carbonate solution, fit a stopper, then shake. Remove the stopper occasionally to relieve the pressure. Allow the mixture to settle, and discard the upper aqueous layer. Wash the impure bromoethane with water, discard the upper layer, and dry it over anhydrous calcium chloride in a stoppered test-tube. Redistil the bromo-ethane, collecting the fraction boiling in the range 35–40° C (Figure 8).

PHYSICAL CONSTANTS

B.p. 38° C; density at 20° C: 1.43 g cm⁻³

4.2. Small-scale Preparation of Bromoethane (Alternative II)

INTRODUCTION

Hydrogen chloride and hydrogen bromide react with alcohols to form alkyl halides:

$$ROH + HCl \rightleftharpoons RCl + H_2O$$
$$ROH + HBr \rightleftharpoons RBr + H_2O$$

The reaction between hydrogen chloride and primary and secondary alcohols is very slow and a catalyst is used, generally anhydrous zinc chloride.

The most effective method for the preparation of alkyl bromides is to use a mixture of solid potassium bromide and concentrated sulphuric acid which yields anhydrous hydrogen bromide.

REAGENTS

Ethanol (6 cm^3)
Concentrated sulphuric acid (7 cm^3)
Potassium (or sodium) bromide (6 g)

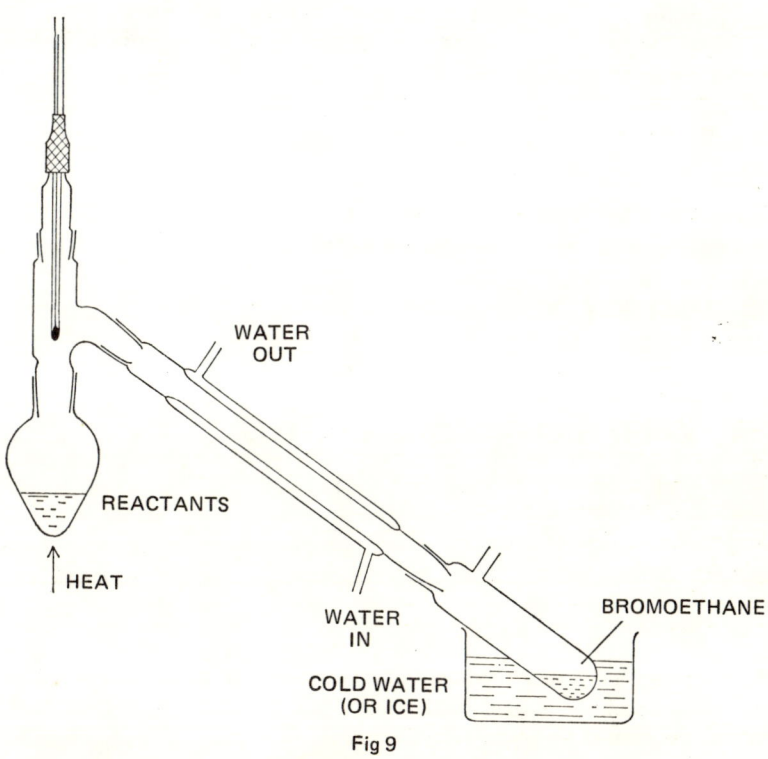

WATER
OUT

REACTANTS

↑ HEAT

WATER
IN

COLD WATER
(OR ICE)

BROMOETHANE

Fig 9

EQUATIONS

$$KBr + H_2SO_4 \longrightarrow KHSO_4 + HBr$$
$$C_2H_5OH + HBr \rightleftharpoons C_2H_5Br + H_2O$$

DETAILS

Place 6 cm^3 of ethanol in a flask. Add slowly, with gentle swirling and cooling under the tap, 7 cm^3 of concentrated sulphuric acid. Add 6 g of powdered potassium (or sodium) bromide and assemble the apparatus as shown in Figure 9. Heat the flask very gently over a gauze, taking care to avoid excessive frothing. Continue heating until no more oily drops of bromoethane distil over. The bromoethane is collected in a receiver surrounded by cold water (or ice).

The distillate contains sulphurous and hydrobromic acid as impurities, and may be purified as described in the first method.

4.3. Small-scale Preparation of 2-Chloro-2-methylbutane

INTRODUCTION

Unlike primary and secondary alcohols which need a catalyst when reacting with hydrogen chloride, tertiary alcohols react readily with concentrated hydrochloric acid at room temperature.

REAGENTS

2-Methylbutan-2-ol (10 cm^3)
Concentrated hydrochloric acid (30 cm^3)
10% solution of sodium hydrogencarbonate (10 cm^3)

EQUATION

$$\underset{\underset{CH_3}{|}}{\overset{\overset{CH_3}{|}}{C_2H_5-C-OH}} + HCl \longrightarrow \underset{\underset{CH_3}{|}}{\overset{\overset{CH_3}{|}}{C_2H_5-C-Cl}} + H_2O$$

DETAILS

Place 10 cm^3 of 2-methylbutan-2-ol and 30 cm^3 of concentrated hydrochloric acid in a separating funnel. Shake for about 10 minutes, and then allow the layers to separate.

Run off the lower acid layer and then add slowly 10 cm^3 of 10% sodium hydrogencarbonate solution to the separating funnel. Again shake, making sure that no excess gas pressure is built up. Again discard the aqueous layer.

Run off the organic layer into a conical flask, and shake the mixture with a few pieces of anhydrous sodium sulphate. Decant the liquid into a distillation flask. Distil the mixture, using a gauze and a very small flame, collecting the fraction boiling between 84–86° C.

PHYSICAL CONSTANTS

B.p. 85° C; density at 20° C: 0.87 g cm^{-3}

4.4. Small-scale Preparation of Iodoethane

This is an example of the substitution of an iodine atom for a hydroxyl group. As phosphorus iodides are unstable, they are prepared during the reaction by the interaction of red phosphorus and iodine.

Iodoethane can be purified by redistillation.

REAGENTS

Ethanol (5 cm^3)
Red phosphorus (0.5 g)
Iodine (5 g)

EQUATIONS

$$2P + 3I_2 \rightleftharpoons 2PI_3$$

$$3C_2H_5OH + PI_3 \longrightarrow 3C_2H_5I + H_3PO_3$$

DETAILS

Place 0.5 g of red phosphorus and 5 g of iodine in a flask. Immerse the flask in a beaker of cold water and introduce, using a dropping pipette, 5 cm^3 of ethanol, in 1 cm^3 portions, down the reflux condenser (Figure 10). When all the alcohol has been added and after the vigour of the reaction has subsided, bring the water in the beaker gently to the boil. Allow the contents of the flask to reflux for an hour.

Allow the apparatus to cool and adjust the condenser for distillation (Figure 9). Bring the water in the bath gently to the boil and maintain at this temperature until no more oily drops of distillate are obtained.

Purify, dry, and redistil the iodoethane (Figure 9). Collect the fraction boiling in the range 68–73° C.

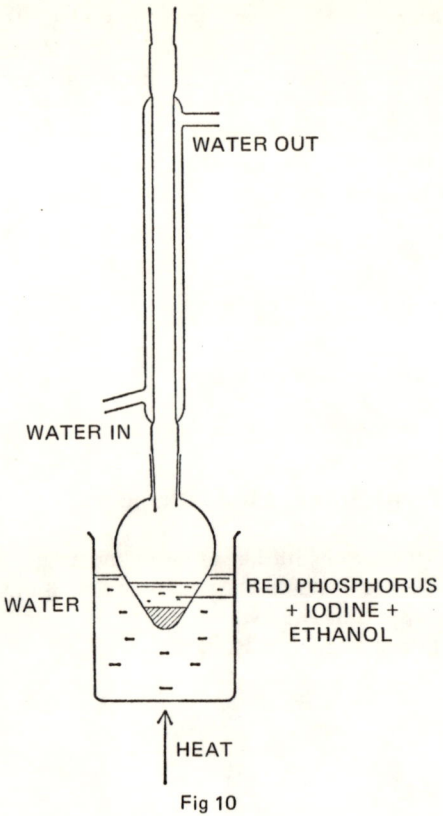

WATER OUT

WATER IN

WATER

RED PHOSPHORUS + IODINE + ETHANOL

HEAT

Fig 10

PHYSICAL CONSTANTS

B.p. $72°$ C; density at $20°$ C: 1.93 g cm^{-3}

4.5. Reactions of Bromoethane

1. Add 2 drops of bromoethane to 1 cm^3 of 5% silver nitrate solution in a test-tube. Shake the mixture and allow it to stand for a few minutes. A slight opalescence, due to the formation of silver bromide, is observed.

   This indicates that hydrolysis has occurred to a slight extent in the cold:

$$C_2H_5Br + H_2O \longrightarrow C_2H_5OH + H^+Br^-$$

$$Ag^+ + Br^- \longrightarrow Ag^+Br^- \downarrow$$

2. Repeat the above test but warm the mixture gently. Note the increased rate of reaction.

   Compare the rate of reaction with that between a solution of potassium bromide and the solution of silver nitrate.

3. To 0.5 cm³ of dilute sodium hydroxide solution (about 8 drops), add 5 drops of ethanol, followed by 2 drops of bromoethane. Shake and warm to boiling. Cool, acidify with dilute nitric acid, and add 2 drops of 5% silver nitrate solution. A precipitate of silver bromide is formed. A more complete reaction has taken place than in reactions 1 and 2.

$$C_2H_5Br + OH^- \longrightarrow C_2H_5OH + Br^-$$

$$Ag^+ + Br^- \longrightarrow Ag^+Br^- \downarrow$$

4. Reaction with magnesium to form a Grignard reagent. An example with an aryl halide is given (Section 22.4).

4.6. Reactions of 1-bromobutane, 2-bromobutane, and 2-bromo-2-methylpropane

Undertake experiment 1 in Section 4.5, substituting these alkyl halides for bromoethane. Note any differences in behaviour between the alkyl halides, suggesting reasons for any you observe.

POLYHALOGEN DERIVATIVES OF ALKANES

4.7. Small-scale Preparation of 1,2-Dibromoethane

INTRODUCTION

As ethene is a gas, it is prepared specially for the subsequent preparation of 1,2-dibromoethane.

Ethene is **unsaturated** and undergoes **addition reactions** readily. This preparation is an example of an addition reaction undergone by alkenes and alkynes.

The purification of 1,2-dibromoethane involves a redistillation.

REAGENTS

Ethanol (5 cm³)

Concentrated sulphuric acid (10 cm³)

Aluminium sulphate, hydrated (1 g)

20% solution of sodium hydroxide (40 cm³)

Bromine (2 cm³)

EQUATIONS

$$CH_3CH_2OH \xrightarrow[\text{dehydrating agent}]{\text{Conc. } H_2SO_4 \text{ as}} H_2C{=}CH_2 + H_2O$$
$$H_2C{=}CH_2 + Br_2 \longrightarrow Br{-}CH_2{-}CH_2{-}Br$$

DETAILS

Prepare ethene by the dehydration of ethanol using concentrated sulphuric acid (Chapter 2). Allow the gas to pass through a 20% sodium hydroxide solution and then through two water-cooled boiling tubes, each containing 1 cm³ of bromine covered with a water layer, 5 cm deep. Prevent the escape of bromine vapour into the atmosphere by absorption in soda-lime (Figure 11).

When the colour of the bromine in the boiling tubes has become much paler, turn the bunsen out and immediately detach the glass tubing at A. Transfer the contents of one of the water-cooled tubes to the other, add a few drops of dilute

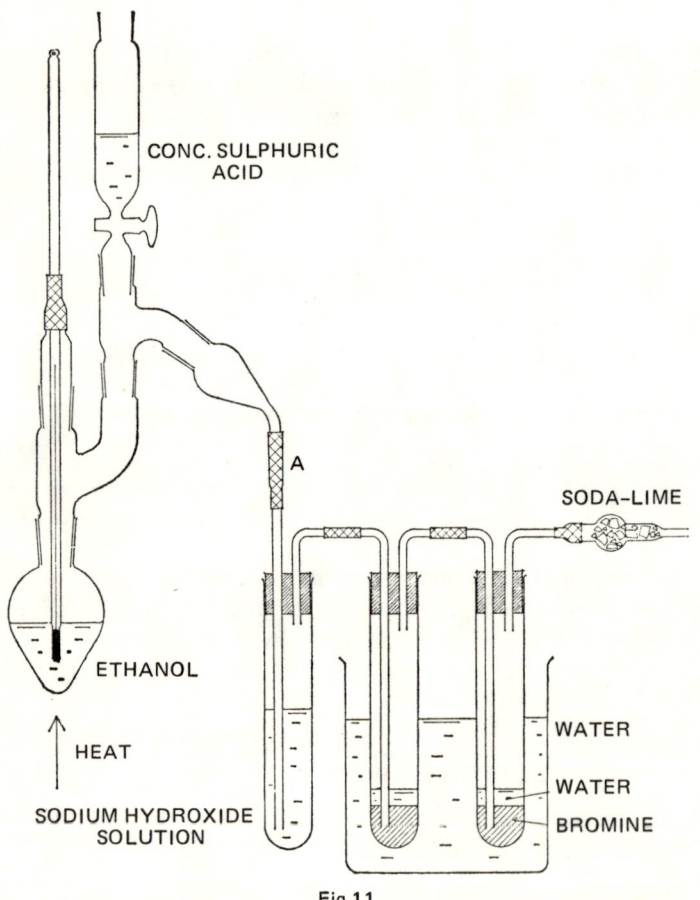

Fig 11

sodium hydroxide solution, fit a stopper, and shake. Continue in this way until the colour of the bromine is just discharged. Pour off as much as possible of the upper aqueous layer, removing the rest with a dropping pipette. Wash the 1,2-dibromoethane with two successive 3 cm³ portions of water, draining off and discarding the upper aqueous layer on each occasion.

Transfer the 1,2-dibromoethane to a test-tube, add 1 or 2 small pieces of anhydrous calcium chloride, fit a cork, and leave until the liquid becomes clear.

Distil the dried product using the apparatus in Figure 5, Plate 1. Collect the distillate within the temperature range 129–132° C.

PHYSICAL CONSTANTS

B.p. 131° C; density at 20° C: 2.18 g cm^{-3}

4.8. Reactions of 1,2-Dichloroethane or 1,2-Dibromoethane

1. Place 1,2-dichloroethane in a test-tube to a depth of 2.5 cm. Add Rocksil wool until the liquid has been absorbed. Place about 1 g of zinc powder half-way along the tube, then arrange the tube as illustrated in Figure 4. Heat the zinc gently and collect 2 test-tubes of ethene.

$$Zn + Cl-CH_2-CH_2-Cl \longrightarrow ZnCl_2 + H_2C=CH_2$$

Carry out experiments 2 and 4 in Section 2.4 for ethene.

2. To 2 drops of 1,2-dichloroethane, add 2 cm³ of distilled water. Shake for about 2 minutes and allow to stand. Note that the liquids are immiscible, the 1,2-dichloroethane forming a lower layer. Withdraw 5 drops of the aqueous layer, add 5 drops of dilute nitric acid, followed by 5 drops of silver nitrate solution. The absence of any precipitate indicates that hydrolysis of the 1,2-dichloroethane has not occurred.

3. Add 2 cm³ of dilute sodium hydroxide solution to 2 drops of 1,2-dichloroethane in a test-tube. Shake and bring gently to the boil. Allow the reagents to cool, acidify with dilute nitric acid, then add silver nitrate solution. A white precipitate of silver chloride indicates that hydrolysis has occurred, yielding chloride ions.

$$Cl-CH_2-CH_2-Cl + 2OH^- \longrightarrow HO-CH_2-CH_2-OH + 2Cl^-$$
$$Ag^+ + Cl^- \longrightarrow Ag^+Cl^- \downarrow$$

4. Add a few pellets (about 0.5 g) of potassium hydroxide to 2 cm³ of ethanol in a test-tube. Warm the test-tube gently until the pellets have dissolved. Add 6 drops of 1,2-dichloroethane to the alcoholic solution of potassium hydroxide. Shake gently, then introduce Rocksil wool plug to absorb the solution. Fit the test-tube with a delivery tube dipping into 2 cm³ of an ammoniacal solution of copper(I) chloride (Section 3.2). Heat the Rocksil plug and observe that, after a short time, a red precipitate of copper(I) dicarbide is obtained.

$$Cl-CH_2-CH_2-Cl + 2KOH \longrightarrow C_2H_2 + 2KCl + 2H_2O$$

$$C_2H_2 + Cu_2Cl_2 + 2NH_4OH \longrightarrow Cu_2C_2 \downarrow + 2NH_4Cl + 2H_2O$$

5. Preparation of a synthetic rubber. Section 30.4.

4.9. Reactions of 1,1-Dichloroethane

1. Repeat experiments 1 and 2 in the previous section (4.8), using 1,1-dichloroethane in place of 1,2-dichloroethane. Note that similar results are obtained.
2. Repeat experiment 3 in the previous section. Note that hydrolysis takes place and that chloride ions are formed. However, ethanal is formed, and can be recognised by its characteristic smell.

$$CH_3CHCl_2 + 2NaOH \longrightarrow CH_3CHO + 2NaCl + H_2O$$

3. Repeat experiment 4 in the previous section. Ethyne is formed and can be tested by passing the gas through an ammoniacal solution of copper(I) chloride.

4.10. Small-scale Preparation of Trichloromethane (Chloroform)

INTRODUCTION

Trichloromethane is generally manufactured by the reduction of tetrachloromethane, hydrogen being generated by iron and steam. However, trichloromethane is prepared in the laboratory from propanone by chlorination, followed by decomposition of the chloro-compound with alkali. The process is inefficient, for there are several side reactions.

The purification of trichloromethane involves redistillation.

REAGENTS

Propanone (4 cm³)
Sodium hypochlorite solution (30 cm³)
Calcium chloride, anhydrous

EQUATIONS

The reactions between propanone and sodium hypochlorite can be represented:

$$CH_3COCH_3 + 3Cl_2 \longrightarrow CCl_3COCH_3 + 3HCl$$

$$CCl_3COCH_3 + NaOH \longrightarrow CHCl_3 + CH_3COONa$$

$$NaOH + HCl \longrightarrow NaCl + H_2O$$

DETAILS

Place 30 cm^3 of sodium hypochlorite solution in the flask and arrange the apparatus (Figure 12, Plate 2). Cool the flask in a beaker of cold water. Introduce carefully, by dropping funnel, a solution of 4 cm^3 of propanone in 2 cm^3 of water. Gently swirl the contents of the flask while immersed in the cold water and allow to stand for about 5 minutes. Raise the temperature of the bath to 55° C and maintain the mixture at that temperature for about 10 minutes to ensure completion of the reaction.

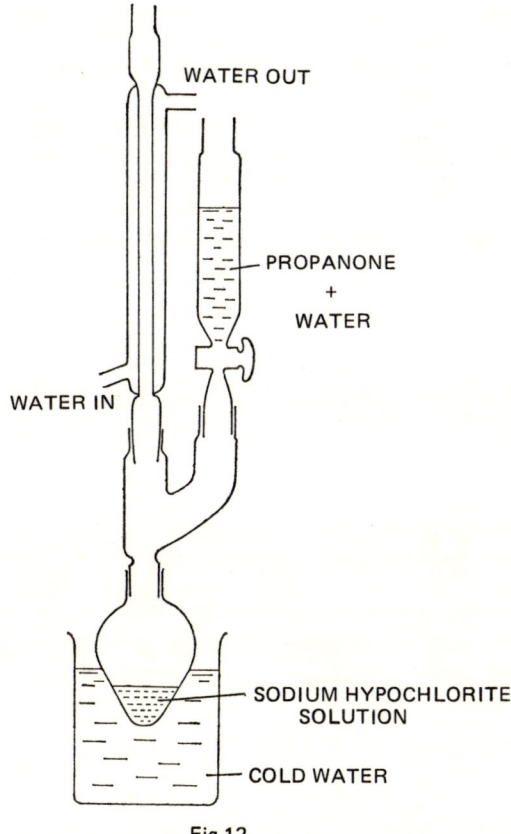

Fig 12

Remove the hot water from the bath and replace with cold water in order to cool the flask. Transfer the contents of the flask to a separating funnel and remove the lower oily layer of trichloromethane.

Combine the yields of about six experiments and place the impure trichloromethane in a clean separating funnel, add an equal volume of water, insert the stopper and shake.

Allow the liquid to settle; remove the lower layer, and discard the upper aqueous layer. Repeat the washing until the aqueous layer no longer gives a white precipitate of silver chloride when treated with silver nitrate solution. Allow the washed trichloromethane to stand in contact with 1 or 2 pieces of anhydrous calcium chloride, in a stoppered test-tube, until the liquid is no longer turbid.

The yields from a number of experiments may be combined and further purified by distillation over a water-bath (Figure 8). Collect the fraction distilling between 60° and 64° C.

PHYSICAL CONSTANTS

B.p. 61° C; density at 20° C: 1.50 g cm^{-3}

4.11. Reactions of Trichloromethane (Chloroform)

1. Place in a test-tube 1 pellet of potassium hydroxide. Add 10 drops of ethanol and 5 drops of trichloromethane. Warm gently while shaking the test-tube all the time:

$$CHCl_3 + 4NaOH \longrightarrow HCOONa + 3NaCl + 2H_2O$$

   Sodium
   methanoate

To show that hydrolysis has taken place and that chloride ions have been formed, acidify the solution with dilute nitric acid and add 2 drops of silver nitrate solution. A white precipitate of silver chloride is formed.

$$Ag^+ + Cl^- \longrightarrow Ag^+Cl^- \downarrow$$

   N.B. Check that trichloromethane itself does not react with silver nitrate to form a precipitate of silver chloride.

2. **The carbylamine reaction.** Place 1 pellet of potassium hydroxide in a test-tube. Add 10 drops of ethanol, 2 drops of trichloromethane, and 2 drops of phenylamine. Warm gently. Note the pungent odour of phenyl isocyanide (carbylamine):

$$CHCl_3 + 3KOH + C_6H_5NH_2 \longrightarrow C_6H_5NC + 3KCl + 3H_2O$$

   Phenylamine   Phenyl
                          isocyanide

N.B. Cool the test-tube, add concentrated hydrochloric acid to convert the poisonous isocyanide to phenylamine, and wash the contents of the test-tube into the sink **with plenty of water. Do this as soon as possible.**

(This test is used to identify not only trichloromethane but also primary amines. The reaction is also used as a laboratory preparation of isocyanides.)

4.12. Small-scale Preparation of Tri-iodomethane (Iodoform)

INTRODUCTION

The iodoform reaction is frequently used in organic chemistry as a test for the

$$CH_3-C-$$
$$\parallel$$
$$O$$

group, or a group that will be oxidised to this group by iodine. Compounds having these groups include propanone, ethanal, ethanol and propan-2-ol.

Tri-iodomethane is purified by recrystallisation from ethanol.

REAGENTS

Ethanol (1 cm^3)
Iodine (1 g)
20% solution of potassium iodide (10 cm^3)
20% solution of sodium hydroxide

EQUATION

$$CH_3CH_2OH + 4I_2 + 6NaOH \longrightarrow CHI_3 \downarrow + HCOONa + 5NaI + 5H_2O$$

DETAILS

Dissolve 1 g of iodine in 10 cm^3 of 20% potassium iodide solution. Add 1 cm^3 of ethanol, then 20% sodium hydroxide solution slowly until the colour of the iodine is discharged. Filter the yellow precipitate of tri-iodomethane using either a small Hirsch funnel or a Willstätter nail filter (Figures 13(a) and 13(b)).

Wash the residue *in situ* with distilled water. Purify the crystals by recrystallising them from ethanol. Dry the crystals, and determine their melting-point (Chapter 31).

If possible, mount 1 or 2 crystals on a microscopic slide. Observe the yellow hexagonal plates.

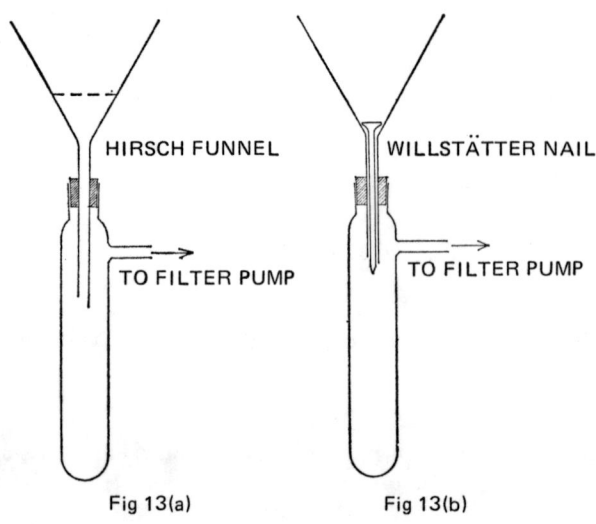

HIRSCH FUNNEL   WILLSTÄTTER NAIL

TO FILTER PUMP   TO FILTER PUMP

Fig 13(a)   Fig 13(b)

PHYSICAL CONSTANT

M.p.119° C.

5

ALCOHOLS

Functional Group — OH

5.1. Preparation of Ethanol by Fermentation

Add 5 g of powdered brewer's yeast to about 50 cm^3 of a 10% solution of sucrose (cane sugar) in a conical flask, and place a plug of cotton wool in the mouth of the flask. Shake the flask and allow it to stand in a warm atmosphere for 2 days. (It is suggested that a fume cupboard in which a bunsen is gently burning provides suitable conditions.)

$$C_{12}H_{22}O_{11} + H_2O \xrightarrow{\text{invertase}} C_6H_{12}O_6 + C_6H_{12}O_6$$
$$\text{Glucose} \quad \text{Fructose}$$

$$C_6H_{12}O_6 \xrightarrow{\text{zymase}} 2C_2H_5OH + 2CO_2$$
$$\text{Glucose or} \qquad \text{Ethanol}$$
$$\text{Fructose}$$

Filter the aqueous solution and distil the filtrate using a bunsen burner. Collect about 20 cm^3 of distillate, and redistil this, collecting the liquid distilling between 75 and 90° C.

5.2. Reactions of Ethanol

A. REACTIONS OF THE —OH GROUP

1. Add a **small** pellet of sodium to 1 cm^3 of ethanol in a test-tube. Note the effervescence. Test for hydrogen with a lighted splint.

$$2C_2H_5OH + 2Na \longrightarrow 2C_2H_5ONa + H_2 \uparrow$$
$$\text{Sodium}$$
$$\text{ethoxide}$$

Note that this is a less vigorous reaction than that between sodium and water.

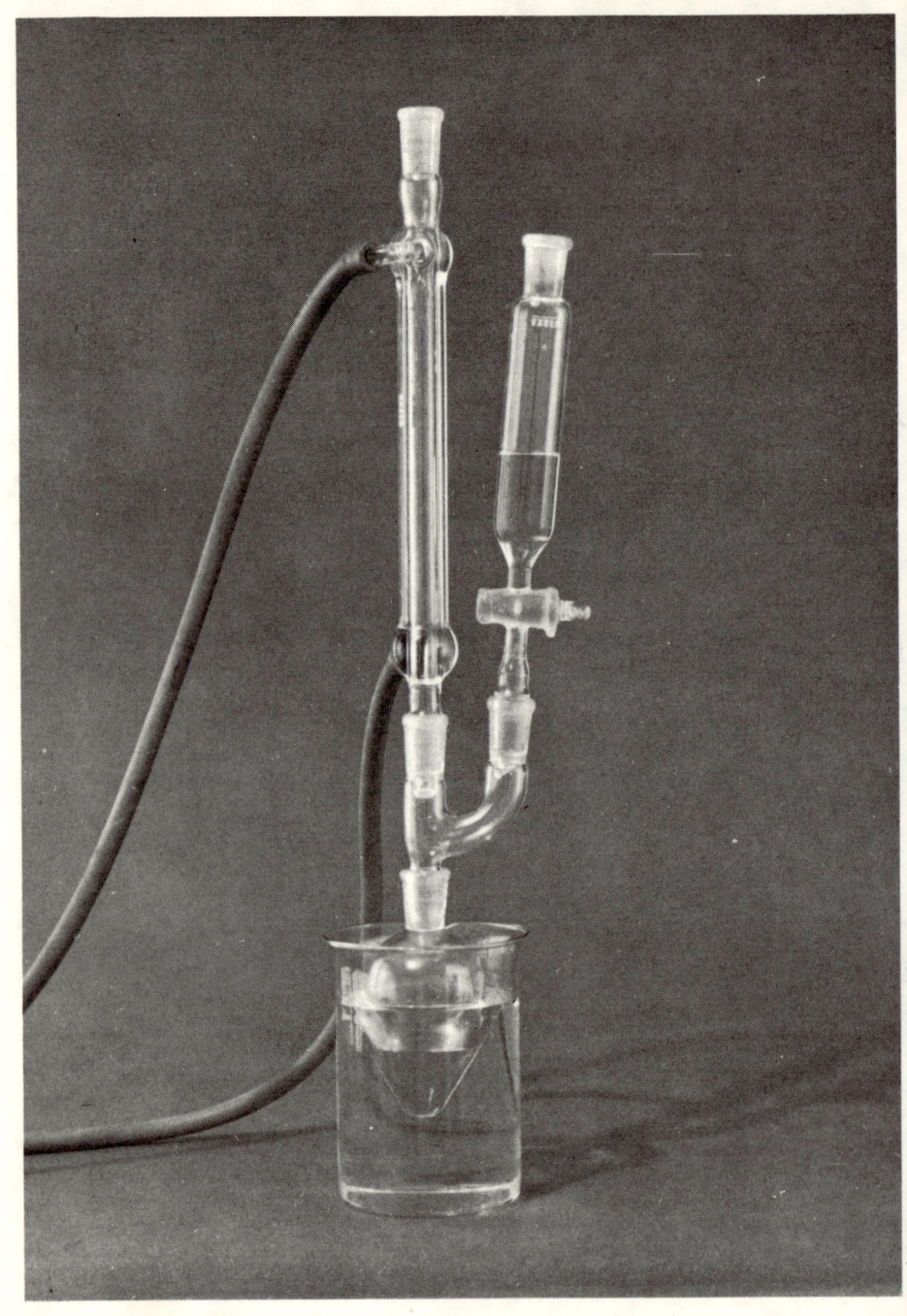

PLATE 2

Preparations of bromoethane (Fig. 7, p. 17), trichloromethane (Fig. 12, p. 27),
1,3-dinitrobenzene (p.104) and phenylamine (Fig. 29, p. 107).

Evaporate to dryness, over a hot water-bath, the solution of sodium ethoxide to obtain a white residue of the salt. Add 3 drops of water to the residue and test the solution with Universal Indicator solution (or with red litmus). It will turn blue, owing to the formation of sodium hydroxide from sodium ethoxide:

$$C_2H_5O^-Na^+ + H_2O \longrightarrow C_2H_5OH + Na^+OH^-$$

(This is an example of the hydrolysis of a salt of a weak acid and strong base.)

2. Warm a mixture of 5 drops of ethanol and 5 drops of ethanoic acid with 1 drop of concentrated sulphuric acid. Note the smell of ethyl ethanoate, which is characteristic of many esters:

$$CH_3COOH + C_2H_5OH \xrightarrow{H^+} CH_3COOC_2H_5 + H_2O$$

Ethanoic acid   Ethyl ethanoate

3. To 5 drops of ethanol, add 1 drop of ethanoyl chloride. A vigorous reaction takes place. Fumes of hydrogen chloride are evolved which become dense when breathed upon, and turn Universal Indicator paper (or blue litmus paper) red.

Dilute the solution with 5 drops of water, and note the smell of the ester, ethyl ethanoate.

$$CH_3COCl + C_2H_5OH \longrightarrow CH_3COOC_2H_5 + HCl$$

Ethanoyl   Ethyl ethanoate
chloride

4. To 1 cm^3 of ethanol in a test-tube, add about 0.1 g of phosphorus pentachloride. Observe the white fumes of hydrogen chloride which become dense when breathed upon, and turn Universal Indicator paper (or blue litmus paper) red.

When the fumes have subsided, smell the residual chloroethane.

$$C_2H_5OH + PCl_5 \longrightarrow C_2H_5Cl + POCl_3 + HCl$$

B. REACTIONS OF THE —CH$_2$OH GROUP

5. To 5 drops of ethanol, add 10 drops of dilute sulphuric acid and 2 drops of dilute potassium dichromate solution. Warm gently. Note that the orange potassium dichromate solution turns green, since chromium(III) sulphate is one of the reduction products. Note also the smell of ethanal.

$$K_2Cr_2O_7 + 4H_2SO_4 + 3CH_3CH_2OH \longrightarrow K_2SO_4$$
$$+ Cr_2(SO_4)_3 + 7H_2O + 3CH_3CHO$$

6. To 5 drops of ethanol, add 10 drops of dilute sulphuric acid and 1 drop of 1% potassium permanganate solution. Warm gently. Note that the purple colour disappears, owing to the reduction of potassium permanganate to manganese(II) sulphate. Note also the smell of ethanal.

$$2KMnO_4 + 3H_2SO_4 + 5CH_3CH_2OH \longrightarrow K_2SO_4$$
$$+ 2MnSO_4 + 8H_2O + 5CH_3CHO$$

7. Half fill an ignition tube with copper(II) oxide. Warm the tube in a bunsen flame and then empty the contents into 5 cm^3 of ethanol in an evaporating basin. Note the smell of ethanal and that the copper(II) oxide is reduced to copper:

$$CH_3CH_2OH + CuO \longrightarrow CH_3CHO + Cu + H_2O$$

C. OTHER REACTIONS

8. **The iodoform reaction**. To 5 drops of ethanol, add 5 drops of iodine solution and then dilute sodium hydroxide solution dropwise until the colour of iodine is discharged. A yellow precipitate of tri-iodomethane (iodoform) is obtained.

If possible, place one drop of the aqueous suspension of tri-iodomethane on a microscopic slide and view it under a microscope. Note the characteristic shape (hexagonal plates) of the crystals.

The reaction may be represented thus:

$$C_2H_5OH + 4I_2 + 6NaOH \longrightarrow CHI_3 + HCOONa + 5NaI + 5H_2O$$

5.3. Reactions of Methanol

A. REACTIONS OF THE —OH GROUP

1. Repeat experiments 1, 2, 3, and 4 in Section 5.2.

2. To 5 drops of methanol in a test-tube, add a drop of concentrated sulphuric acid. Shake after cooling. Add a few crystals of 2-hydroxybenzoic acid (salicylic acid) and warm gently for half a minute. The odour of the methyl ester (Oil of Wintergreen) is detectable.

B. REACTIONS OF THE —CH_2OH GROUP

3. Repeat experiments 5, 6 and 7 in Section 5.2, using methanol instead of ethanol. Note the smell of methanol.

4. Introduce about 10 cm^3 of methanol into a 100 cm^3 beaker. Warm a spiral of platinum wire, wound on a glass rod, to red-heat in a bunsen flame. Introduce the spiral above the methanol by placing the glass rod across the beaker

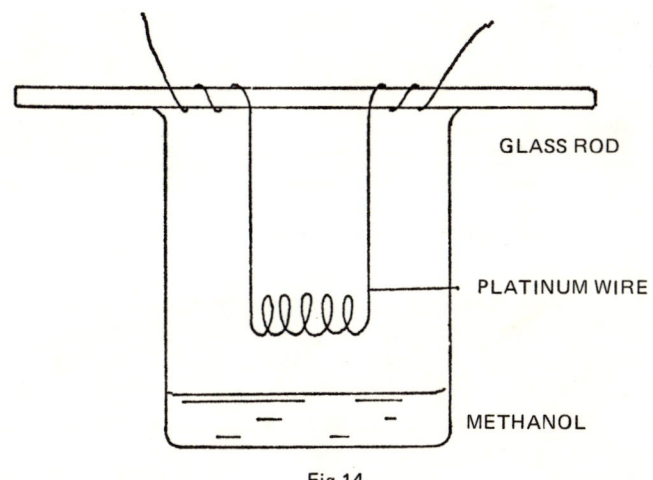

Fig 14

(Figure 14). The spiral continues to glow and the pungent odour of methanal can be noted. This is a demonstration of the manufacture of methanal.

$$2CH_3OH + O_2 \xrightarrow[\text{catalyst}]{\text{Pt as a}} 2HCHO + 2H_2O$$

Methanol   Methanal

C. OTHER REACTIONS

5. Pure methanol does not undergo the iodoform reaction (experiment 8 in Section 5.2).

5.4. Reactions of Propan–2–ol

A. REACTIONS OF THE —OH GROUP

1. Repeat experiments 1, 2, 3, and 4 in Section 5.2.

B. REACTIONS OF THE CHOH GROUP

2. Repeat experiments 5, 6, and 7 in Section 5.2, noting that propanone, a ketone, is formed.

C. OTHER REACTIONS

3. Propan-2-ol undergoes the iodoform reaction (experiment 8 in Section 5.2).

5.5. Reactions of Propan-1-ol

A. REACTIONS OF THE —OH GROUP

1. Repeat experiments 1, 2, 3, and 4 in Section 5.2.

B. REACTIONS OF THE —CH$_2$OH GROUP

2. Repeat experiments 5, 6, and 7 in Section 5.2, noting that propanal, an aldehyde, is formed.

C. OTHER REACTIONS

3. Repeat experiment 8 in Section 5.2. Tri-iodomethane is not precipitated.

6

ETHERS

Functional Group —O—

6.1. Small-scale Preparation of Diethyl Ether

INTRODUCTION

This reaction is another example of the action of concentrated sulphuric acid as a dehydrating agent (cf. Section 2.1).

The purification of diethyl ether involves the neutralisation of acids (by sodium hydroxide), the removal of alcohol (by calcium chloride solution) and of excess water (by anhydrous calcium chloride). The final purification is by redistillation.

Ethyl hydrogensulphate is formed from ethanol and concentrated sulphuric acid (2.1). The ester reacts with excess of the alcohol to form diethyl ether:

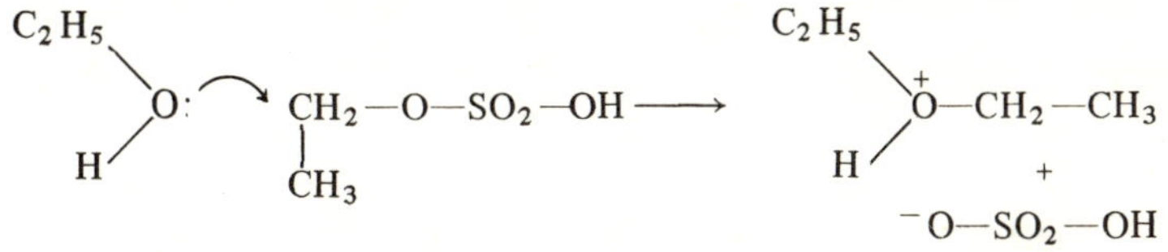

$$
\begin{array}{c}
C_2H_5 \\
\diagdown \\
O: \quad CH_2-O-SO_2-OH \longrightarrow \\
\diagup \qquad | \\
H \qquad CH_3
\end{array}
\qquad
\begin{array}{c}
C_2H_5 \\
\diagdown \; + \\
O-CH_2-CH_3 \\
\diagup \qquad + \\
H \\
\\
{}^-O-SO_2-OH
\end{array}
$$

$$\longrightarrow \quad C_2H_5-O-C_2H_5 \; + \; H_2SO_4$$

REAGENTS

Ethanol (20 cm^3)
Concentrated sulphuric acid (8 cm^3)
10% solution of sodium hydroxide (5 cm^3)
Calcium chloride, anhydrous

EQUATION

$$2C_2H_5OH \xrightarrow[\text{dehydrating agent}]{\text{Conc. } H_2SO_4 \text{ as}} C_2H_5-O-C_2H_5 \; + \; H_2O$$

Great care must be taken that there are no flames nearby when ether is prepared or used.

DETAILS

Place 10 cm³ of ethanol in a flask, and add slowly 8 cm³ of concentrated sulphuric acid in small portions. Cool the flask under the tap and gently swirl the contents. When all the acid has been added set up the apparatus as in Figure 15 and
Plate 3. Place 10 cm³ of ethanol in the dropping funnel and connect a piece of

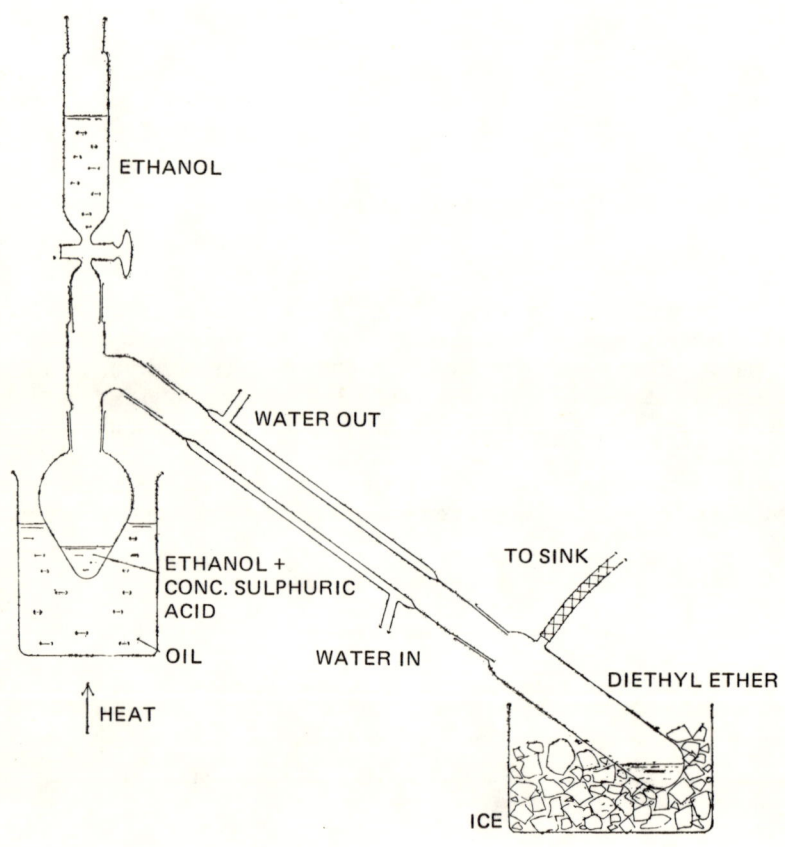

ETHANOL

WATER OUT

TO SINK

ETHANOL +
CONC. SULPHURIC
ACID

OIL

WATER IN

DIETHYL ETHER

HEAT

ICE

Fig 15

rubber tubing to the side arm of the receiver in order to convey highly inflamm-
able vapour of ether to the sink outlet. It is advisable to keep water from the tap
running gently to wash down the sink outlet during the course of the experiment.

Bring the temperature of the oil-bath slowly to 150–155° C, stirring the oil
occasionally. When the ether begins to distil over, introduce into the flask
ethanol from the dropping funnel at the same rate as the distillate collects in the
receiver. Maintain the temperature of the bath at 155° C until no more ether
distils. About 7–8 cm³ of crude ether will have collected in the receiver.

Turn out the bunsen, disconnect the receiver, and transfer its contents to a
separating funnel. Add 5 cm³ of a 10% sodium hydroxide solution, replace the

stopper, and shake to remove sulphurous acid. Owing to the high volatility of ether, the stopper should be removed carefully from the funnel to release the vapour under pressure. Run off and discard the lower aqueous layer.

To the top layer in the separating funnel, add 5 cm^3 of a saturated calcium chloride solution and shake to remove ethanol. Again, separate and discard the lower aqueous layer. Transfer the ether to a boiling-tube or small flask, add 2 or 3 small pieces of fused calcium chloride, cork and leave to stand for about 1 hour. The calcium chloride removes not only water but also ethanol.

Decant the ether into a flask and set up the apparatus for distillation from a hot water-bath (Figure 8). The water-bath should be heated to 60° C, well away from the apparatus for safety. Immerse the flask in the hot water and collect the fraction distilling in the range 34–39° C.

PHYSICAL CONSTANTS

B.p. 35° C; density at 20° C: 0.71 g cm^{-3}

7

ALDEHYDES AND KETONES

Functional Groups

$$\overset{O}{\underset{||}{-C-H}} \quad \text{and} \quad \overset{O}{\underset{||}{-C-}}$$

7.1. Small-scale Preparation of Ethanal (Acetaldehyde)

INTRODUCTION

Acidified potassium or sodium dichromate solution is frequently used in organic chemistry as an oxidising agent. In this example, the primary alcohol group, $-CH_2OH$, is oxidised to the aldehyde group, $-CHO$. Care must be taken that the aldehyde is not oxidised to the acid, $-COOH$.

The purification of ethanal is by redistillation.

REAGENTS

Ethanol (4 cm^3)
Sodium dichromate (5 g)
Concentrated sulphuric acid (2 cm^3)

EQUATION

$3C_2H_5OH + Na_2Cr_2O_7 + 4H_2SO_4 \longrightarrow$

Ethanol

$Na_2SO_4 + Cr_2(SO_4)_3 + 4H_2O + 3CH_3CHO$

Ethanal

DETAILS

Set up the apparatus shown in Figure 16.

In a clean test-tube, dissolve 5 g of sodium dichromate in 5 cm^3 of water, and then add 4 cm^3 of ethanol.

Place 6 cm^3 of water in the flask and add slowly 2 cm^3 of concentrated sulphuric acid, swirling gently and cooling under the tap. Heat the dilute acid slowly until it is boiling, and then turn out the bunsen flame. Add the alcohol mixture, using the dropping funnel, at such a rate that the liquid is maintained at the boiling point. The receiver should be surrounded by ice, or by very cold water.

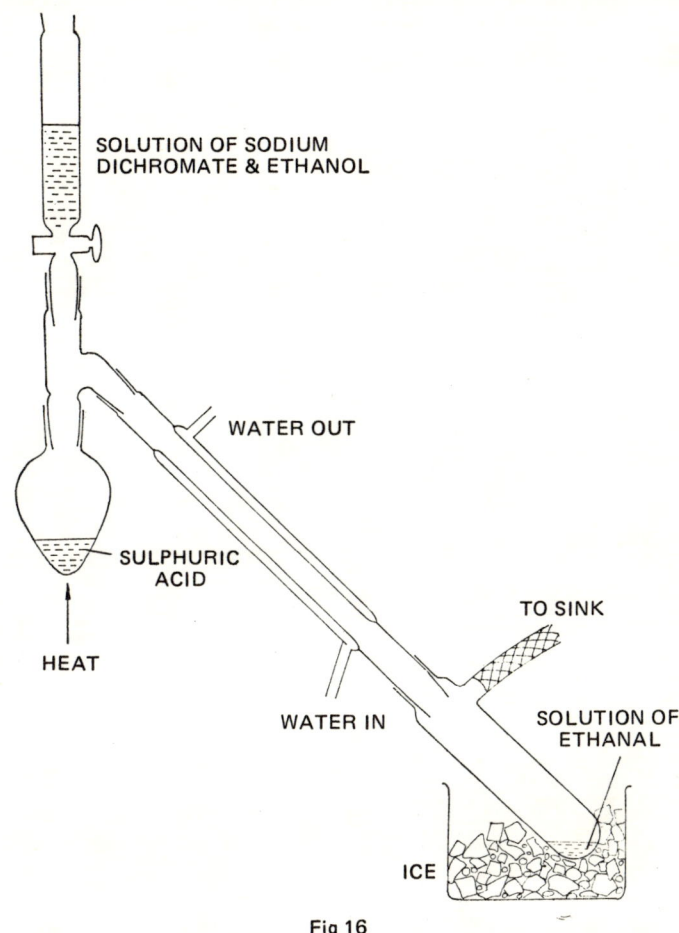

SOLUTION OF SODIUM DICHROMATE & ETHANOL

WATER OUT

SULPHURIC ACID

TO SINK

HEAT

WATER IN

SOLUTION OF ETHANAL

ICE

Fig 16

A colourless distillate is obtained, containing ethanal, ethanol, ethanoic acid, and water.

Transfer the impure ethanal to a clean flask and redistil the mixture (Figure 8) over a warm water-bath. Collect the fraction boiling between 20° C and 23° C, keeping the receiver surrounded by ice.

PHYSICAL CONSTANT

B.p. 21° C

7.2. Test-tube Preparation of Ethanal

A. FROM ETHANOL, BY THE 'WET-ROCKSIL' METHOD

Place ethanol in a test-tube to a depth of about 2 cm. Push Rocksil wool down the tube until the alcohol has been absorbed. Add copper turnings to a depth of 5 cm and set up an apparatus similar to that shown in Figure 17. Warm the

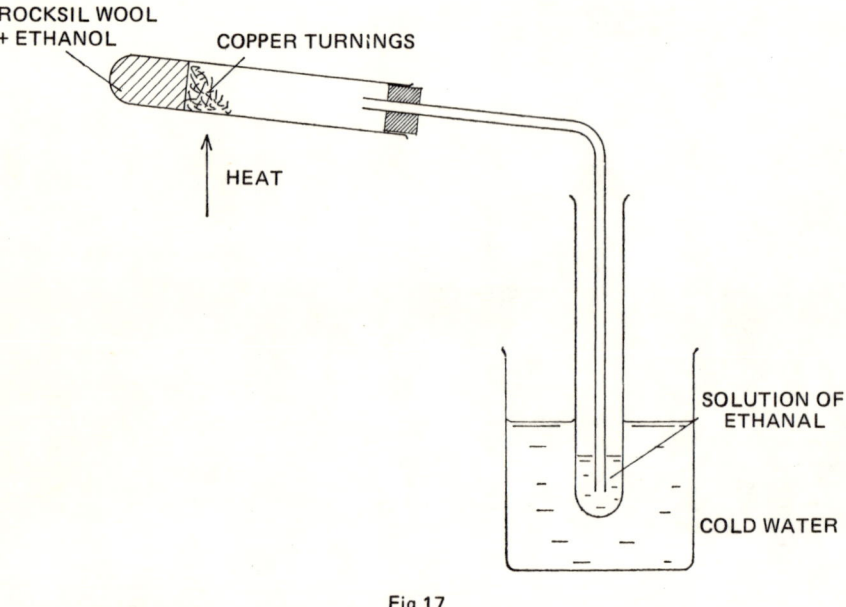

Fig 17

copper turnings and collect some ethanal in the test-tube in which some cold water is present. The test-tube is allowed to stand in a beaker of cold water. Note the characteristic odour of ethanal.

$$CH_3 CH_2 OH \xrightarrow{\quad Cu \quad} CH_3 CHO + H_2$$

The presence of ethanal can also be demonstrated by passing the vapour directly into a solution of Schiff's reagent (Section 7.6, experiment 3).

B. MANUFACTURE FROM ETHYNE

This experiment illustrates the manufacture of ethanal from ethyne.

Generate ethyne by adding water to calcium dicarbide, either in a test-tube (Figure 18(a)) **or** in a flask (Figure 18(b)). Allow the gas to pass through a test-tube containing 10 cm^3 of (1:3) sulphuric acid, 2 cm^3 of mercury(II) chloride

43

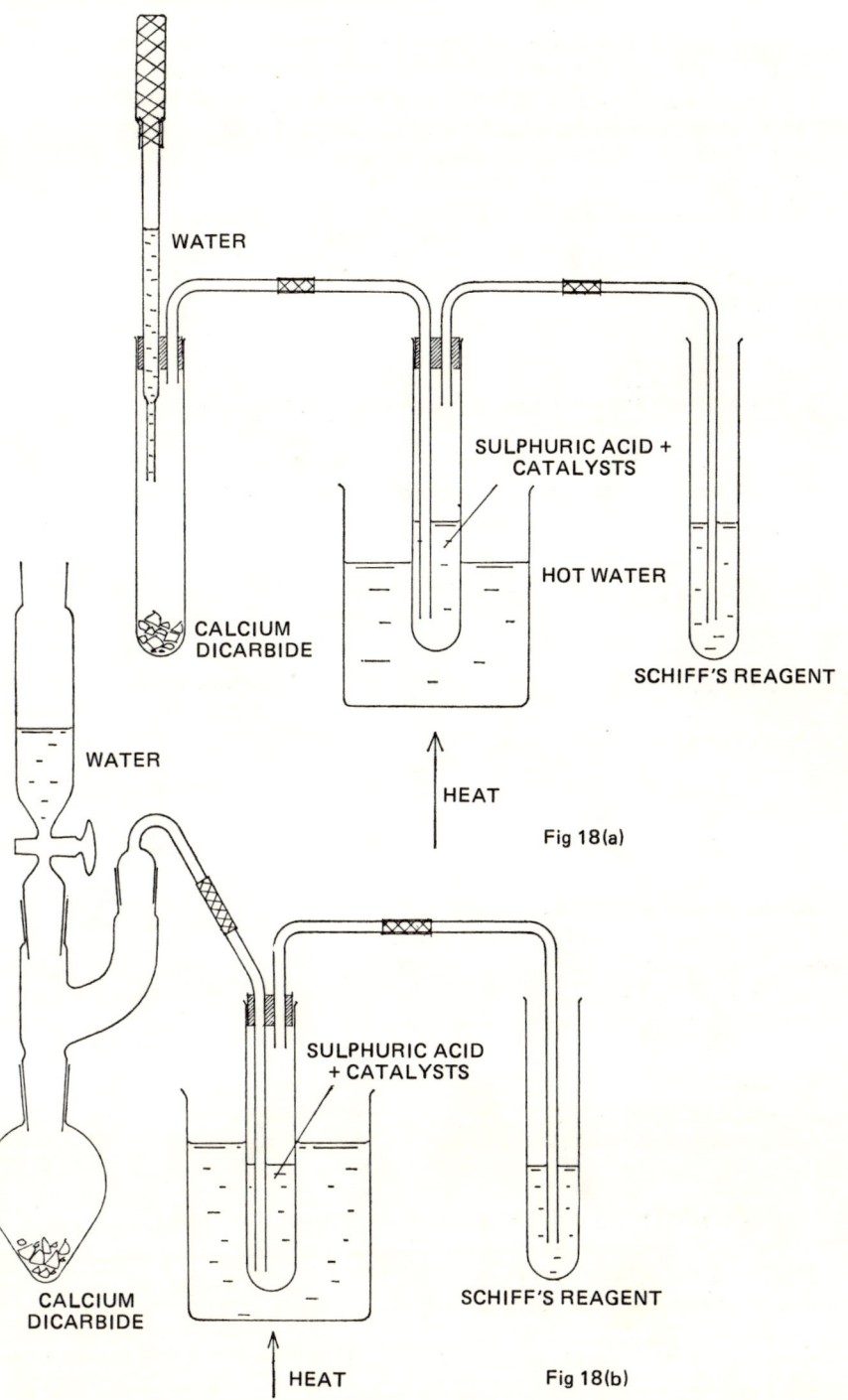

WATER

CALCIUM
DICARBIDE

SULPHURIC ACID +
CATALYSTS

HOT WATER

SCHIFF'S REAGENT

HEAT

Fig 18(a)

WATER

CALCIUM
DICARBIDE

SULPHURIC ACID
+ CATALYSTS

SCHIFF'S REAGENT

HEAT

Fig 18(b)

.

solution, and a small crystal of iron(III) sulphate. Keep the solution at about 80° C by immersing the test-tube in a beaker of hot water.

Ethanal is evolved and passes into a third test-tube, containing cold water. The aldehyde can be detected by Schiff's reagent (Section 7.6, experiment 3).

$$CaC_2 + 2H_2O \longrightarrow C_2H_2 + Ca(OH)_2$$
$$C_2H_2 + H_2O \xrightarrow[Fe_2(SO_4)_3]{H_2SO_4 + HgSO_4} CH_3CHO$$

7.3. Test-tube Preparation of Methanal (Formaldehyde)

Repeat experiment A in Section 7.2, using methanol instead of ethanol. The presence of methanal can be demonstrated by the action of Fehling's solution (Section 7.6, experiment 2).

7.4. Small-scale Preparation of Propanone (Acetone)

INTRODUCTION

This is an example of the oxidation of a secondary alcohol group, $>$CHOH, to the carbonyl group $>$C=O. Acidified potassium or sodium dichromate solution is used as the oxidising agent.

Propanone is purified by redistillation.

REAGENTS

Propan-2-ol (4 cm^3)
Sodium dichromate (5 g)
Concentrated sulphuric acid (2 cm^3)

EQUATIONS

$$Na_2Cr_2O_7 + 4H_2SO_4 + 3(CH_3)_2CHOH \longrightarrow$$
Propan-2-ol

$$Na_2SO_4 + Cr_2(SO_4)_3 + 4H_2O + 3CH_3COCH_3$$
Propanone

DETAILS

Set up the apparatus shown in Figure 16.

In a clean test-tube, dissolve 5 g of sodium dichromate in 5 cm^3 of water, and then add 4 cm^3 of propan-2-ol.

Place 6 cm^3 of water in the flask and add slowly 2 cm^3 of concentrated sulphuric acid, swirling gently and cooling under the tap. Heat the dilute acid slowly until it is boiling, and then turn out the bunsen flame. Add the mixture of propan-2-ol, sodium dichromate, and water from the dropping funnel at such a rate that the liquid in the flask is maintained at the boiling-point.

A colourless distillate is obtained, containing propanone, propan-2-ol and water.

Transfer the impure ketone to a clean flask and redistil the mixture (Figure 9). Collect the fraction boiling between 54° C and 56° C, keeping the receiver surrounded by ice or cold water.

PHYSICAL CONSTANTS

B.p. 56° C; density at 20° C: 0.79 g cm^{-3}

7.5. Test-tube Preparation of Propanone

A. FROM PROPAN-2-OL, BY THE 'WET-ROCKSIL' METHOD

Repeat experiment A described in Section 7.2, using propan-2-ol instead of ethanol (cf. Figure 17).

$$CH_3-\underset{\underset{H}{|}}{\overset{\overset{OH}{|}}{C}}-CH_3 \xrightarrow{Cu} CH_3-\overset{\overset{O}{||}}{C}-CH_3 + H_2$$

Test for propanone by adding 2,4-dinitrophenylhydrazine solution (Section 7.6, experiment 8).

B. FROM ETHANOIC ACID, BY THE 'WET-ROCKSIL' METHOD

Repeat experiment A described in Section 7.2, using ethanoic acid instead of ethanol, and aluminium oxide as the catalyst.

$$2CH_3COOH \xrightarrow{Al_2O_3} CH_3-\overset{\overset{O}{||}}{C}-CH_3 + CO_2 + H_2O$$

7.6. Reactions of Ethanal

A. ETHANAL ACTING AS A REDUCING AGENT

1. **Silver mirror test.** Aldehydes reduce an ammoniacal solution of silver nitrate to silver. To 1 cm³ of a solution of silver nitrate, add 1 drop of dilute sodium hydroxide solution to form a precipitate of silver oxide. Add dilute ammonia solution, drop by drop, until the brown precipitate just redissolves. (This solution is known as Tollen's reagent.) Pour the ammoniacal solution into a clean test-tube. (The test-tube should have been thoroughly washed with water, then with propanone, and then dried.) Add 3 drops of ethanal and warm the test-tube in a beaker of boiling water. A silver mirror is deposited on the inside of the test-tube:

$$CH_3CHO + Ag_2O \longrightarrow CH_3COOH + 2Ag$$

Tollen's reagent should never be stored but made up as fresh solution. Explosive products are likely to be formed on standing.

2. **Reaction with Fehling's solution.** Fehling's solution is freshly prepared by adding solution II (or B) to 1 cm³ of solution I (or A) until the blue precipitate just redissolves to give a deep blue solution.

Solution I is made up by dissolving copper(II) sulphate in water while Solution II is an alkaline solution of sodium potassium 2,3-dihydroxybutanedioate (tartrate).

Add 3 drops of ethanal to the solution and boil the mixture for a few minutes. The red precipitate of copper(I) oxide shows that a reducing agent is present. The reaction can be represented by the equation:

$$CH_3CHO + 2CuO \longrightarrow CH_3COOH + Cu_2O$$

3. **Schiff's reagent.** (Schiff's reagent is prepared by decolorising and a red solution of fuchsine with sulphur dioxide.)

Place about 3 drops of ethanal in a test-tube. Add 2 drops of Schiff's reagent and the red colour of fuchsine is rapidly restored.

4. To 1 cm³ of dilute sulphuric acid, add 2 drops of a 1% solution of potassium permanganate. Add 2 or 3 drops of ethanal. Warm gently. Note the decolorising of the permanganate.

$$2KMnO_4 + 3H_2SO_4 + 5CH_3CHO \longrightarrow K_2SO_4$$
$$+2MnSO_4 + 3H_2O + 5CH_3COOH$$

5. Repeat the above experiment using acidified potassium dichromate solution. Note the colour change from orange to green, owing to the reduction of potassium dichromate to chromium(III) sulphate:

$$K_2Cr_2O_7 + 4H_2SO_4 + 3CH_3CHO \longrightarrow K_2SO_4$$
$$+ Cr_2(SO_4)_3 + 4H_2O + 3CH_3COOH$$

B. ADDITION REACTIONS OF ETHANAL

6. Saturate 2 cm^3 of water with sodium hydrogensulphite (metabisulphite). Pass sulphur dioxide through the solution. Add 3 drops of ethanal to the solution, shake, and leave for 1–2 hours. Crystals of the addition product, ethanal hydrogensulphite, are formed:

$$CH_3-\overset{\displaystyle H}{\underset{\displaystyle |}{C}}=O + NaHSO_3 \longrightarrow CH_3-\overset{\displaystyle H}{\underset{\displaystyle |}{\underset{\displaystyle |}{C}}}-OH$$
$$SO_3^-Na^+$$

Ethanal hydrogensulphite

7. **Preparation of ethanal-ammonia.** Place 10 cm^3 of concentrated ammonia solution (S.G. 0.880) in a test-tube, surrounded by a freezing mixture. Add 5 cm^3 of ethanal dropwise with continuous shaking. White crystals should appear after about 45 minutes. These can be filtered, washed with ether, and dried.

The molecule of ethanal-ammonia has a cyclic structure. However, the equation is often represented as:

$$CH_3-\overset{\displaystyle H}{\underset{\displaystyle |}{C}}=O + NH_3 \longrightarrow CH_3-\overset{\displaystyle H}{\underset{\displaystyle |}{\underset{\displaystyle |}{C}}}-OH$$
$$NH_2$$

Ethanal-ammonia

C. CONDENSATION REACTIONS OF ETHANAL

8. To 5 drops of a solution of 2,4-dinitrophenylhydrazine in a test-tube, add 3 drops of ethanal. (Instructions for the preparation of the reagent are given in Appendix I.) A yellow precipitate is formed, which can be centrifuged (or filtered), washed with water, and recrystallised from ethanoic acid or from ethanol. Separate (or filter) and wash again. Dry the crystals and take the melting-point of ethanal 2,4-dinitrophenylhydrazone (m.p. 168° C.).

9. Dissolve 0.5 g of semicarbazide hydrochloride and 0.5 g of sodium ethanoate in 3 cm^3 of water in a test-tube; warm to obtain a clear solution. Dissolve 0.5 cm^3 of ethanal in 3 cm^3 and add this solution to the first one.

Allow to stand, scratching the interior of the test-tube with a glass rod until crystals are formed. Centrifuge (or filter) the crystals. Separate them and then wash with water. Recrystallise from ethanol, dry, and find the melting-point. (M.p. of ethanal semicarbazone is 162° C.)

$$CH_3-\overset{\displaystyle H}{\underset{\displaystyle |}{C}}=O + H_2N-NH-CO-NH_2 \longrightarrow CH_3-\overset{\displaystyle H}{\underset{\displaystyle |}{C}}=N-NH-CO-NH_2 + H_2O$$

Ethanal semicarbazone

D. POLYMERISATION REACTIONS OF ETHANAL

10. To 3 drops of ethanal in a test-tube, add, cautiously, concentrated sodium hydroxide solution drop by drop. A brown resin is formed with a characteristic smell.

11. Place 10 drops of ethanal in a test-tube, and surround the tube with an ice-salt mixture. Add 1 drop of concentrated sulphuric acid and stir with a thermometer. Note the rise in temperature and the liquid trimer, $(CH_3CHO)_3$, rising to the surface.

12. Dissolve 1 cm^3 of ethanal in 2 cm^3 of dry ether in a test-tube. Cool the tube in an ice-salt mixture and pass dry hydrogen chloride through the solution. (Generate hydrogen chloride by adding concentrated sulphuric acid to sodium chloride. Dry the gas by passage through concentrated sulphuric acid.)
    A solid ethanal tetramer, $(CH_3CHO)_4$, crystallises out after 1–3 minutes.

E. OTHER REACTIONS OF ETHANAL

13. **The iodoform reaction.** To 5 drops of ethanal in a test-tube, add 5 drops of iodine solution and then dilute sodium hydroxide solution dropwise until the brown colour is just discharged. Warm if necessary. Observe the yellow precipitate of tri-iodomethane (iodoform).

7.7. Reactions of Methanal

Carry out the following experiments with a 40% aqueous solution of methanal (known as formalin).

1. Carry out experiments 1, 2, 3, 4, and 5 in Section 7.6, using formalin in place of ethanal. Similar results are obtained in each case. The oxidising agents used in experiments 4 and 5 oxidise methanal first to methanoic acid and finally to carbon dioxide and water.

2. Place 10 cm^3 of formalin in a small beaker. Add 10 cm^3 of 0.880 ammonia solution and evaporate the solution gently to dryness on a boiling water-bath. A white residue of a condensation product, hexamethylenetetramine, is obtained:

$$6HCHO + 4NH_3 \longrightarrow (CH_2)_6N_4 + 6H_2O$$

Contrast this reaction with that which takes place between ethanal and ammonia (in Section 7.6).

3. Carry out experiment 8 in Section 7.6, using formalin in place of ethanal. Methanal 2,4-dinitrophenylhydrazone melts at $168°$ C.

4. Repeat experiment 9 in Section 7.6, using formalin in place of ethanal. Methanal semicarbazone melts at $169°$ C with decomposition.

5. **Action with alkalis.** Carry out experiment 10 in Section 7.6, using formalin in place of ethanal. Note that methanal does not yield a resin in the presence of aqueous sodium hydroxide but instead undergoes the Cannizzaro reaction. (See also Section 26.2, experiment 9.)

$$2HCHO + NaOH \longrightarrow HCOONa + CH_3OH$$

6. Carry out experiment 13 in Section 7.6, using formalin instead of ethanal. Methanal does not undergo the iodoform reaction.

7. Place some formalin on a watch-glass, evaporating it to dryness by resting the glass on a beaker containing gently boiling water in a fumes cupboard. A white solid residue of a polymer, polymethanal $(HCHO)_n$, is obtained.

7.8. Reactions of Propanone

A. TO SHOW THAT PROPANONE IS NOT A STRONG REDUCING AGENT

1. Repeat experiments 1, 2 and 3 in Section 7.6, using propanone instead of ethanal. Propanone is not a strong reducing agent and will not undergo these reactions.

   Propanone will restore the colour to Schiff's reagent very slowly.

2. Repeat experiments 4 and 5 in Section 7.6, using propanone instead of ethanal. Propanone does not undergo these reactions so readily as the aldehydes. However, propanone will decolorise acidified potassium permanganate solution slowly.

B. ADDITION REACTION OF PROPANONE

3. Repeat experiment 6 in Section 7.6, using propanone instead of ethanal. Propanone undergoes an addition reaction with sodium hydrogensulphite.

C. CONDENSATION REACTIONS OF PROPANONE

4. Repeat experiment 8 in Section 7.6, using propanone instead of ethanal. Propanone forms a derivative. The melting-point of propanone 2,4-dinitrophenylhydrazone is 128° C.

   Experiment 8 in Section 7.6 is used to show whether or not the molecule contains a reactive carbonyl group (aldehyde or ketone). Experiments 1 and 2 in Section 7.6 can then be used to distinguish between an aldehyde and a ketone.

5. Preparation of propanone oxime. Dissolve 1 g of hydroxylamine hydrochloride in 2 cm^3 of water in a test-tube. Add 0.5 g of sodium hydroxide dissolved in 2 cm^3 of water. Cool the solution in ice. Add 10 drops of propanone, and leave the solution in a freezing mixture overnight. If no crystals should separate, shake the mixture vigorously.

Filter the crystals and dry them between filter papers. Recrystallise from petroleum ether (b.p. 40–60° C). M.p. of propanone oxime is 60°C.

$$\underset{CH_3}{\overset{CH_3}{>}}C{=}O + H_2NOH \longrightarrow \underset{CH_3}{\overset{CH_3}{>}}C{=}NOH + H_2O$$

Propanone oxime

6. Repeat experiment 9 in Section 7.6, above, using propanone instead of ethanal. M.p. of propanone semicarbazone is 187° C.

D. PROPANONE DOES NOT READILY UNDERGO POLYMERISATION REACTIONS

7. Repeat experiments 10, 11, and 12 in Section 7.6, using propanone instead of ethanal. Propanone does not undergo polymerisation reactions under these conditions.

E. OTHER REACTIONS OF PROPANONE

8. The iodoform reaction. Repeat experiment 13 in Section 7.6, using propanone instead of ethanal. Note that the precipitate appears readily in the cold.

The iodoform test is a general test for compounds whose molecules contain the CH_3CO-group attached to a hydrogen atom, an alkyl radical or an aryl radical and for substances readily oxidised to such compounds (e.g. ethanol and propan–2–ol).

8

CARBOXYLIC ACIDS AND THEIR SALTS

Functional Group $\quad -\overset{\displaystyle O}{\underset{\displaystyle \|}{C}}-O-H$

8.1. Preparation of Ethanoic Acid (Acetic Acid)

INTRODUCTION

Primary alcohols contain the $-CH_2OH$ group. Oxidation of primary alcohols yields aldehydes at first (experiment 5 in Section 5.2) and finally, with excess of the oxidising agent, carboxylic acids (experiments 4 and 5 in Section 7.6).

In this experiment ethanol is oxidised to ethanoic acid by means of a mixture of sodium dichromate and dilute sulphuric acid. In the preparation of ethanal (Section 7.1) oxidation was arrested at the aldehyde stage by adding a mixture of ethanol and aqueous sodium dichromate to hot dilute sulphuric acid. The volatile ethanal distilled over before further oxidation could take place. However if an aqueous solution of ethanol is added slowly to a solution of sodium dichromate in dilute sulphuric acid, the mixture being refluxed to prolong contact between the reactants, further oxidation to ethanoic acid occurs.

REAGENTS

Ethanol (1.5 cm^3)
Sodium dichromate (5 g)
Concentrated sulphuric acid (3.5 cm^3)

DETAILS

Place 6 cm^3 of water in a 50 cm^3 pear-shaped flask and add slowly 3.5 cm^3 of concentrated sulphuric acid in small portions. Cool the flask under the tap and gently swirl the contents. Add 5 g of sodium dichromate to the diluted acid and repeat the gentle swirling action until it has all dissolved. Introduce a few anti-bumping granules into the flask, then set up the apparatus as in Figure 19 and Plate 2. Place 1.5 cm^3 of ethanol and 5 cm^3 of water in the dropping funnel. Add the mixture dropwise to the flask which should be cooled at first in a cold water-bath. When all of the aqueous solution of ethanol has been added bring the water in the beaker gently to the boil and allow the contents of the flask to reflux for 15 minutes.

Remove the hot water-bath and arrange the flask for distillation using the apparatus shown in Figure 5 and Plate 1. The thermometer is not required and should be replaced by a stopper. Heat the flask gently over a gauze and collect about 5 cm^3 of aqueous ethanoic acid in the receiver.

Confirm the presence of ethanoic acid in the distillate by carrying out experiments 1 and 2 in Section 8.3.

There may be a small quantity of ethanal in the distillate. Carry out experiment 3 in Section 7.6 to see if this is so.

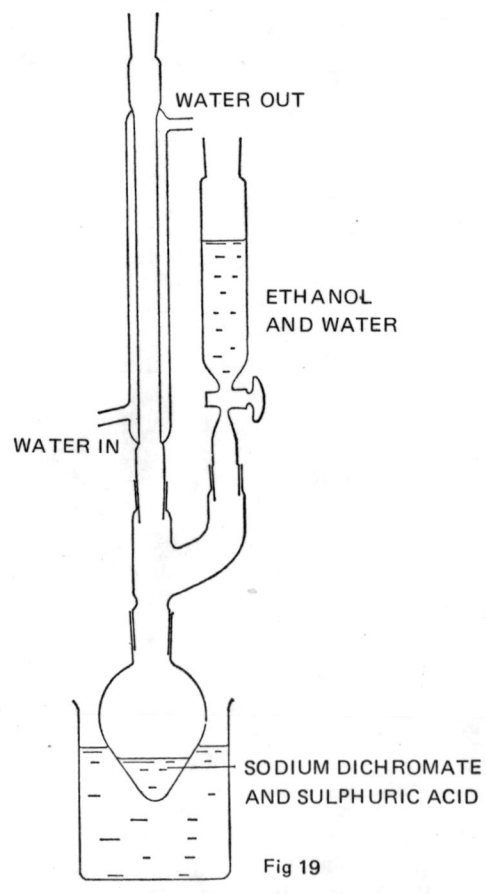

WATER OUT

ETHANOL AND WATER

WATER IN

SODIUM DICHROMATE AND SULPHURIC ACID

Fig 19

8.2. Reactions of Methanoic Acid and Methanoates

A. METHANOIC ACID AS AN ACID

1. **The iron(III) chloride test**. Make up a neutral solution of iron(III) chloride by adding a dilute solution of ammonia to 5 cm^3 of iron(III) chloride solution, until a precipitate just appears. Add the original iron(III) chloride solution, dropwise, until the precipitate just disappears.

   Place 5 drops of methanoic acid in a clean test-tube. Add a dilute solution of ammonia until just alkaline, and boil off the excess ammonia. To this neutral solution, add 5 drops of the neutral iron(III) chloride solution. Note the characteristic red colour of the iron(III) salt.

$$FeCl_3 + 3HCOONH_4 \longrightarrow (HCOO)_3\,Fe + 3NH_4\,Cl$$

Dilute the red solution of the iron(III) methanoate with an equal volume of water, then boil. Observe the brown precipitate of basic methanoate.

$$(HCOO)_3\,Fe + 2H_2\,O \longrightarrow (HCOO)Fe(OH)_2 + 2HCOOH$$

2. Place about 0.1 g of solid sodium hydrogencarbonate in a test-tube and add 3 drops of methanoic acid. Test for carbon dioxide with lime water.

$$NaHCO_3 + HCOOH \longrightarrow HCOONa + H_2\,O + CO_2$$

B. METHANOIC ACID AS A REDUCING AGENT

3. To 1 cm^3 of methanoic acid in a test-tube, add 1 cm^3 of dilute sulphuric acid and warm gently. Add a 1% solution of potassium permanganate drop by drop. Note that potassium permanganate is decolorised and that bubbles of gas (carbon dioxide) are formed:

$$2KMnO_4 + 3H_2\,SO_4 + 5HCOOH \longrightarrow$$
$$K_2\,SO_4 + 2MnSO_4 + 8H_2\,O + 5CO_2$$

4. Repeat experiment 3, using acidified potassium dichromate solution. Note that the orange colour of potassium dichromate is changed to the green colour of chromium(III) sulphate:

$$K_2\,Cr_2\,O_7 + 4H_2\,SO_4 + 3HCOOH \longrightarrow$$
$$K_2\,SO_4 + Cr_2(SO_4)_3 + 7H_2\,O + 3CO_2$$

5. To 1 cm^3 of ammoniacal silver nitrate solution (for preparation see Section 7.6, experiment 1), add 3 drops of methanoic acid. If the tube is immersed in hot water, a deposit of silver *slowly* appears.

$$Ag_2\,O + 2HCOOH \longrightarrow 2HCOOAg + H_2\,O$$
$$2HCOOAg \longrightarrow HCOOH + 2Ag + CO_2 \uparrow$$

6. To 1 cm^3 of a solution of mercury(II) chloride, add 4 drops of methanoic acid and warm gently. A white precipitate of mercury(I) chloride is slowly formed.

$$2HgCl_2 + HCOOH \longrightarrow Hg_2Cl_2 + 2HCl + CO_2$$

C. OTHER REACTIONS OF METHANOIC ACID

7. Place sodium methanoate crystals in a test-tube to a depth of 1 cm. Heat and test for hydrogen with a lighted splint.

$$\begin{matrix} H \vdots COONa \\ + \\ H \vdots COONa \end{matrix} \longrightarrow \begin{matrix} COONa \\ | \\ COONa \end{matrix} + H_2 \uparrow$$

Allow the residue to cool. Add 2 cm^3 of concentrated sulphuric acid and warm the test-tube. Test the gases evolved with (a) lime water (for carbon dioxide) and (b) a lighted splint (for carbon monoxide).

$$\begin{matrix} COONa \\ | \\ COONa \end{matrix} + H_2SO_4 \longrightarrow \begin{matrix} COOH \\ | \\ COOH \end{matrix} + Na_2SO_4$$

$$\begin{matrix} COOH \\ | \\ COOH \end{matrix} \longrightarrow H_2O + CO \uparrow + CO_2 \uparrow$$

8. To 1 cm^3 of methanoic acid in a test-tube, add 1 cm^3 of concentrated sulphuric acid and warm. Carbon monoxide is evolved, and will burn with a blue flame when ignited by a burning splint.

$$HCOOH \xrightarrow{\text{Conc. } H_2SO_4 \text{ as dehydrating agent}} CO \uparrow + H_2O$$

9. **Decomposition of methanoic acid vapour over metals.** Place methanoic acid to a depth of 2.5 cm in a test-tube and push down a plug of Rocksil wool to the bottom of the tube. Set up an apparatus similar to that in Figure 1, excluding the beaker, and having some nickel foil or copper turnings half-way along the tube. Warm the catalyst, and collect the gases in test-tubes, both by downward and upward displacement of air.

$$HCOOH \longrightarrow H_2 + CO_2$$

Test for hydrogen (with a lighted splint) and for carbon dioxide (with lime water).

8.3. Reactions of Ethanoic Acid and Ethanoates

A. ETHANOIC ACID AS AN ACID

1. **The iron(III) chloride test.** Repeat experiment 1 in Section 8.2, using ethanoic acid instead of methanoic acid. Note the red colour of iron(III) ethanoate.

2. Repeat experiment 2 in Section 8.2, using ethanoic acid instead of methanoic acid. Again, carbon dioxide is evolved.

$$NaHCO_3 + CH_3COOH \longrightarrow CH_3COONa + H_2O + CO_2 \uparrow$$

3. Esterification. Repeat experiment 2 in Section 5.2. Note the characteristic smell of ethyl ethanoate.

$$CH_3COOH + C_2H_5OH \xrightarrow{\text{H+}} CH_3COOC_2H_5 + H_2O$$

B. ETHANOIC ACID IS NOT A REDUCING AGENT

4. Repeat experiment 3, 4, 5, and 6 in Section 8.2, using ethanoic acid instead of methanoic acid. Note that ethanoic acid does not undergo these reactions, showing that it is not a reducing agent.

C. OTHER REACTIONS OF ETHANOIC ACID

5. Mix equal amounts of anhydrous sodium ethanoate and soda-lime. Place the mixture in a test-tube to a depth of about 5 cm. Set up the apparatus as in Figure 20.

Warm the test-tube and collect the gas.

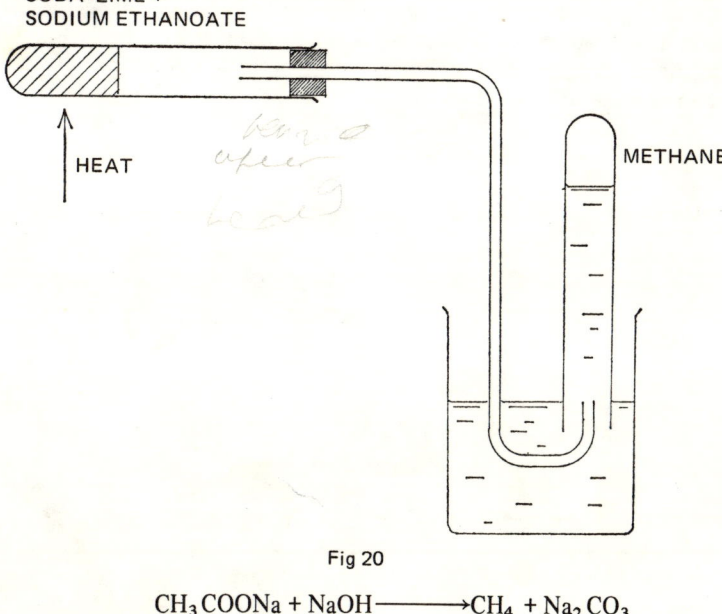

SODA–LIME + SODIUM ETHANOATE

HEAT

METHANE

Fig 20

$$CH_3COONa + NaOH \longrightarrow CH_4 + Na_2CO_3$$

Sodium ethanoate   Methane

Carry out tests for methane as described in Section 1.4.

9

DERIVATIVES OF THE CARBOXYLIC ACIDS–I, ESTERS, ACID CHLORIDES, ANHYDRIDES AND AMIDES

9.1. Small-scale Preparation of Ethyl Ethanoate

INTRODUCTION

This is an example of an **esterification**:

$$\text{Alcohol} + \text{Acid} \rightleftharpoons \text{Ester} + \text{Water.}$$

It is a reversible reaction. Under normal conditions, equilibrium is reached when only about two-thirds of the acid and alcohol have been consumed. Concentrated sulphuric acid is added, both to catalyse the reaction and to displace the equilibrium to the right, by absorbing the water formed in the reaction.

The mechanism of reaction is considered to be:

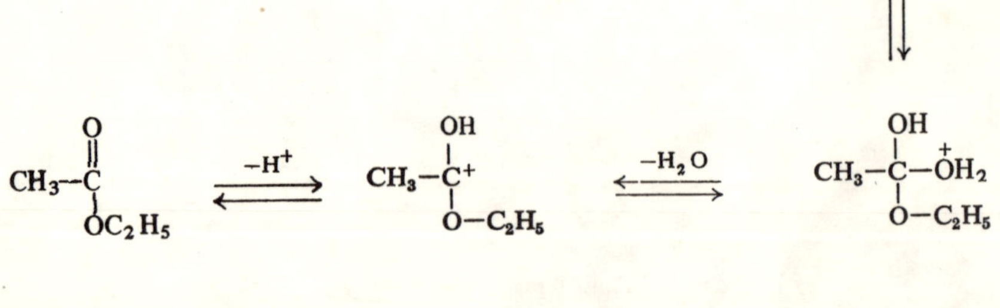

The ester is purified by neutralising excess acid (with alkali), by removing excess alcohol (with calcium chloride solution) and water (with anhydrous calcium chloride). Final purification is by redistillation.

DETAILS

Place 5 cm^3 of ethanol in the flask, immersing the latter in oil. Add slowly, and with gentle swirling, 5 cm^3 of concentrated sulphuric acid. Set up the apparatus as shown in Figure 21.

Place a mixture of 5 cm^3 of ethanol and 5 cm^3 of ethanoic acid in the dropping funnel. Raise the temperature of the oil-bath to 140° C., and then run the mixture dropwise into the flask. Add the mixture at the same rate at which the ethyl ethanoate distils over. Maintain the temperature of the oil-bath at 140° C until all of the mixture has been added.

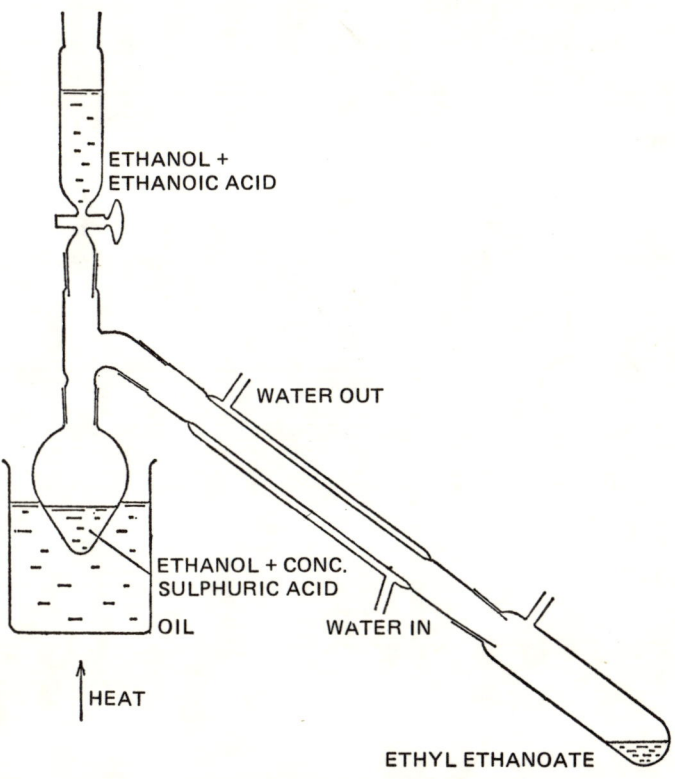

ETHANOL +
ETHANOIC ACID

WATER OUT

ETHANOL + CONC.
SULPHURIC ACID

OIL

WATER IN

HEAT

ETHYL ETHANOATE

Fig 21

After a few minutes, when the rate of distillation slackens, remove the receiver and transfer the distillate to a separating funnel or to a test-tube. Add 5 cm^3 of 30% sodium carbonate solution and shake. Remove the stopper from time to time to relieve the pressure. Test the liquid with Universal Indicator paper (or red litmus paper) to ensure that all of the ethanoic and sulphurous acids have been removed. Remove and discard the lower aqueous layer.

Dissolve 5 g of calcium chloride in 5 cm^3 of water, and add the solution to the ethyl ethanoate and shake to remove ethanol. Allow the mixture to separate.

Remove and discard the lower aqueous layer. Dry the ethyl ethanoate by allowing it to stand over 2 or 3 small pieces of anhydrous calcium chloride in a small stoppered flask or test-tube. When this liquid is no longer turbid, decant it into a dry flask.

Distil the dry ester from a water-bath (or oil-bath). Use the apparatus shown in Figure 8, gradually raising the temperature of the bath by adding hotter water, and distil off the ether, present as an impurity, over the range 34–39° C. Change the receiver and collect the fraction distilling between 75° and 79° C.

PHYSICAL CONSTANTS

B.p. 77° C; density at 20° C: 0.90 g cm^{-3}

9.2. Reactions of Esters

1. **Saponification.** Place 2 cm^3 of ethyl ethanoate and 20 cm^3 of sodium hydroxide solution (made up by dissolving 5 g of sodium hydroxide in 20 cm^3 of water) in a flask, and reflux the mixture for 30 minutes (Figure 22).

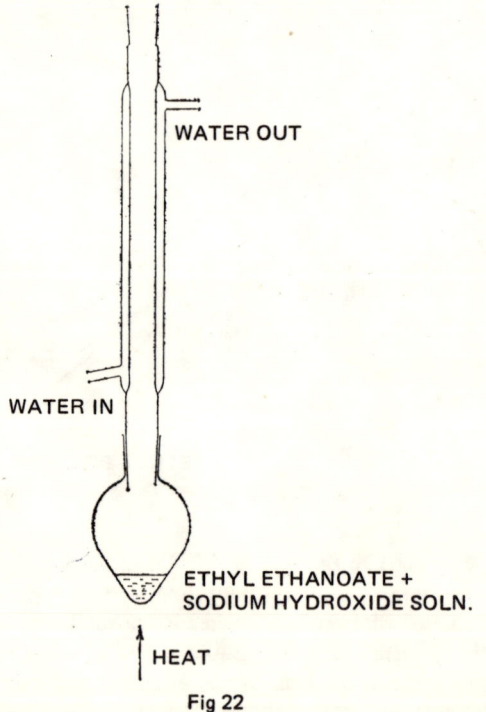

WATER OUT

WATER IN

ETHYL ETHANOATE + SODIUM HYDROXIDE SOLN.

HEAT

Fig 22

$$CH_3COOC_2H_5 + NaOH \longrightarrow CH_3COONa + C_2H_5OH$$

Distil the mixture (Figure 23, Plate 4), collecting 4–5 cm^3 of distillate. Carry out some tests for ethanol (Section 5.2, experiments 2, 5, 6, 8).

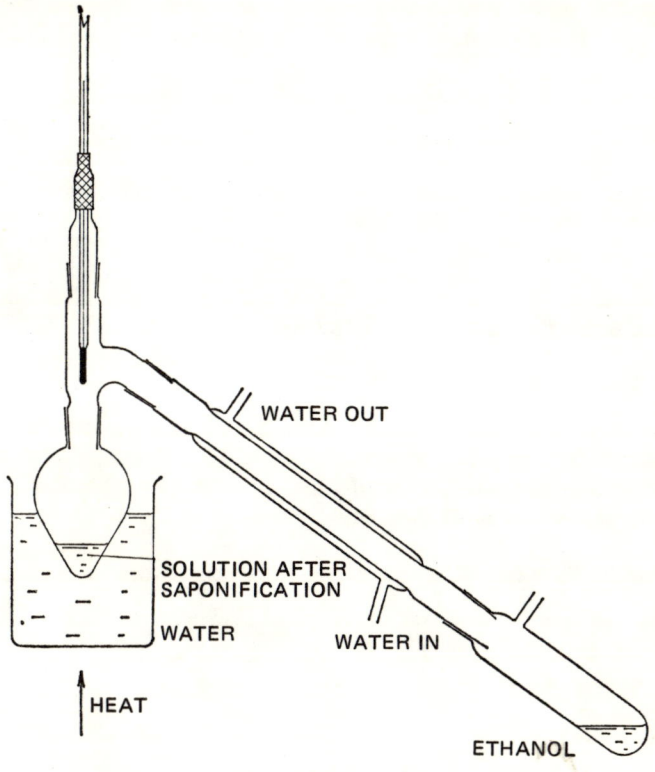

WATER OUT

SOLUTION AFTER
SAPONIFICATION

WATER

WATER IN

HEAT

ETHANOL

Fig 23

Transfer the liquid remaining to an evaporating basin, and evaporate carefully to dryness. Allow the basin to cool and add 10 cm^3 of dilute sulphuric acid to the residue. Note the smell of ethanoic acid:

$$2CH_3COONa + H_2SO_4 \longrightarrow 2CH_3COOH + Na_2SO_4$$

This solution may be distilled, and the first 5 cm^3 of distillate can be tested with neutral iron(III) chloride solution (Section 8.2, experiment 1).

2. **Hydroxamic acid test for esters.** Place 1 drop of ethyl ethanoate in a test-tube, and add 3 drops of a saturated solution of hydroxylamine hydrochloride in methanol followed by 3 drops of a saturated solution of potassium hydr-oxide in methanol. Warm the mixture until it boils, and acidify with dilute hydrochloric acid.

$$CH_3COOC_2H_5 + H_2N-OH \longrightarrow CH_3-CO-NH-OH + C_2H_5OH$$

To this solution, add one drop of iron(III) chloride solution. A red or violet coloration indicates that an ester is present.

The hydroxamic acid exhibits tautomerism:

$$R-\overset{\overset{\displaystyle O}{\|}}{C}-\overset{\overset{\displaystyle H}{|}}{N}-O-H \longleftrightarrow R-\overset{\overset{\displaystyle OH}{|}}{C}=N-O-H$$

Keto form   Enol form

Iron(III) chloride gives a characteristic colour with compounds containing the enol group (Section 24.2, experiment 3).

9.3. Small-scale Preparation of Ethanoyl Chloride

INTRODUCTION

This is another example of the substitution of a halogen atom for a hydroxyl group, using a phosphorus halide (cf. Section 4.1). Phosphorus trichloride is used for it is easily separated, by distillation, from ethanoyl chloride.

Ethanoyl chloride is purified by redistillation.

REAGENTS

Ethanoic acid (8 cm^3)
Phosphorus trichloride (4 cm^3)
Calcium chloride, anhydrous

EQUATION

$$3CH_3COOH + PCl_3 \longrightarrow 3CH_3COCl + H_3PO_3$$

DETAILS

Place 8 cm^3 of ethanoic acid in a flask, and set up the apparatus (in a fume cupboard, if possible) (Figure 24). Add 4 cm^3 of phosphorus trichloride very slowly from the dropping funnel. When all the phosphorus trichloride has been added, light the bunsen burner and raise the temperature of the water-bath to 40–45° C. Maintain the bath at this temperature until the rate of evolution of hydrogen chloride slackens. Raise the temperature of the bath to 80–90° C and maintain this temperature until distillation ceases.

Transfer the distillate to a clean flask and redistil the ethanoyl chloride. Use the apparatus as shown in Figure 24, replacing the dropping funnel by a thermometer. Slowly raise the temperature of the bath and collect the fraction distilling between 53° and 75° C.

The anhydrous calcium chloride tube is used to prevent any moisture from entering the flask, and thus reacting with the ethanoyl chloride. The ethanoyl chloride must be stored in a dry, stoppered bottle.

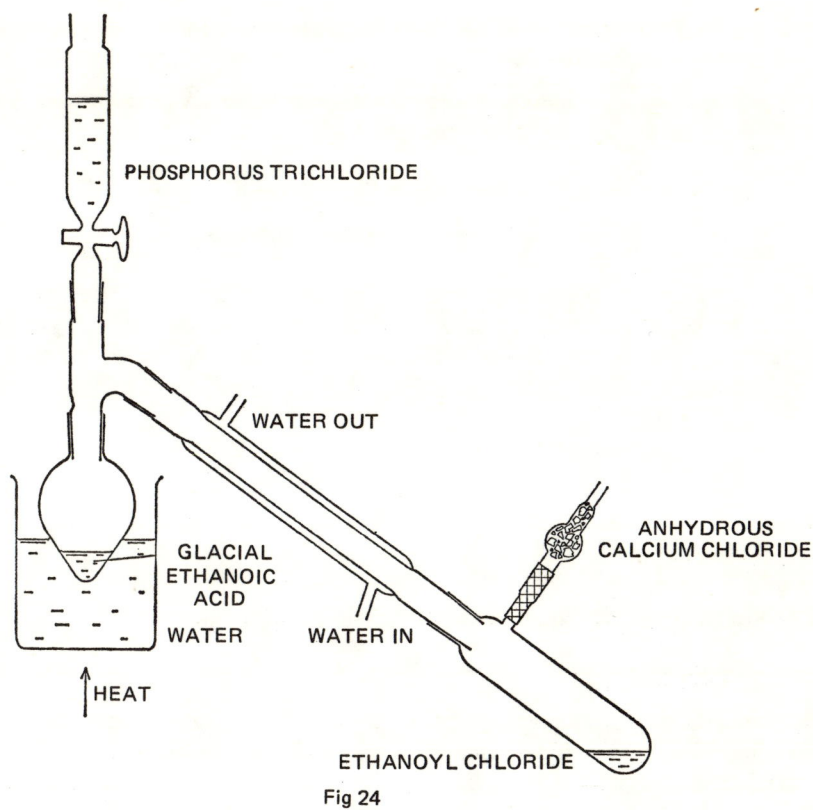

Fig 24

PHYSICAL CONSTANTS

B.p. 55° C; density at 20° C: 1.1 g cm^{-3}

9.4. Reactions of Acid Chlorides

1. Place 5 drops of ethanoyl chloride in a test-tube. Add 5 drops of water carefully. Note the vigorous reaction and the characteristic odour of ethanoic acid:

$$CH_3COCl + H_2O \longrightarrow CH_3COOH + HCl$$

Ethanoyl chloride   Ethanoic acid

Note also the fumes of hydrogen chloride, which become denser when breathed upon.

62

2. Repeat the esterification of ethanol with ethanoyl chloride. (For details, see Section 5.2, experiment 3.)

3. Ethanoylate phenylamine with ethanoyl chloride to form *N*-phenylethanamide. (For details, see Section 20.2, experiment 4.)

$$CH_3COCl + C_6H_5NH_2 \longrightarrow CH_3-CO-NH-C_6H_5 + HCl$$

Phenylamine   *N*-phenylethanamide

4. Place 10 cm³ of 0.880 ammonia solution in a beaker, then add carefully a few drops of ethanoyl chloride. A vigorous reaction takes place, yielding fumes of ammonium chloride and hydrogen chloride, together with a residue of ethanamide. This reaction should be carried out in a fume cupboard.

$$CH_3COCl + NH_3 \longrightarrow CH_3CONH_2 + HCl$$

$$HCl + NH_3 \longrightarrow NH_4Cl$$

9.5. Small-scale Preparation of Ethanoic Anhydride

INTRODUCTION

Acid anhydrides can be prepared by the dehydration of carboxylic acids. However, 'mixed' acid anhydrides cannot be prepared by this method.

The method described here, the interaction of the sodium salt of an acid and an acid chloride, can be used for the preparation of 'simple' and 'mixed' anhydrides.

Ethanoic anhydride is purified by redistillation.

REAGENTS

Sodium ethanoate (5 g if anhydrous; 10 g if crystalline)
Ethanoyl chloride (4 cm³)
Calcium chloride, anhydrous

EQUATION

$$CH_3COONa + CH_3COCl \longrightarrow (CH_3CO)_2O + NaCl$$

DETAILS

(If no anhydrous sodium ethanoate is available, heat about 10 g of crystalline sodium ethanoate in an evaporating basin. Melt the crystals to drive off the water of crystallisation. When the water has vaporised, the molten salt solidifies, melting again when the temperature is raised. After the second melting, allow to cool and grind the solid to a powder in a mortar.)

Set up an apparatus similar to that in Figure 24 (if possible, in a fume cupboard), placing 5 g of anhydrous sodium ethanoate in a dry flask and 4 cm^3 of ethanoyl chloride in the dropping funnel.

Partly immerse the flask in cold water, and add ethanoyl chloride slowly with gentle shaking. Remove the water-bath, dry the outside of the flask and heat carefully in a small, luminous bunsen flame. Collect the distillate in a dry receiver.

Transfer the distillate to a clean, dry flask. Redistil the ethanoic anhydride (cf. Figure 25) and collect the fraction distilling in the range 135–140° C in a clean, dry receiver.

PHYSICAL CONSTANTS

B.p. 138° C; density at 20° C: 1.08 g cm^{-3}

9.6. Reactions of Ethanoic Anhydride

1. To 5 drops of ethanoic anhydride in a test-tube, add 5 drops of water. Note that the reaction is very slow compared with the action of water on ethanoyl chloride.

$$(CH_3CO)_2O + H_2O \longrightarrow 2CH_3COOH$$

2. Ethanoylate phenylamine with ethanoic anhydride to form N-phenylethanamide (Section 20.2, experiment 5).

$$(CH_3CO)_2O + C_6H_5NH_2 \longrightarrow CH_3{-}CO{-}NH{-}C_6H_5 + CH_3COOH$$

3. Ethanoylate phenol, dissolved in sodium hydroxide solution, with ethanoic anhydride to form phenyl ethanoate.

$$(CH_3CO)_2O + C_6H_5ONa \longrightarrow CH_3{-}CO{-}OC_6H_5 + CH_3COONa$$

Place 0.5 g of phenol in a test-tube and add 4 cm^3 of dilute sodium hydroxide solution followed by 1 cm^3 of ethanoic anhydride. Fit a cork to the test-tube, then shake for a few minutes. An emulsion of phenyl ethanoate is obtained. Note the odour of the ester.

9.7. Small-scale Preparation of Ethanamide

INTRODUCTION

Acid amides are generally prepared by the dehydration of the ammonium salts of the corresponding acids. In the preparation of ethanamide, dehydration of ammonium ethanoate is carried out by heating in the presence of ethanoic acid. The acid not only assists in the removal of the elements of water from ammonium ethanoate but also prevents thermal dissociation of the ammonium salt:

$$CH_3COONH_4 \rightleftharpoons CH_3COOH + NH_3$$

Excess ethanoic acid alters the position of equilibrium to the left so that the ethanoic acid and ammonia remain combined as ammonium ethanoate.

The ammonium salt is prepared during the preparation by the reaction between ethanoic acid and ammonium carbonate.

Ethanamide is purified by redistillation.

REAGENTS

Ammonium carbonate (3 g)
Ethanoic acid (6 cm^3)

EQUATIONS

$$2CH_3COOH + (NH_4)_2CO_3 \longrightarrow 2CH_3COONH_4 + CO_2 + H_2O$$

$$CH_3COONH_4 \longrightarrow CH_3CONH_2 + H_2O$$

DETAILS

Place 3 g of ammonium carbonate in the flask. Add ethanoic acid carefully. Boil gently under reflux for half an hour (cf. Figure 22) to convert the ammonium ethanoate into ethanamide.

Allow the apparatus to cool and arrange the apparatus for distillation, using a bunsen burner (cf. Figure 25 and Plate 1).

Heat the flask but do not allow the thermometer reading to exceed 180° C. Reject the distillate, which consists mainly of water and ethanoic acid. Clean and dry the receiver and attach it to the condenser again. Continue the distillation, using the condenser as an air condenser. Collect the fraction in the range 210–225° C.

The distillate solidifies on cooling and may be purified by recrystallisation from propanone.

PHYSICAL CONSTANTS

M.p. 82° C; B.p. 222° C.

9.8. Reactions of Acid Amides

1. To about 0.1 g of ethanamide in a test-tube, add 2 cm^3 of dilute sodium hydroxide solution. Boil, and test the vapour evolved with moist Universal Indicator paper (or red litmus paper). Note also the smell of ammonia.

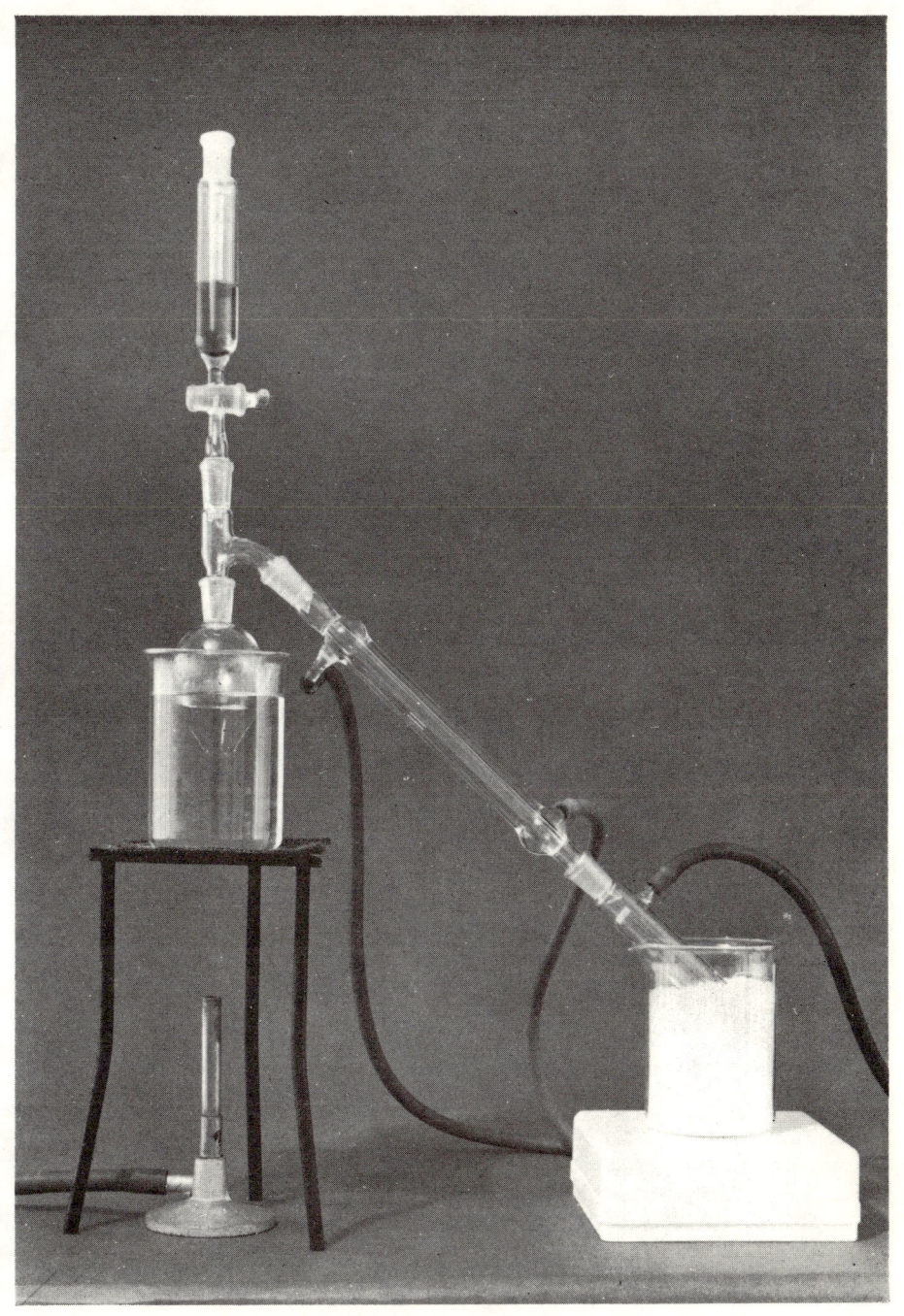

PLATE 3
Preparation of diethyl ether (Fig. 15, p. 38).

$$CH_3CONH_2 + H_2O \longrightarrow CH_3COONH_4$$

Ethanamide   Ammonium ethanoate

$$CH_3COONH_4 + NaOH \longrightarrow CH_3COONa + H_2O + NH_3 \uparrow$$

2. To about 0.1 g of ethanamide in a test-tube, add 3 drops of bromine (CARE). Add 2 cm^3 of dilute sodium hydroxide solution. Cork the test-tube and shake for about 2 minutes. Remove the cork, add 1 pellet of sodium hydroxide, and boil the solution gently. Note the fishy, ammoniacal smell of methylamine. Test the vapour with moist Universal Indicator paper (or red litmus paper):

$$CH_3CONH_2 + Br_2 + 4NaOH \longrightarrow CH_3NH_2 + Na_2CO_3 + 2NaBr + 2H_2O$$

Ethanamide   Methylamine

In this reaction the molecule of the amine contains 1 carbon atom less than the molecule of the parent amide. The reaction is known as the **Hofmann degradation.**

3. Dissolve 0.1 g of ethanamide in 1 cm^3 of water. Add 0.2 g of sodium nitrite and shake until it has dissolved. Add dilute hydrochloric acid dropwise until the solution is just acid to litmus. Note the evolution of nitrogen, together with a small amount of nitrogen dioxide formed by decomposition of some of the nitrous acid.

$$CH_3CONH_2 + HNO_2 \longrightarrow CH_3COOH + N_2 + H_2O$$

$$(3HNO_2 \longrightarrow HNO_3 + H_2O + 2NO; \; 2NO + O_2 \longrightarrow 2NO_2)$$

When effervescence has ceased, make the solution just alkaline with aqueous ammonia. Boil the solution to expel excess ammonia, allow to cool and add neutral iron(III) chloride solution dropwise (Section 8.2, experiment 1). Note the blood-red solution of iron(III) ethanoate.

4. **Ethanamide is amphoteric.** It will react as an acid with mercury(II) oxide, a basic oxide.

    Dissolve 1 g of ethanamide in 2 cm^3 of water. Add a few grains of yellow mercury(II) oxide. Warm gently. The oxide dissolves to form a soluble salt.

$$2CH_3CONH_2 + HgO \longrightarrow (CH_3CONH)_2Hg + H_2O$$

Ethanamide also reacts with strong acids to form unstable salts, e.g. $[CH_3CONH_3]^+Cl^-$, which decompose in the presence of water.

10

DERIVATIVES OF THE CARBOXYLIC ACIDS–II, ACID NITRILES (Alkyl cyanides)

10.1 Small-scale Preparation of Ethanonitrile (Methyl Cyanide)

INTRODUCTION

Acid nitriles can be prepared by the dehydration of acid amides. Phosphorus(V) oxide is often used as the dehydrating agent.

The acid nitriles is purified by distillation over phosphorus(V) oxide, which decomposes excess acid amide.

REAGENTS

Ethanamide
Phosphorus(V) oxide (8.5 g)
Potassium carbonate, anhydrous

EQUATIONS

$$CH_3 CONH_2 \xrightarrow[\text{dehydrating agent}]{P_4 O_{10} \text{ as a}} CH_3 CN + H_2 O$$

$$(P_4 O_{10} + 2H_2 O \longrightarrow 4HPO_3)$$

DETAILS

Place 4 g of dry ethanamide into the clean, dry flask. Weigh out about 8 g of phosphorus(V) oxide; transfer it immediately to the flask and shake to mix the solids. Fit the flask with a water condenser and a dry receiver (Figure 25 and Plate 1).

Heat the flask gently with a naked, luminous bunsen flame so that the ethanonitrile distils slowly. Frothing occurs during the reactions.

Transfer the crude ethanonitrile to a separating funnel or test-tube, add 1 cm³ of water and enough powdered anhydrous potassium carbonate to saturate the lower aqueous layer. Stopper the dropping funnel (or test-tube), shake, and leave for about 15 minutes. Remove the stopper from time to time to release carbon dioxide formed when ethanoic acid, present as an impurity, reacts with the potassium carbonate. Remove and discard the lower aqueous layer.

68

Transfer the ethanonitrile to a clean, dry flask, add 0.5 g of phosphorus(V) oxide, and distil (cf. Figure 25). Collect the fraction distilling in the range 80–82° C.

PHYSICAL CONSTANTS

B.p. 81° C; density at 20° C: 0.79 g cm^{-3}

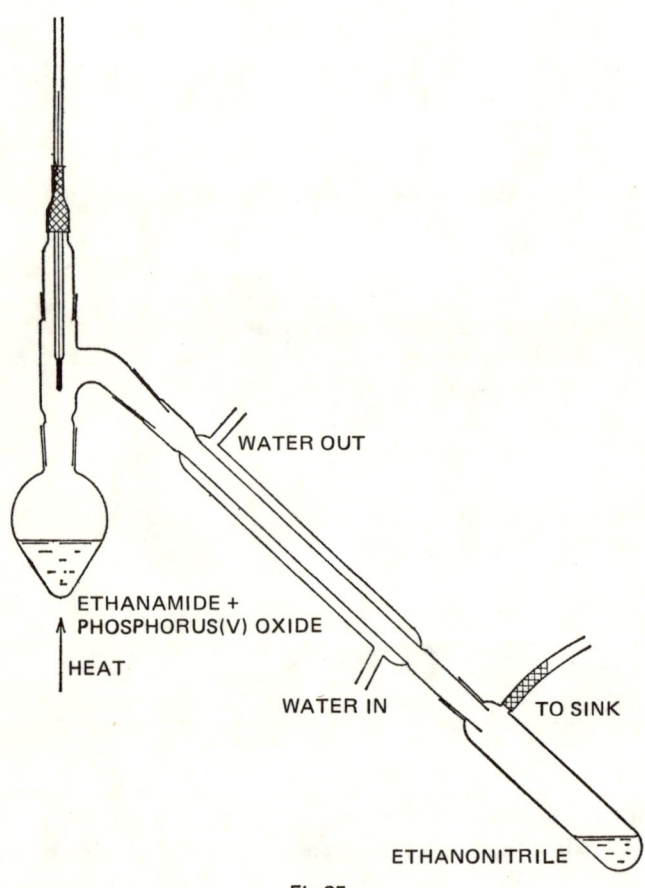

Fig 25

10.2. Reactions of Ethanonitrile

Both the following reactions indicate the **unsaturated** nature of the nitrile group.

1. To 5 drops of ethanonitrile, add 5 drops of dilute sodium hydroxide solution. Warm. Test the gas evolved with Universal Indicator paper (or with red litmus paper).

$$CH_3CN + H_2O \longrightarrow CH_3CONH_2$$
Ethanamide

$$CH_3CONH_2 + H_2O \longrightarrow CH_3COONH_4$$
Ammonium ethanoate

$$CH_3COONH_4 + NaOH \longrightarrow CH_3COONa + H_2O + NH_3 \uparrow$$

2. **Mendius's reaction.** To 5 drops of ethanonitrile, add 0.1 g of zinc dust and 5 drops of concentrated hydrochloric acid.

$$CH_3CN + 2H_2 \longrightarrow CH_3CH_2NH_2$$
Ethylamine

$$CH_3CH_2NH_2 + HCl \longrightarrow [CH_3CH_2NH_3]^+Cl^-$$
Ethyl ammonium
chloride

When the evolution of hydrogen has subsided, add dilute sodium hydroxide solution until the solution is alkaline. Warm, to liberate ethylamine.

Note the characteristic odour of ethylamine and test the gas with moist Universal Indicator paper (or red litmus paper).

$$[CH_3CH_2NH_3]^+Cl^- + NaOH \longrightarrow CH_3CH_2NH_2 + NaCl + H_2O$$
Ethylamine

11

ALIPHATIC AMINES

Functional Groups $-NH_2$; $>NH$; $\geqslant N$

11.1 Small-scale Preparation of Methylamine and Methylammonium chloride

INTRODUCTION

Amines can be prepared from acid amides by the **Hofmann degradation**. The molecule of the amine contains 1 carbon atom less than that of the acid amide. The reaction is thus used in the descent of the homologous series.

REAGENTS

Ethanamide (2 g)
Bromine (2 cm^3)
Sodium hydroxide (6 g) *or* potassium hydroxide (8 g)
Dilute hydrochloric acid (20 cm^3)

EQUATIONS

The reactions involved may be represented thus:

$$CH_3CONH_2 + Br_2 + 4NaOH \longrightarrow CH_3NH_2 + 2NaBr + Na_2CO_3 + 2H_2O$$

$$CH_3NH_2 + HCl \longrightarrow [CH_3NH_3]^+Cl^-$$

$$[CH_3NH_3]^+Cl^- + NaOH \longrightarrow CH_3NH_2 + NaCl + H_2O$$

DETAILS

Place 2 g of ethanamide and 2 cm^3 of bromine in a boiling-tube. Add 2 g of sodium (or potassium) hydroxide dissolved in 10 cm^3 of water, shaking the tube gently under a stream of cold water. A pale yellow solution of sodium bromo-ethanamide is formed.

Dissolve 4 g of sodium hydroxide (or 6 g of potassium hydroxide) in 10 cm^3

of water in a second boiling-tube and pour the solution of sodium hydroxide into the flask (Figure 26).

Place the solution of sodium bromoethanamide in the dropping funnel.

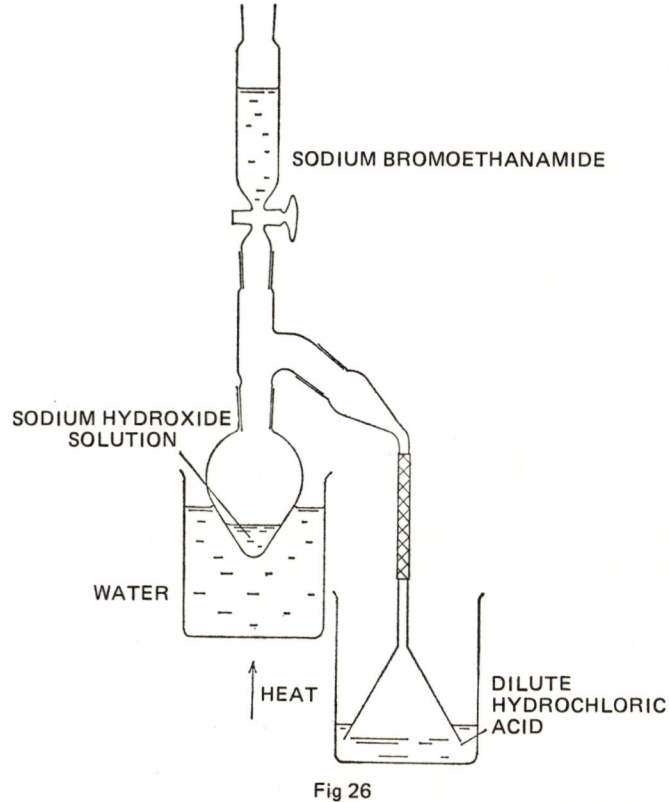

Fig 26

Heat the flask to 70° C in a water-bath, and add the sodium bromoethanamide solution carefully so that the temperature of the bath does not rise above 75° C. When all the solution has been added, maintain the mixture at about 70° C for a further 15 minutes.

Remove the water-bath and boil the solution to drive over the methylamine, which is absorbed in dilute hydrochloric acid. An inverted funnel is used to prevent sucking back.

Transfer the solution of methylammonium chloride to an evaporating basin, and evaporate the solution just to dryness on a water-bath.

Dissolve the crystals in a minimum of ethanol and filter the hot solution. (The insoluble solid impurities contain ammonium chloride formed as a by-product owing to the alkaline hydrolysis of ethanamide.) Allow the alcoholic solution to cool. Filter off the crystals of methylammonium chloride, using a Hirsch funnel (Figure 13(a)).

To liberate free methylamine, add dilute sodium hydroxide solution to a few crystals in a test-tube. Warm and note the characteristic fishy odour of the amine. Note that the vapour turns Universal Indicator paper (or red litmus paper) blue.

PHYSICAL CONSTANTS

Methylamine: B.p.–7° C.
Methylammonium chloride: M.p. 225° C.

11.2. Test-tube Preparation of Methylamine

For details, see Section 9.8, experiment 2.

11.3. Reactions of Methylamine and Ethylamine

Note the similarity of ammonia to the primary amines, methylamine and ethylamine. **Do each experiment with both a primary amine and with ammonia.**

1. Place about 2 cm^3 of an aqueous solution of methylamine or ethylamine in a beaker. Test the vapour with moist Universal Indicator paper (or red litmus paper).

$$CH_3NH_2 + H_2O \longrightarrow [CH_3NH_3]^+ + OH^-$$
$$cf. \ NH_3 + H_2O \longrightarrow [NH_4]^+ + OH^-$$

2. Hang a drop of concentrated hydrochloric acid, on a glass rod, above the solution of the amine. Note the white fumes of the alkylammonium chloride.

$$CH_3NH_2 + HCl \longrightarrow [CH_3NH_3]^+Cl^-$$
$$cf. \ NH_3 + HCl \longrightarrow [NH_4]^+Cl^-$$

3. To 1 g of methylammonium chloride in a test-tube, add 5 cm^3 of dilute sodium hydroxide solution. Boil gently. Test the vapour with moist Universal Indicator paper (or red litmus paper). Note the smell of the gas.

$$[CH_3NH_3]^+Cl^- + NaOH \longrightarrow CH_3NH_2 + NaCl + H_2O$$

Apply a lighted splint to the vapour and note that it burns in air. Contrast the behaviour of ammonia which burns only in oxygen.

4. To a solution of methylammonium chloride (1 g in 5 cm^3 of water), add a few crystals of sodium nitrite. Note the evolution of nitrogen.

$$CH_3NH_2 + HNO_2 \longrightarrow CH_3OH + N_2 + H_2O$$

(Only a small amount of methanol is formed. There are several side reactions.)

5. To 1 cm^3 of an aqueous solution of either methylamine or ethylamine, in a test-tube add ethanoyl chloride drop by drop. **Care, use a fume cupboard.**

$$CH_3NH_2 + CH_3COCl \longrightarrow CH_3{-}NH{-}CO{-}CH_3 + HCl$$

The solid product is a substituted amide, N-methylethanamide.

6. To 5 cm^3 of a copper(II) sulphate solution in a test-tube, add an aqueous solution of either methylamine or ethylamine, dropwise. A pale blue precipitate is first formed, which dissolves in excess amine solution to give a deep blue solution, containing complex copper(II) ions.

11.4. Reactions of Secondary Amines

1. To 1 cm^3 of water in a test-tube, add 2 drops of diethylamine. Note that the amine is completely miscible with water and that the solution is alkaline to Universal Indicator paper (or red litmus paper):

$$(C_2H_5)_2NH + H_2O \longrightarrow [(C_2H_5)_2NH_2]^+ + OH^-$$

2. Hang a drop of concentrated hydrochloric acid, on a glass rod, above the solution. Note the white fumes of the dialkylammonium chloride:

$$(C_2H_5)_2NH + HCl \longrightarrow [(C_2H_5)_2NH_2]^+Cl^-$$

3. To 1 g of diethylammonium chloride in a test-tube, add 5 cm^3 of dilute sodium hydroxide solution. Boil gently. Test the vapour with moist Universal Indicator paper (or red litmus paper). Note also the smell of the gas.

$$[(C_2H_2)_2NH_2]^+Cl^- + NaOH \longrightarrow (C_2H_5)_2NH + NaCl + H_2O$$

4. To a solution of diethylammonium chloride (1 g in 5 cm^3 of water), add a few crystals of sodium nitrite. A yellow oil separates and no nitrogen is evolved:

$$(C_2H_5)_2NH + HNO_2 \longrightarrow (C_2H_5)_2N{-}N{=}O + H_2O$$

N,N-Diethylnitrosamine

5. To an aqueous solution of diethylamine in a test-tube, add ethanoyl chloride dropwise. A white precipitate is formed:

$$(C_2H_5)_2NH + CH_3COCl \longrightarrow (C_2H_5)_2-N-CO-CH_3 + HCl$$

N, N-diethylethanamide

11.5. Reactions of Tertiary Amines

1. Repeat experiments 1, 2, and 3 in Section 11.4, using triethylamine instead of diethylamine. Similar results are obtained, showing that the tertiary amine is a base.

2. Repeat experiment 4 in Section 11.4, using triethylamine instead of diethylamine. Neither nitrogen nor a nitrosamine is formed.

3. Repeat experiment 5 in Section 11.4, using triethylamine instead of diethylamine. No substituted amide can be formed.

12

NITROALKANES

Functional Group $-N\overset{\displaystyle O}{\underset{\displaystyle O}{\diagup}}$

12.1 Reactions of Nitroethane

1. To 10 drops of nitroethane in a test-tube, add 1 cm^3 of dilute sodium hydroxide solution and a small quantity (0.5 cm on the end of a wooden splint) of powdered aluminium or Devarda's alloy. Warm gently to start the reaction.

   When the evolution of hydrogen ceases, warm the solution and note the characteristic smell of ethylamine, and that the vapour turns moist Universal Indicator paper (or red litmus paper) blue.

$$C_2H_5NO_2 + 3H_2 \longrightarrow C_2H_5NH_2 + 2H_2O$$

2. To 10 drops of water in a test-tube, add 2 drops of nitroethane. Allow the liquid to settle and note that the nitroalkane is not very soluble in water.

3. To 10 drops of dilute sodium hydroxide solution in a test-tube, add 2 drops of nitroethane. Note that the nitroalkane readily dissolves.

   In common with other nitroalkanes, nitroethane exhibits tautomerism.

$$CH_3-CH_2-N\overset{\displaystyle O}{\underset{\displaystyle O}{\diagup}} \rightleftharpoons CH_3-CH=N\overset{\displaystyle OH}{\underset{\displaystyle O}{\diagup}}$$

aci-form

The sodium hydroxide reacts with the aci-form, displacing the equilibrium to the right.

$$CH_3-CH=N\overset{\displaystyle OH}{\underset{\displaystyle O}{\diagup}} + Na^+ + OH^- \longrightarrow \left[CH_3-CH=N\overset{\displaystyle O}{\underset{\displaystyle O}{\diagup}}\right]^- Na^+ + H_2O$$

4. To 0.5 cm^3 of an alcoholic solution of potassium hydroxide in a test-tube, add 10 drops of nitroethane. To 1 drop of this solution, add 3 drops of iron(III) chloride solution.

Note the red coloration and compare this with the test for an enol group (Section 24.2, experiment 3).

13

CARBAMIDE (Urea)

$$O=C \begin{matrix} \diagup N \diagdown \begin{matrix} H \\ H \end{matrix} \\ \diagdown N \diagdown \begin{matrix} H \\ H \end{matrix} \end{matrix}$$

The structure of carbamide is a resonance hybrid of the canonical structures:

$$\bar{O}-C \begin{matrix} \diagup \overset{+}{N}H_2 \\ \diagdown NH_2 \end{matrix} \qquad O=C \begin{matrix} \diagup NH_2 \\ \diagdown NH_2 \end{matrix} \qquad \bar{O}-C \begin{matrix} \diagup NH_2 \\ \diagdown \overset{+}{N}H_2 \end{matrix}$$

$$\text{I} \qquad\qquad \text{II} \qquad\qquad \text{III}$$

Structures I and III account for carbamide being a monoacidic base, and, owing to the polarity of the molecules, a crystalline solid.

13.1 Reactions of Carbamide

1. Carbamide acts as a monoacidic base.
    To 1 cm^3 of water in a test-tube, add a few crystals of carbamide, warming the solution. Add more crystals until the solution is just saturated. Cool and decant the solution into a clean test-tube. Add concentrated nitric acid dropwise to the solution. A white precipitate of carbamide nitrate is formed:

$$CO(NH_2)_2 + HNO_3 \longrightarrow CO(NH_2)_2 . HNO_3$$

      Carbamide   Carbamide nitrate

2. Carbamide undergoes hydrolysis.

(a) Place about 0.1 g of carbamide in a test-tube. Add 1 cm^3 of dilute sodium hydroxide solution and bring gently to the boil. Test the vapour evolved with moist Universal Indicator paper (or red litmus paper). Note the smell of ammonia:

$$CO(NH_2)_2 + 2NaOH \longrightarrow Na_2CO_3 + 2NH_3$$

This reaction demonstrates the presence of an amide group, $-CONH_2$. Carbamide is hydrolysed to carbon dioxide and ammonia but the carbon dioxide is absorbed by the alkali to form sodium carbonate.

(b) Action of the enzyme, urease. To an aqueous solution of carbamide in a test-tube, add a tablet of urease (or some soya flour, which contains urease) and stand the test-tube in a beaker of water at 40° C for a minute. Test the gas evolved with moist Universal Indicator paper (or red litmus paper) to show the presence of ammonia.

$$H_2N-CO-NH_2 + H_2O \xrightarrow{\text{Urease}} 2NH_3 + CO_2$$

In both these examples, the molecule of carbamide has been decomposed:

$$H_2N-\overset{\overset{\displaystyle O}{\|}}{C}-NH_2 \atop H-O-H \longrightarrow NH_3 + CO_2 + NH_3$$

3. The carbamide molecule contains two amino groups ($-NH_2$). It, therefore, reacts with nitrous acid to yield nitrogen:

$$H_2N.CO.NH_2 + 2HNO_2 \longrightarrow CO_2 + 2N_2 + 3H_2O$$

Place about 0.1 g of carbamide in a test-tube and add 3 cm^3 of dilute hydrochloric acid. Add a few crystals of sodium nitrite, and note the liberation of a colourless gas.

4. Carbamide can be oxidised. To 1 cm^3 of a saturated aqueous solution of carbamide, add sodium hypochlorite solution dropwise. Nitrogen is evolved but not carbon dioxide, which reacts with the sodium hydroxide present to form sodium carbonate.

$$H_2NCONH_2 + 3NaOCl + 2NaOH \longrightarrow 3NaCl + Na_2CO_3 + 3H_2O + N_2$$

5. **Action of heat.** Place about 0.1 g of carbamide in a dry test-tube and heat. The solid melts and after a short time, ammonia is evolved. This can be identified by its smell and by its action on moist Universal Indicator paper (or red litmus paper). Continue to heat the residue gently:

$$H_2N-CO-NH_2 + H_2N-CO-NH_2 \longrightarrow$$

$$H_2N-CO-NH-CO-NH_2 + NH_3$$
Biuret

Allow the tube to cool, and dissolve the residue in about 5 drops of water. Add 2 drops of copper(II) sulphate solution followed by dilute sodium hydroxide solution dropwise, until the solution is alkaline. A violet coloration confirms the presence of biuret. **The Biuret test** is used to confirm the presence of the peptide link, $-CO-NH-$, in a molecule (for example, to show the presence of a protein) (Section 14.4).

6. If the carbamide is heated strongly, a white sublimate of cyanuric acid is deposited in the cooler regions of the test-tube:

$$3H_2N-CO-NH_2 \longrightarrow (HOCN)_3 + 3NH_3$$
Cyanuric
acid

14

AMINO ACIDS AND PROTEINS

14.1 Preparation of Glycine (Aminoethanoic acid)

Make a solution of ammonia by adding 4 cm^3 of concentrated ammonia solution to 4 cm^3 of water. Add 2 g of monochloroethanoic acid:

$$Cl-CH_2-COOH + 3NH_3 \longrightarrow H_2N-CH_2-COONH_4 + NH_4Cl$$

Shake the mixture well and leave for about an hour. Add solid copper(II) carbonate until no more will react and there is excess copper(II) carbonate.

$$2H_2N-CH_2-COONH_4 + CuCO_3 \longrightarrow$$
$$(H_2N-CH_2-COO)_2Cu + 2NH_3 + CO_2 + H_2O$$

Using a Hirsch funnel (Figure 13(a)), filter at the pump, evaporate and crystallise out copper(II) glycine. Dissolve the crystals in water and pass hydrogen sulphide through the solution.

$$(H_2N-CH_2-COO)_2Cu + H_2S \longrightarrow 2H_2N-CH_2-COOH + CuS \downarrow$$

Filter the precipitate (or separate by centrifuge) and evaporate the filtrate to obtain crystals of glycine.

14.2 Reactions of Glycine

Amino acids are white crystalline compounds which dissolve in water but do not dissolve in organic solvents. They have high melting-points.

Their structure is a dipolar ion (a zwitter ion). For example, glycine has the structure:

$$H_3\overset{+}{N}-CH_2-COO^-$$

1. Test the solubility of glycine in (a) ethanol, (b) diethyl ether. Glycine, being a highly polar compound, is almost insoluble in these solvents.

2. Dissolve a small amount of glycine in water. Add Universal Indicator solution. Although glycine yields a neutral aqueous solution it will, nevertheless, react with both acids and bases to form salts.

3. To form a salt with an acid, dissolve 1 g of glycine in a very small quantity (a few drops) of concentrated hydrochloric acid that has been previously heated just to the boiling-point without much loss of hydrogen chloride. Cool the mixture. A salt separates out.

$$H_3\overset{+}{N}-CH_2-COO^- + H^+ + Cl^- \longrightarrow [H_3\overset{+}{N}-CH_2-COOH]\,Cl^-$$

4. To form a salt with a base, dissolve 1 g of glycine in 10 cm^3 of water and heat the solution. Stir in copper(II) carbonate until effervescence stops. Copper(II) glycine is produced.

$$CuCO_3 + 2H_2N-CH_2COOH \longrightarrow (H_2N-CH_2COO)_2Cu + H_2O + CO_2$$

Boil the mixture and decant the solution into a test-tube. Blue crystals of copper(II) glycine separate out.

5. Glycine dissolves slowly in 5% sodium hydrogencarbonate solution. Carbon dioxide is not evolved so readily as by monocarboxylic acids (Section 8.2, experiment 2).

6. Dissolve 0.1 g of glycine in 1 cm^3 of water in a test-tube. Place 1 cm^3 of water in a second test-tube. To each of the tubes, add 5 drops of iron(III) chloride solution. Contrast the deeper orange-red colour of the solution in the first test-tube.

7. To about 1 cm^3 of ice-cold solution of sodium nitrite, add 1 cm^3 of dilute hydrochloric acid. Some decomposition of the nitrous acid formed will occur. When the effervescence has subsided, introduce a few crystals (or a few drops of a concentrated aqueous solution) of glycine. Effervescence occurs again as nitrogen is evolved:

$$H_2N-CH_2-COOH + HNO_2 \longrightarrow HO-CH_2-COOH + H_2O + N_2$$
$$\text{Hydroxyethanoic acid}$$

8. Glycine will undergo the carbylamine reaction, characteristic of the amino group (Section 4.11, experiment 2).

9. Heat a mixture of about 0.5 g of glycine and 1 g of soda-lime in a Pyrex test-tube. Decarboxylation of the glycine occurs while methylamine vapour is evolved. Test for the latter by holding a piece of moist Universal Indicator paper (or red litmus paper) in the vapour:

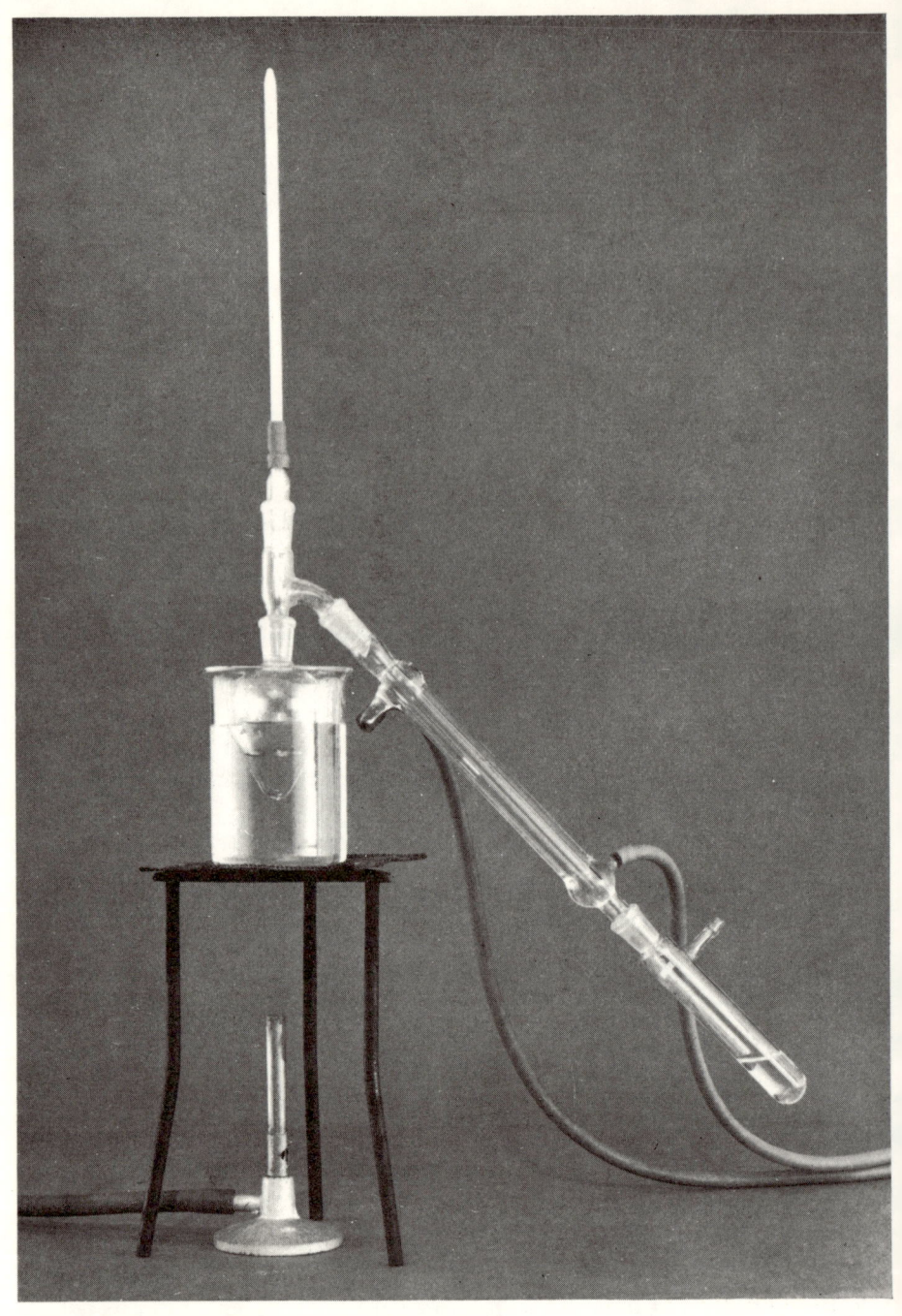

PLATE 4

Apparatus to collect ethanol following the saponification of an ester (Fig. 21, p. 57 and p. 142).

$$H_2N—CH_2—COOH + NaOH \longrightarrow H_2N—CH_2—COONa + H_2O$$

$$H_2N—CH_2—COONa + NaOH \longrightarrow CH_3NH_2 + Na_2CO_3$$

Charring occurs, and other vapours are evolved.

10. Separation of amino acids by paper chromatography (Section 32.5).

14.3. Preparation of a Protein Solution

A. PREPARATION OF AN EGG ALBUMEN SOLUTION

Dissolve the white of an egg in 5 times its own volume of water, adding about 1 g of sodium chloride. The salt helps the albumen to dissolve. Filter the solution (preferably through a muslin cloth).

B. PREPARATION OF A BLOOD SERUM SOLUTION

For a large number of experiments, mix a pint of fresh blood with a solution of 1.5 g of sodium ethanedioate in 100 cm^3 of water to remove calcium ions. Either filter or centrifuge the solution, and dilute the solution to about 10 times its volume for the tests in Section 14.4.

14.4. Reactions of a Protein Solution

1. **Denaturing of proteins.** Test 2 cm^3 portions for precipitation by (a) boiling, (b) adding dilute sulphuric acid, (c) adding dilute sodium hydroxide solution, (d) adding ethanol.

2. **Biuret test.** To a 2 cm^3 portion of egg albumen solution, add 2 cm^3 of sodium hydroxide solution, followed by 2 drops of copper(II) sulphate solution. Note the violet colour, showing the presence of the peptide link (Section 13.1, experiment 5).

3. **Arginine test.** Many proteins contain arginine

$$\overset{\displaystyle NH_2}{\underset{\displaystyle |}{}} \qquad \overset{\displaystyle NH_2}{\underset{\displaystyle |}{}}$$
$$HN\!=\!C—NH—CH_2—CH_2—CH_2—CH—COOH$$

Add dilute sodium hydroxide solution to 1 cm^3 of the protein solution in a test-tube, until it is alkaline. Add 2 drops of a 2% solution of naphthanen-1-ol in ethanol and 2 drops of sodium hypochlorite solution. Note a bright-red coloration, indicating the presence of arginine.

4. Test for sulphur. Place 5 drops of lead(II) ethanoate solution in a test-tube. Add dilute sodium hydroxide solution dropwise until the first-formed white precipitate of lead(II) hydroxide just dissolves. Add 1 cm^3 of protein solution and boil. A black precipitate of lead(II) sulphide indicates the presence of sulphur.

14.5. Test for Presence of Nitrogen in Meat

To a small piece of meat, add 2 or 3 pellets of sodium hydroxide and a few drops of water. Warm. Note the smell of ammonia. Test the gas with (a) moist Universal Indicator paper (or red litmus paper), (b) a piece of filter paper on which a spot of Nessler's reagent has been placed from a dropping pipette.

14.6. Dyeing a Protein

To 4 test-tubes, 2 containing 5 cm^3 of a solution of eosin and 2 containing 5 cm^3 of a solution of methylene blue, add a little white rabbit wool or a white feather. To each set of dyes, add 3 drops of ethanoic acid to one solution and 3 drops of concentrated ammonia solution to the other. Wash the wool or feather after about 10 minutes and note which solutions give the fast dye.

14.7. Preparation of Polymers containing the Peptide Link

The preparation of nylon is described in Section 30.1, experiments 3 and 4.

15

POLYHYDRIC ALCOHOLS

Those alcohols having molecules which contain more than one **hydroxyl group** are known as **polyhydric alcohols**. They have a sweet taste and are either solids or colourless viscous liquids. They are soluble in water but only sparingly soluble in ether. Dihydric alcohols are known as **diols** (glycols).

15.1 Reactions of Ethane-1,2-Diol (Ethylene Glycol)

1. Add a small pellet of sodium to 2 cm^3 of ethane-1,2-diol in a test-tube. Note the effervescence and test for hydrogen with a lighted splint. The mono-sodium salt is obtained.

$$2 \begin{array}{c} CH_2OH \\ | \\ CH_2OH \end{array} + 2Na \longrightarrow 2 \begin{array}{c} CH_2OH \\ | \\ CH_2ONa \end{array} + H_2$$

Only 1 of the 2 replaceable hydrogen atoms in the molecule of the diol is replaced by sodium at room temperature.

2. To 1 cm^3 of the diol in a test-tube, add a little phosphorus pentachloride (**CARE**). Observe the fumes of hydrogen chloride:

$$\begin{array}{c} CH_2OH \\ | \\ CH_2OH \end{array} + 2PCl_5 \longrightarrow \begin{array}{c} CH_2Cl \\ | \\ CH_2Cl \end{array} + 2POCl_3 + 2HCl$$

1,2-Dichloroethane

3. To 1 cm^3 of the diol in a crucible or small evaporating basin, add ethanoyl chloride dropwise (**CARE**). A reaction ensues and fumes of hydrogen chloride are evolved:

$$\begin{array}{c} CH_2OH \\ | \\ CH_2OH \end{array} + 2CH_3COCl \longrightarrow \begin{array}{c} CH_2O - CO - CH_3 \\ | \\ CH_2O - CO - CH_3 \end{array} + 2HCl$$

4. Add 5 drops of ethane-1,2-diol to 1 cm^3 of dilute acidified potassium permanganate solution. Shake to dissolve the diol, then warm gently over a bunsen flame. The colour of the permanganate is quickly discharged, showing that the diol is a reducing agent:

$$\begin{array}{c} CH_2OH \\ | \\ CH_2OH \end{array} \longrightarrow \begin{array}{c} CH_2OH \\ | \\ CHO \end{array} \begin{array}{c} CHO \\ | \\ CHO \end{array} \begin{array}{c} CHO \\ | \\ CH_2OH \\ | \\ COOH \end{array} \begin{array}{c} CHO \\ | \\ COOH \end{array} \longrightarrow \begin{array}{c} COOH \\ | \\ COOH \end{array} \longrightarrow 2CO_2 + H_2O$$

5. Dissolve a few crystals of disodium(I) tetraborate(III)-10-water (borax) in 2 cm^3 of distilled water and add 1 drop of phenolphthalein. The colour of the indicator turns pink since the solution is alkaline by hydrolysis.

$$2Na^+ + B_4O_7{}^{2-} + 7H_2O \longrightarrow 2Na^+ + 2OH^- + 4H_3BO_3$$

Add ethane-1,2-diol dropwise to the solution and shake. Note that the pink colour is discharged 1,2 and 1,3 diols react with boric(III) acid to form acids that are stronger than boric(III) acid:

$$2\begin{array}{c} CH_2OH \\ | \\ CH_2OH \end{array} + H_3BO_3 \longrightarrow \left[\begin{array}{c} H_2C-O \qquad O-CH_2 \\ | \qquad \diagdown \diagup \qquad | \\ \qquad \qquad B \\ | \qquad \diagup \diagdown \qquad | \\ H_2C-O \qquad O-CH_2 \end{array} \right]^- + H^+ + 3H_2O$$

Dilute the solution of the complex with water and note that the pink colour is restored.

6. Fill a Pyrex test-tube to a depth of 1 cm with ethane-1,2-diol. Push a plug of Rocksil wool to the bottom of the tube to absorb the diol and cover the plug with a 1 cm layer of potassium hydrogensulphate crystals. Heat the plug (Figure 27) and pass the vapour which contains ethanal into 2–3 cm^3 of Schiff's reagent for about a minute:

$$HO-CH_2-CH_2-OH \longrightarrow CH_3CHO + H_2O$$

The pink colour of the reagent is restored.

7. Redistil a sample of car anti-freeze fluid. Collect the fraction (ethane-1,2-diol) boiling between 190° C and 200° C. To 1 cm^3 samples in different test-tubes, add 3, 4, 5, . . . 10 cm^3 of water, and cool the tubes in an ice-salt mixture to show that the liquid has lowered the freezing-point of water and is an effective anti-freeze.

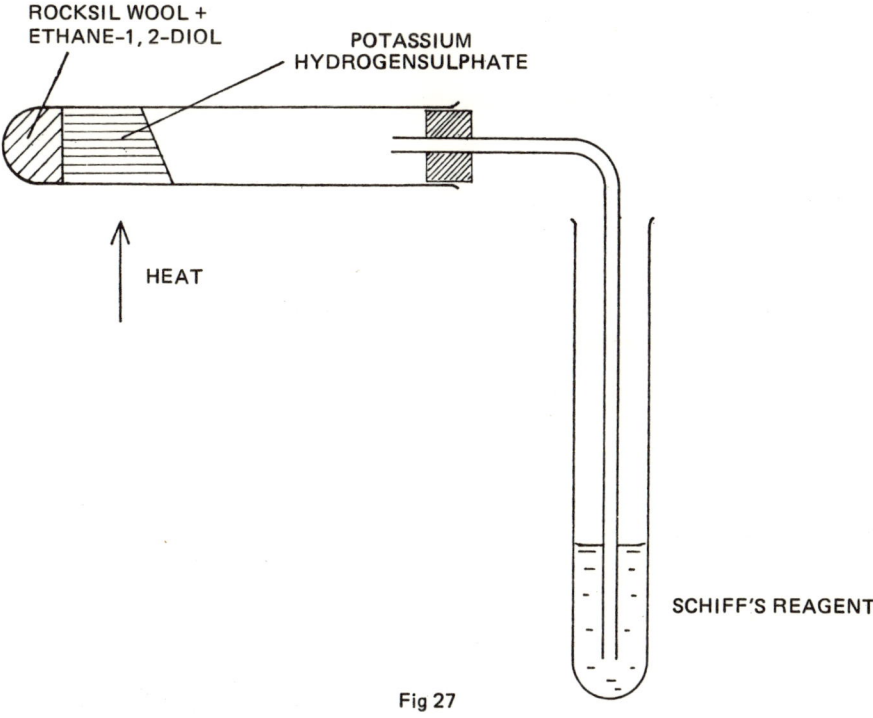

ROCKSIL WOOL +
ETHANE-1, 2-DIOL

POTASSIUM
HYDROGENSULPHATE

HEAT

SCHIFF'S REAGENT

Fig 27

15.2. Reactions of Propane-1,2,3-Triol (Glycerol)

Repeat the experiments described in the previous section using propane-1, 2, 3-triol in place of ethane-1, 2-diol.

1. Hydrogen is evolved slowly. Only 1 hydrogen atom per molecule is replaced by sodium at ordinary temperatures.

$$2HOCH_2{-}CHOH{-}CH_2OH + 2Na \longrightarrow$$

$$2HOCH_2{-}CHOH{-}CH_2ONa + H_2$$

2. The reaction between the triol and phosphorus pentachloride is slow at first but, after a few seconds, it becomes vigorous:

$$HOCH_2{-}CHOH{-}CH_2OH + 3PCl_5 \longrightarrow$$

$$ClCH_2{-}CHCl{-}CH_2Cl + 3POCl_3 + 3HCl$$

The product is 1,2,3-trichloropropane.

3. The reaction of the triol with ethanoyl chloride is little less vigorous than that of ethane-1,2-diol. Fumes of hydrogen chloride are evolved.

$$HOCH_2{-}CHOH{-}CH_2OH + 2CH_3COCl \longrightarrow$$

$$CH_3{-}CO{-}O{-}CH_2{-}CH(O{-}CO{-}CH_3){-}CH_2Cl + H_2O + HCl$$

4. Repeat experiment 4 described in Section 15.1, using propane-1,2,3-triol instead of ethane-1,2-diol.

5. Repeat experiment 5 in the previous section, using propane-1,2,3-triol.

6. Repeat experiment 6 in the previous section, using propane-1,2,3-triol (Figure 27). The vapour evolved contains propenal (acrolein) which has a characteristic irritating odour.

$$HOCH_2{-}CHOH{-}CH_2OH \longrightarrow H_2C{=}CH{-}CHO + 2H_2O$$
Propenal

Test for propenal in the following manner:
(a) Pass the vapour directly into 1 cm³ of bromine dissolved in tetrachloromethane contained in a test-tube. Bromine is decolorised.

$$H_2C{=}CH{-}CHO + Br_2 \longrightarrow BrCH_2{-}CHBr{-}CHO$$

(b) Pass the vapour into 1 cm³ of distilled water for about 1 minute. Cool the solution if necessary, then add a few drops of Schiff's reagent. The red colour is restored.

16

DICARBOXYLIC ACIDS

16.1 Reactions of Ethanedioic Acid (Oxalic Acid) and Ethanedioates (Oxalates)

1. Heat about 0.5 g of ethanedioic acid crystals in a test-tube fitted with a delivery tube dipping into lime water (cf. Figure 27). Note the evolution of carbon dioxide.

$$(COOH)_2 . 2H_2O \longrightarrow (COOH)_2 + 2H_2O$$
$$(COOH)_2 \longrightarrow HCOOH + CO_2$$

Some of the methanoic acid may decompose, yielding carbon monoxide.

$$HCOOH \longrightarrow CO + H_2O$$

2. Repeat the previous test using sodium ethanedioate. Test for carbon dioxide and carbon monoxide. A charred residue remains, which contains some sodium carbonate.

   The reaction can be represented by the equation

$$7(COONa)_2 \longrightarrow 7Na_2CO_3 + 3CO + 2CO_2 + 2C$$

Allow the tube to cool, and then add dilute hydrochloric acid to the residue. Test for the carbon dioxide evolved.

3. In 2 test-tubes place 0.5 g each of ethanedioic acid crystals and of sodium ethanedioate respectively. Add enough concentrated sulphuric acid to cover the crystals and warm gently. Test for carbon dioxide by hanging a drop of lime water in the evolved gases, then apply a lighted splint to ignite the carbon monoxide.

$$\begin{matrix} COOH \\ | \\ COOH \end{matrix} \xrightarrow[\text{dehydrating agent}]{\text{Conc. } H_2SO_4 \text{ as a}} CO + CO_2 + H_2O$$

4. Dissolve a few crystals of ethanedioic acid or of sodium ethanedioate in 1 cm^3 of water. Add 1 cm^3 of dilute sulphuric acid, followed by 2 or 3 drops of potassium permanganate solution. The permanganate remains unaffected in the cold. Warm the solution gently; the colour of the permanganate is discharged.

$$2KMnO_4 + 3H_2SO_4 + 5(COOH)_2 \longrightarrow K_2SO_4 + 2MnSO_4 + 8H_2O + 5CO_2$$

5. To 1 cm^3 of ethanedioic acid solution, add dilute ammonia solution until the solution is just alkaline to litmus. Add 5% calcium chloride solution dropwise and observe the white precipitate of calcium ethanedioate.

$$\begin{array}{l} COOH \\ | \\ COOH \end{array} \xrightarrow{NH_3\,(aq)} \begin{array}{l} COO^-NH_4^+ \\ | \\ COO^-NH_4^+ \end{array} \xrightarrow{CaCl_2} \begin{array}{l} COO^- \\ | \quad Ca^{2+} \\ COO^- \end{array}$$

Separate (or filter) the mixture, and divide the precipitate into 3 portions. Add dilute hydrochloric acid, dilute nitric acid, and dilute ethanoic acid to these portions, respectively.

6. Add calcium chloride solution to sodium ethanedioate solution. Calcium ethanedioate is again precipitated.

7. Fill a dry test-tube to a depth of 1 cm with iron(II) ethanedioate crystals. Heat the tube and note the colour change from yellow to black. Carbon dioxide and carbon monoxide are evolved. Test for these gases as in experiment 3.

$$\begin{array}{l} COO^- \\ | \quad Fe^{2+} \longrightarrow FeO + CO + CO_2 \\ COO^- \end{array}$$

Invert the test-tube so that the hot residue falls onto a crucible lid. The residue becomes incandescent due to formation of iron(II) diiron(III) oxide (magnetic oxide of iron).

$$6FeO + O_2 \longrightarrow 2Fe_3O_4$$

8. Heat strongly a mixture of sodium ethanedioate and soda-lime in a test-tube. Ignite the hydrogen evolved. Allow the tube to cool, and add dilute hydrochloric acid to the residue. Test for carbon dioxide.

$$\begin{array}{l} COO^-Na^+ \\ | \qquad\qquad + 2NaOH \longrightarrow 2Na_2CO_3 + H_2 \\ COO^-Na^+ \end{array}$$

$$Na_2CO_3 + 2HCl \longrightarrow 2NaCl + H_2O + CO_2$$

16.2. Reactions of Propanedioic Acid (Malonic Acid)

1. Heat some crystals of propanedioic acid in an apparatus similar to that in Figure 28. The crystals melt, then decompose, yielding carbon dioxide and

ethanoic acid. The latter is condensed in a water-cooled test-tube and may be detected by its smell.

PROPANEDIOIC ACID

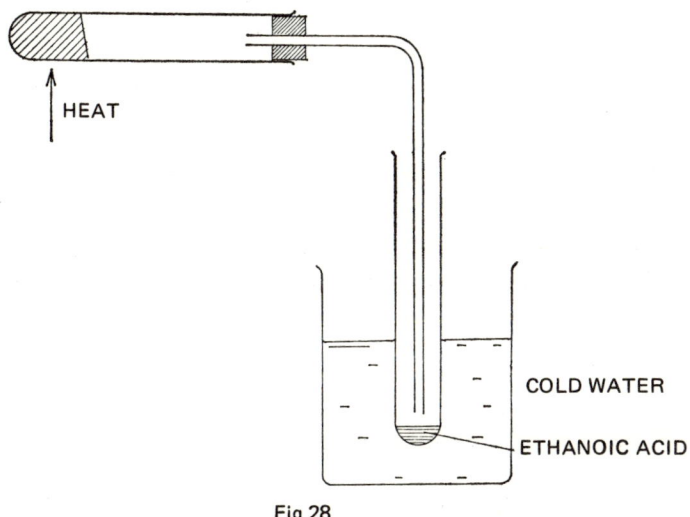

Fig 28

$$\begin{array}{c} COOH \\ | \\ CH_2 \\ | \\ COOH \end{array} \longrightarrow CH_3COOH + CO_2$$

Test for carbon dioxide with lime water.

2. Repeat experiment 5 in the previous section, using propanedioic acid in place of ethanedioic acid. A white precipitate of the calcium salt is obtained on standing for a minute or two. Scratching with a glass rod hastens the precipitation. The precipitate dissolves in dilute hydrochloric acid, in dilute nitric acid, and in dilute ethanoic acid.

3. Add 1 cm³ of bromine water to 0.1 g of propanedioic acid in a test-tube. Warm the tube gently and shake. The bromine water is decolorised and bubbles of carbon dioxide are evolved. The propanedioic acid is converted into tribromoethanoic acid.

$$\begin{array}{c} COOH \\ | \\ CH_2 \\ | \\ COOH \end{array} + 3Br_2 \longrightarrow Br_3C{-}COOH + CO_2 + 3HBr$$

4. Suspend 0.1 g of propanedioic acid in 2 cm^3 of ether, then add a drop of bromine. Fit a cork to the tube, then shake gently for about 1 minute. The bromine is slowly decolorised and 2-bromopropanedioic acid is formed.

$$
\begin{array}{c}
\text{COOH} \\
| \\
\text{CH}_2 \\
| \\
\text{COOH}
\end{array}
+ \text{Br}_2 \longrightarrow
\begin{array}{c}
\text{COOH} \\
| \\
\text{CHBr} \\
| \\
\text{COOH}
\end{array}
+ \text{HBr}
$$

This reaction illustrates the reactivity of the methylene group in the acid molecule.

5. Repeat experiment 4 in the previous section, using propanedioic acid in place of ethanedioic acid. The colour of the permanganate is discharged slowly in the cold but rapidly on warming.

16.3. Reactions of Butanedioic Acid (Succinic Acid)

1. Heat a few crystals of butanedioic acid in a ignition tube. A white sublimate of butanedioic anhydride is obtained.

$$
\begin{array}{c}
\text{CH}_2\,\text{COOH} \\
| \\
\text{CH}_2\,\text{COOH}
\end{array}
\xrightarrow{\ \text{heat}\ }
\begin{array}{c}
\overset{\displaystyle O}{\overset{\|}{}} \\
\text{H}_2\text{C}-\text{C} \\
| \qquad\quad \diagdown \\
\qquad\qquad\quad O + \text{H}_2\text{O} \\
| \qquad\quad \diagup \\
\text{H}_2\text{C}-\text{C} \\
\underset{\displaystyle O}{\underset{\|}{}}
\end{array}
$$

Butanedioic anhydride

The vapours evolved have a pungent odour.

2. Place 0.1 g each of butanedioic acid and of sodium butanedioate in separate test-tubes. Add 1 cm^3 of concentrated sulphuric acid to each and warm. The butanedioic acid and the sodium salt dissolve in the sulphuric acid without charring. No gases are evolved.

3. Repeat experiment 4 in Section 16.1, using butanedioic acid and sodium butanedioate. The colour of the permanganate is not discharged.

4. Repeat experiments 5 and 6 in Section 16.1, using butanedioic acid and sodium butanedioate. In each case a white crystalline precipitate of the calcium salt is obtained on boiling. This precipitate is soluble in dilute ethanoic acid (contrast with calcium ethanedioate).

5. Make 1 cm^3 of an aqueous solution of butanedioic acid just alkaline by adding a dilute solution of ammonia. Boil off the excess ammonia and to the neutral solution add neutral iron(III) chloride solution. A buff precipitate of basic iron(III) butanedioate is obtained.

6. Repeat experiment 8 in Section 16.1, using sodium butanedioate. Ignite the ethane evolved.

$$\begin{array}{l} CH_2COO^{--}Na^+ \\ | \\ CH_2COO^-Na^+ \end{array} + 2NaOH \longrightarrow 2Na_2CO_3 + C_2H_6$$

16.4. Preparation of Hexanedioic Acid (Adipic Acid) from Cyclohexene (see Section 2.5)

16.5. Geometric Isomerism of Butenedioic Acids (Maleic and Fumaric Acids)

Dissolve 10 g of butenedioic anhydride in 12 cm^3 of boiling water in a small beaker. A solution of *cis*-butenedioic acid is formed:

Butenedioic anhydride   *cis*-Butenedioic acid

Cool the solution by placing the beaker in a larger beaker of cold water. Filter the solid acid, using a Hirsch funnel (Figure 13(a)). Do not wash the solid with water. Collect the solid and dry it between pads of filter papers. Find the melting point (Section 31.1).

Collect the filtrate and add 20 cm^3 concentrated hydrochloric acid. Place the mixture in a flask and reflux it for about 20 minutes. Crystals of *trans*-butenedioic acid separate out. Filter these off, again using a Hirsch funnel. Recrystallise the acid from boiling water. Dry the crystals between pads of filter paper, and find the melting point.

PHYSICAL CONSTANTS

M.p. of *cis*-butenedioic acid 130° C; m.p. of *trans*-butenedioic acid 287° C (sublimes).

Hydrogen chloride adds on to the *cis*-butenedioic acid molecule to form an intermediate in which there is unrestricted rotation about the C—C bond:

$$
\begin{array}{ccccccc}
& \overset{\displaystyle O}{\underset{\displaystyle \|}{}} & & & & \overset{\displaystyle \overset{Cl}{|}\quad O}{} & \\
H-C-\overset{\|}{C}-O-H & & \text{HCl} & \longrightarrow & & H-C-C-OH & \\
\| & & & & & | & \\
H-C-C-O-H & & & & & H-C=C-OH & \\
& \underset{\displaystyle O}{\underset{\displaystyle \|}{}} & & & & \underset{\displaystyle OH}{|} &
\end{array}
$$

restricted rotation   free rotation   restricted rotation

17

CARBOHYDRATES

17.1. Reactions of Monosaccharides

A. GLUCOSE, $C_6H_{12}O_6$

1. Heat about 1 g of glucose in a test-tube. It melts, and some water may be expelled. The residue finally chars to form carbon. There is a smell of burnt sugar.

2. Place about 0.5 g of glucose in a test-tube and add 1.5 cm^3 of concentrated sulphuric acid. Warm the mixture gently. Note that there is charring and that carbon is formed.

$$C_6H_{12}O_6 \xrightarrow{\text{Conc. } H_2SO_4 \text{ as dehydrating agent}} 6C + 6H_2O$$

Glucose contains an aldehyde group, and thus has reducing properties. These are demonstrated by reactions 3 and 4.

3. It undergoes the silver mirror test. (For details, see Section 7.6, experiment 1.) Use about 0.1 g of glucose in place of the aldehyde.

4. Glucose also shows its reducing properties by reducing Fehling's solution to copper(I) oxide. (For details, see Section 7.6, experiment 2.) Use about 0.1 g of glucose in place of the aldehyde. This reaction is often used to prepare a pure sample of copper(I) oxide.

5. **Formation of an osazone.** Dissolve 0.5 g of glucose in 5 cm^3 of water. Dissolve 1 g of phenylhydrazine in 1 cm^3 of ethanoic acid, and dilute to 10 cm^3 with water. Mix the 2 solutions, and warm gently in a beaker of hot water. Crystals of glucosazone are formed which can be filtered, washed with water and then with ethanol. Recrystallise the glucosazone from ethanol. Separate the crystals by filtration, wash with water and dry. Study the crystalline structure of the osazone under a microscope. M.p. of glucosazone is 204° C.

6. **Molisch's test.** Dissolve about 0.05 g of glucose in 1 cm^3 of water. Add 2 drops of a 20% solution of naphthalen-1-ol in ethanol followed by 1 cm^3 of

concentrated sulphuric acid. The latter should be added slowly down the side of the test-tube, using a dropping pipette, to form a lower layer. An interfacial violet coloration indicates the presence of a carbohydrate.

7. **Barfoed's test.** This test is specific for monosaccharides and serves to distinguish them from disaccharides.

  Dissolve 0.1 g of copper(II) ethanoate in 2 cm^3 of a 1% aqueous solution of ethanoic acid. Add a very small amount (*ca*. 2 mg) of glucose and boil the mixture gently for about 1 minute. A red precipitate of copper(I) oxide is formed.

B. FRUCTOSE, $C_6H_{12}O_6$

8. Repeat experiment 1, using fructose instead of glucose. Note the charring and the formation of carbon.

9. Repeat experiment 2, using fructose instead of glucose. Note the formation of carbon.

10. Repeat experiments 3 and 4. Although fructose contains a keto group, the compound can undergo the silver mirror test and reduce Fehling's solution. This is characteristic of compounds that have a keto group adjacent to a hydroxyl group.

11. Repeat experiment 5, using fructose instead of glucose. Examine the crystals under the microscope and take the m.p. of the osazone. It will be found that the osazone from glucose and from fructose are identical.

12. Repeat experiment 6. Again, note the interfacial violet coloration.

13. Repeat experiment 7. Again, note the red precipitate, showing that fructose is a monosaccharide.

17.2. Reactions of Disaccharides

SUCROSE (Cane Sugar), $C_{12}H_{22}O_{11}$

1. Repeat experiments 1 and 2 in Section 17.1, using sucrose instead of glucose. Note the formation of carbon.

$$C_{12}H_{22}O_{11} \xrightarrow{\text{Conc. H}_2\text{SO}_4 \text{ as dehydrating agent}} 12C + 11H_2O$$

2. Repeat experiment 3 in Section 17.1, using sucrose instead of glucose. Sucrose is not a reducing agent. (It contains the residues of glucose and fructose joined by the aldehyde group; thus sucrose does not contain an aldehyde group and is not a reducing agent.)

3. **Inversion of sucrose.** Dissolve 2 g of sucrose in 10 cm^3 of water, and divide into 2 portions.

(a) Boil one portion with Fehling's solution (Section 7.6, experiment 2). Note that no reduction occurs, unlike the reaction with glucose (Section 17.1, experiment 4).

(b) Boil the other part with 5 drops of dilute sulphuric acid. Neutralise by adding dilute sodium hydroxide solution dropwise. Boil this solution with Fehling's solution. The solution is reduced to red copper(I) oxide, for the sucrose has been hydrolysed by sulphuric acid to glucose and fructose, both reducing agents.

$$C_{12}H_{22}O_{11} + H_2O \xrightarrow{\quad H^+ \quad} C_6H_{12}O_6 + C_6H_{12}O_6$$
$$\text{Glucose} \qquad \text{Fructose}$$

4. Preparation of ethanol by fermentation (Section 5.1).

5. **Molisch's test.** Repeat experiment 6 in Section 17.1. A similar result is obtained.

6. **Barfoed's test.** Repeat experiment 7 in Section 17.1. A precipitate of copper(I) oxide is *not* obtained.

17.3. Reactions of Polysaccharides

STARCH, $(C_6H_{10}O_5)_n$

1. Repeat experiments 3 and 4 in Section 17.1, using starch instead of glucose. Starch is not a reducing agent.

   Make a paste with about 0.1 g of soluble starch and about 1 cm^3 of water. Pour the paste into about 10 cm^3 of boiling water and continue boiling for 2 minutes. Divide the solution into 3 portions.

2. To the first portion add 2 drops of iodine solution. Note the blue coloration.

3. To the second portion add 5 drops of dilute sulphuric acid and boil for a few minutes. Neutralise the solution by adding dilute sodium hydroxide solution drop by drop. Divide this solution into 2 parts.

   (a) To the first part, add 2 drops of iodine; there should be no blue coloration.

   (b) To the second part, add Fehling's solution to show the presence of a reducing agent (glucose).

These experiments show that starch has been hydrolysed by sulphuric acid to glucose:

$$(C_6H_{10}O_5)_n + nH_2O \xrightarrow{\quad H^+ \quad} nC_6H_{12}O_6$$
$$\text{Starch} \qquad\qquad\qquad \text{Glucose}$$

4. Add a little saliva to the third portion of the starch solution in a test-tube, and warm in a beaker of water at about 70° C.

Test the solution as in experiment 3(a) in Section 17.2.

5. **Molisch's test.** Repeat experiment 6 in Section 17.1. As in the case of the previous carbohydrates, a violet coloration is obtained.

17.4. Small-scale Preparation of Cellulose Ethanoate

INTRODUCTION

The fibres in cotton, wool, flax, wood, and some other materials are composed chiefly of cellulose. Cellulose is a natural polymer which has unbranched long-chain molecules consisting of β-glucose units. The molecular formula of cellulose is $(C_6H_{10}O_5)_n$ where n has a value in the region 100–200. The formula may be represented structurally:

By treatment with acids cellulose yields esters, the most important of which are the ethanoates, and nitrates. In the following experiment, each of the three hydroxyl groups in the cellulose ring is replaced by an ethanoate group

$$\underset{(H_3C-\overset{\displaystyle O}{\overset{\displaystyle \|}{C}}-O-)}{}$$ to give the tri-ethanoate.

Cellulose ethanoate is used in the manufacture of films, fibres (Tricel, rayon), and lacquers. In conjunction with a plasticiser, it is used in the moulding of such articles as screwdriver handles.

REAGENTS

Cotton wool (0.5 g)
Ethanoic acid (20 cm³)
Ethanoic anhydride (5 cm³)
Trichloromethane (15 cm³)
Concentrated sulphuric acid
Calcium chloride, anhydrous

DETAILS

Mix 20 cm^3 of ethanoic acid, 5 cm^3 of ethanoic anhydride and 2 drops (from a dropping pipette) of concentrated sulphuric acid in a beaker. Then add, with stirring, 0.5 g of cotton wool, which has been finely shredded by tearing.

Continue to stir so that the cotton wool is evenly distributed throughout the mixture and there are no air bubbles. Then leave the mixture for about a day, stirring occasionally. The mixture gradually becomes less viscous, ending in a clear liquid, which is easy to pour.

Pour the reaction mixture slowly into a large beaker containing 500 cm^3 of water. A precipitate of cellulose ethanoate separates out.

Filter the ester, using a Hirsch funnel (Figure 13(a)), wash it well with water and transfer it to a filter paper. Use pads of filter paper to dry it.

Take about a quarter of the ester and dissolve it in about 15 cm^3 of trichloromethane in a boiling tube. If the solution is turbid, place some anhydrous calcium chloride in the tube and shake the solution. Decant the solution into a basin and allow it to evaporate **in a fume cupboard**. Remove the solid cellulose ethanoate film.

18

AROMATIC HYDROCARBONS

18.1 Reactions of Benzene

1. To 5 drops of benzene in a test-tube, add 1 cm^3 of bromine in tetrachloromethane. Shake well. Note that the bromine is not decolorised. Contrast this with the behaviour of ethene (Chapter 2) and ethyne (Chapter 3) with bromine.

2. Place 5 drops of benzene in each of 2 test-tubes. To one of these, add some iron filings. Add 3 drops of bromine to both, and note that more hydrogen bromide is evolved from the one with iron filings present. It may take a few minutes before fumes of hydrogen bromide are detected.

$$C_6H_6 + Br_2 \longrightarrow C_6H_5Br + HBr$$

Iron acts as a catalyst and is known in this reaction as a halogen carrier.

3. Preparation of hexachlorocyclohexane (Section 22.6).

4. To 1 cm^3 of acidified potassium permanganate solution, add 5 drops of benzene. Shake. No reaction takes place in the cold (contrast the reactions of ethene (Chapter 2) and ethyne (Chapter 3) with acidified potassium permanganate solution). Warm the solution; the permanganate is slowly decolorised. The benzene is **slowly** oxidised to a mixture of substances of lower relative molecular masses.

5. Place 0.5 cm^3 of *concentrated* nitric acid in a test-tube, and add 0.5 cm^3 of *concentrated* sulphuric acid, shaking and cooling the test-tube under a stream of cold water. Add the mixed acids to 5 drops of benzene in another test-tube. Shake the mixture under a stream of cold water. Allow the mixture to stand for a few minutes. Observe the dense, pale-yellow drops of nitrobenzene. Note also the smell of almonds.

$$C_6H_6 + HNO_3 \xrightarrow{\text{Conc. } H_2SO_4} C_6H_5NO_2 + H_2O$$
$$\text{Nitrobenzene}$$

6. Place 4 drops of benzene in a test-tube, and then add 10 drops of *concentrated* sulphuric acid. Warm the test-tube gently, until the benzene has dissolved

into the acid layer. Pour the mixture into a small beaker containing 10 cm^3 of a cold saturated solution of salt. White crystals of sodium benzenesulphonate are formed.

$$C_6H_6 + H_2SO_4 \longrightarrow C_6H_5SO_3H + H_2O$$
$$\text{Benzenesulphonic}$$
$$\text{acid}$$

$$C_6H_5SO_3H + NaCl \rightleftharpoons C_6H_5SO_3Na\downarrow + HCl$$

18.2. Reactions of Methylbenzene (Toluene)

1. Repeat the experiments 1, 2, 3, 4, and 5 in Section 18.1 using methylbenzene instead of benzene.

2. Place 10 drops of methylbenzene, 10 cm^3 of water, 0.1 g of sodium carbonate, and 1 g of potassium permanganate crystals in a 50 cm^3 flask. Reflux the mixture (cf. Figure 22) until the purple colour disappears.

    Cool the mixture, and acidify with dilute sulphuric acid. Add sodium hydrogensulphite to remove manganese(IV) oxide. Filter the white crystals of benzoic acid.

    Benzoic acid can be recrystallised from hot water. M.p. 121°C.

18.3. Preparation and Reactions of the Triphenylmethyl Radical

Generally, free radicals have a very short lifetime (c $10^{-8} - 10^{-10}$ s). However, triphenylmethyl is stable, and can be prepared in solution:

(a) Dissolve about 0.5 g of triphenylchloromethane in 5 cm^3 of dry benzene in a test-tube. Add a small pinch of zinc powder and cork the test-tube. Shake the mixture for about 5 minutes and decant the solution above the zinc into a clean test-tube.

(b) Shake the solution, removing and replacing the cork, noting the changes in colour.

(c) Allow to stand without shaking for a few minutes.

(d) Repeat the procedures (b) and (c) 2 or 3 times.

(e) Allow the test-tube to stand for a further 10 minutes.

Comment on the results you obtain. What products do you consider have been formed and what tests would you perform to confirm your predictions?

19

AROMATIC NITRO COMPOUNDS

19.1. Small-scale Preparation of Nitrobenzene

INTRODUCTION

The conditions used in the nitration of an aromatic compound depend on the structure of the compound. Concentrated nitric acid, with concentrated sulphuric acid as catalyst, is used to nitrate benzene. Nitrobenzene is purified by distillation.

The reaction is thought to occur in several stages:

$$H_2SO_4 + H\!-\!O\!-\!NO_2 \rightleftharpoons HSO_4^- + \overset{H}{\underset{H}{>}}\overset{+}{O}\!-\!NO_2$$

The protonated nitric acid decomposes to form the nitronium ion, $\overset{+}{N}O_2$, which reacts with benzene:

$$\overset{H}{\underset{H}{>}}O^+\!-\!NO_2 \longrightarrow H_2O + \overset{+}{N}O_2$$

(The positive charge is delocalised over three of the carbon atoms, in the 2-, 4-, 6- positions). The proton is removed by the hydrogensulphate anion:

$$+ HSO_4^- \longrightarrow C_6H_5NO_2 + H_2SO_4$$

REAGENTS

Benzene (6 cm^3)
Concentrated nitric acid (7 cm^3)
Concentrated sulphuric acid (9 cm^3)
Dilute solution of sodium carbonate
Calcium chloride, anhydrous

EQUATION

$$C_6H_6 + HNO_3 \xrightarrow{\text{Conc. } H_2SO_4} C_6H_5NO_2 + H_2O$$

DETAILS

Place 7 cm^3 of concentrated nitric acid in a flask and add **slowly** 9 cm^3 of concentrated sulphuric acid, swirling gently, and cooling the flask under the tap. Partly immerse the flask in a beaker of cold water and introduce, in small portions, 6 cm^3 of benzene, using the dropping pipette. Swirl the mixture gently after each addition and do **not** allow the temperature to rise above $50\,^\circ\text{C}$ at this stage. When all the benzene has been added, maintain the flask at $60\,^\circ\text{C}$ in a water-bath for 30 minutes. Gently swirl the contents of the flask occasionally, to ensure proper mixing of the reactants.

Allow the flask to cool, and transfer the contents to the separating funnel. Remove and discard the lower layer. Wash the nitrobenzene with successive 10 cm^3 quantities of water, dilute sodium carbonate solution, and then water. In each case, separate and retain the lower layer.

Transfer the nitrobenzene to a stoppered test-tube, and add a few small lumps of anhydrous calcium chloride. When the liquid clears, decant and distil the nitrobenzene, using the condenser as an air condenser. Collect the fraction boiling between $207\,^\circ\text{C}$ and $211\,^\circ\text{C}$ (cf. Figure 25).

PHYSICAL CONSTANTS

B.p. $210\,^\circ\text{C}$; density at $20\,^\circ\text{C}$: 1.2 g cm^{-3}

19.2. Reactions of Nitrobenzene

1. Place 3 drops of nitrobenzene in a test-tube. Add 1 cm^3 of water and then 1 cm^3 of *concentrated* hydrochloric acid, followed by 2 or 3 small pieces of tin. Warm. The phenylamine formed goes into solution as soluble phenylammonium chlorostannate(IV)

$$2C_6H_5-NO_2 + Sn + 6HCl \longrightarrow$$
$$(C_6H_5-\overset{+}{N}H_3)_2 \ SnCl_6{}^{2-} + 2H_2O$$

104

Make alkaline with dilute sodium hydroxide solution, to liberate the phenyla-mine as an oil. Add enough alkali to dissolve the tin(IV) oxide formed as sodium stannate(IV).

$$(C_6H_5-\overset{+}{N}H_3)_2\ SnCl_6^{2-} + 8NaOH \longrightarrow$$
$$2C_6H_5NH_2 + Na_2SnO_3 + 5H_2O + 6NaCl$$

Test for phenylamine by adding 1 drop of the oil to an aqueous suspension of bleaching powder. If phenylamine is present, a blue colour will appear.

2. Repeat the reduction of nitrobenzene, using zinc dust and glacial ethanoic acid instead of tin and hydrochloric acid. There is no necessity for heating. Note that the reduction of nitrobenzene is much easier.

19.3. Preparation of 1,3-Dinitrobenzene

INTRODUCTION

The effect of the nitro-group in the molecule of nitrobenzene is to withdraw electrons from the benzene ring, rendering the 2- and 4-positions electron deficient. The NO_2^+ ion, formed from nitric acid (19.1), reacts at the 3-position, as it is the position of highest electron density. However, the electron density, even at the 3-position, is lower than that for benzene itself, and nitration will be more difficult for nitrobenzene than it is for benzene.

REAGENTS

Nitrobenzene (6 cm^3)
Concentrated nitric acid (8 cm^3)
Concentrated sulphuric acid (10 cm^3)
Ethanol (methylated spirit)

EQUATION

DETAILS

Place 8 cm^3 of concentrated nitric acid in a flask. Add *slowly* 10 cm^3 of concen-trated sulphuric acid, swirling gently, and cooling the flask under the tap. Arrange the apparatus as shown in Figure 29, placing 6 cm^3 of nitrobenzene in the dropping funnel and using the condenser as an air condenser.

Introduce the nitrobenzene *slowly* into the flask, swirling gently after the addition of each portion of approximately 1 cm^3. When all of the nitrobenzene has been added, bring the water in the bath to the boil and allow the contents of the flask to reflux at this temperature for 40 minutes. Gently swirl the reactants occasionally to ensure thorough mixing.

Pour the mixture into 150 cm^3 of cold water contained in a beaker. Allow the beaker to stand, preferably in cold water, for about 15 minutes, stirring the contents from time to time. Filter the solid 1,3-dinitrobenzene (Figures 13(a) and 13(b)) and wash it with distilled water. At this stage, the 1,3-dinitrobenzene contains a small quantity of 1,2- and 1,4-isomers as well as some unreacted nitrobenzene. — Pg 30

Transfer the crude product to a while tile or to a filter paper and press gently with a pad of two or three filter papers to absorb liquid impurities.

Place the 1,3-dinitrobenzene in a 100 cm^3 beaker, add 40 cm^3 of ethanol (methylated spirit), and heat in a warm water-bath until it dissolves. (If there are solid impurities, filter these off.) Allow the solution to cool and filter the crystalline product (Figure 13(a)).

Transfer the crystals to a filter paper or a watch-glass and dry them in a warm oven. Determine the melting point of 1,3-dinitrobenzene.

PHYSICAL CONSTANT

M.p. 90 °C.

20

AROMATIC AMINES

20.1. Small-scale Preparation of Phenylamine (Aniline)

INTRODUCTION

Aromatic amines are often prepared by the reduction of the corresponding aromatic nitro compounds in acid solution. In the laboratory, tin and concentrated hydrochloric acid are generally used.

The main product is the involatile salt, phenylammonium chlorostannate(IV). The free base is liberated by addition of excess alkali.

As phenylamine is only slightly soluble in water, it can be purified from involatile impurities by steam distillation. To improve the separation of phenylamine and water in the distillate, salt is added. The base is displaced from the water layer. Final purification is by distillation.

REAGENTS

Nitrobenzene (2 cm^3)
Tin, granulated (4.5 g)
Concentrated hydrochloric acid (10 cm^3)
Sodium hydroxide (10 g)
Sodium chloride (3 g)
Diethyl ether

EQUATIONS

$$2C_6H_5-NO_2 + Sn + 6HCl \rightarrow (C_6H_5 - \overset{+}{N}H_3)_2 \, SnCl_6^{2-} + 2H_2O$$

$$(C_6H_5-\overset{+}{N}H_3)_2 SnCl_6{}^{2-} + 8NaOH \rightarrow 2C_6H_5-NH_2 + Na_2SnO_3 + 5H_2O + 6NaCl$$

DETAILS

To 4.5 g of tin and 2 cm³ of nitrobenzene (Figure 29, Plate 2), add slowly 10 cm³ of concentrated hydrochloric acid, from a dropping funnel.

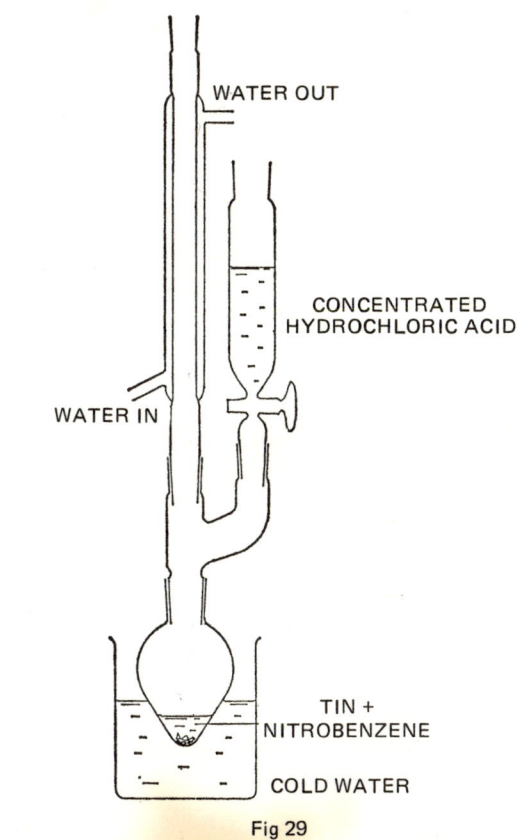

WATER OUT

CONCENTRATED
HYDROCHLORIC ACID

WATER IN

TIN +
NITROBENZENE

COLD WATER

Fig 29

When all the acid has been added, and the vigour of the reaction has subsided, remove the flask head, and heat the open flask on a boiling water-bath for 30 minutes. This completes the reduction of the nitrobenzene to phenylamine by tin(II) chloride, and also removes excess nitrobenzene by steam distillation.

If there is a residue of metal, add concentrated hydrochloric acid, dropwise, until it has dissolved. The phenylamine is present as phenylammonium chlorostannate(IV), which is soluble in water.

Cool the flask, and add slowly, with gentle shaking, excess sodium hydroxide solution (7.5 g in 10 cm³ of water). This liberates phenylamine as the free base, and dissolves tin compounds as soluble sodium stannate(IV). There should be a clear solution. If there is a precipitate, add sodium hydroxide solution, dropwise, until it has dissolved.

Set up the flask for steam distillation (Figure 30, Plate 5). Warm the flask to prevent undue condensation of steam. Continue to distil until no more oily drops of phenylamine can be detected in the condensate.

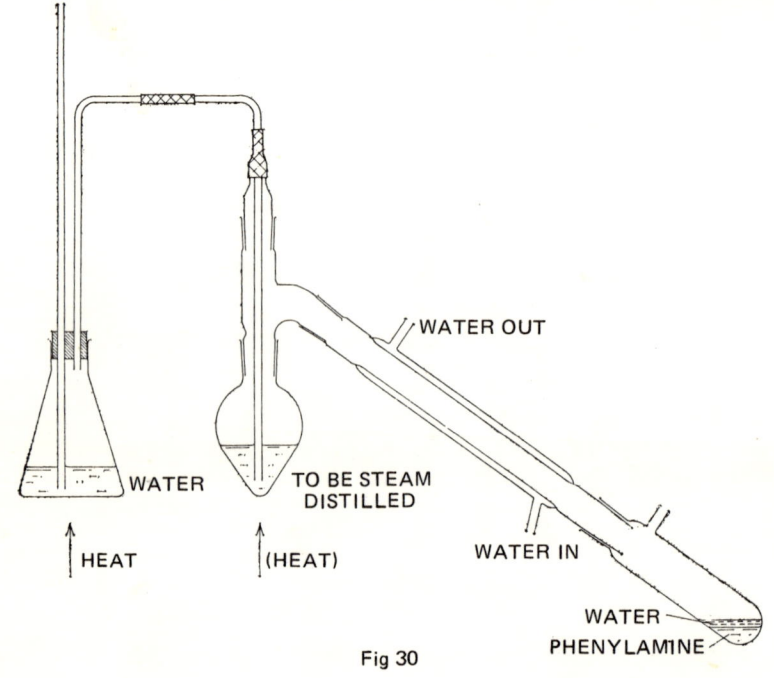

Fig 30

Transfer the distillate to the separating funnel, add 3 g of sodium chloride, and shake. This reduces the solubility of the amine in water. Run off the crude phenylamine into a test-tube. Add a few pellets of sodium hydroxide to remove moisture, and allow to stand in a stoppered test-tube until the turbidity disappears.

Redistil the amine, using an air condenser (cf. Figure 25, Plate 1). Collect the fraction distilling between $181\,^{\circ}C$ and $185\,^{\circ}C$.

PHYSICAL CONSTANTS

B.p. $183\,^{\circ}C$; density at $20\,^{\circ}C$: 1.02 g cm^{-3}

20.2. Reactions of Phenylamine

A. REACTIONS OF THE AMINO, $-NH_2$, GROUP

1. To 2 drops of phenylamine in a test-tube, add 5 drops of water. Insert a piece of Universal Indicator paper (or red litmus paper) and shake. The paper is

unaffected. Contrast this with the behaviour of aliphatic amines (Section 11.3, experiment 1).

2. Place 1 cm^3 of dilute sulphuric acid in a test-tube. Add 3 drops of phenylamine and shake. A white precipitate of phenylammonium sulphate is formed:

$$2C_6H_5NH_2 + H_2SO_4 \longrightarrow (C_6H_5\overset{+}{N}H_3)_2SO_4{}^{2-}$$

3. Place 5 drops of phenylamine in a test-tube, and add 5 drops of water. Shake the mixture. An oily suspension is formed as phenylamine is insoluble in water. Then add concentrated hydrochloric acid dropwise until the solution is clear. Phenylammonium chloride is soluble in water. Boil off the water; the residue is a white solid. *+ $\subseteq$ NOCH*

$$C_6H_5NH_2 + HCl \longrightarrow (C_6H_5\overset{+}{N}H_3)Cl^-$$

$$\text{cf. } NH_3 + HCl \longrightarrow (\overset{+}{N}H_4)Cl^-$$

4. To 5 drops of phenylamine in a test-tube, add 2 drops of ethanoyl chloride **(CARE)**. A vigorous reaction takes place, and a white precipitate of *N*-phenylethanamide is deposited. It can be recrystallised, by adding excess water and boiling. Decant the solution carefully into a clean test-tube (filter if the solution is not clear) and cool the solution under a running cold tap. White crystals are deposited. M.p. 113 °C.

$$CH_3COCl + C_6H_5NH_2 \longrightarrow CH_3-CO-NH-C_6H_5 + HCl$$
$$\textit{N}\text{-Phenylethanamide}$$

5. The ethanoylation of phenylamine can also be carried out with ethanoic anhydride. To 5 drops of phenylamine in a test-tube, add concentrated hydrochloric acid dropwise until the amine dissolves; add 3 drops of water, then 7 drops of ethanoic anhydride. Add saturated sodium ethanoate solution dropwise until a white crystalline precipitate of *N*-phenylethanamide is obtained. Filter the precipitate and purify by recrystallisation from hot water. Dry the crystals and determine the melting-point. M.p. 113°C

$$(CH_3CO)_2O + C_6H_5NH_2 \longrightarrow$$

$$CH_3-CO-NH-C_6H_5 + CH_3COOH$$

The detailed preparation of *N*-phenylethanamide is given at the end of the chapter (Section 20.4).

6. **Schotten-Baumann reaction.** Place 3 drops of phenylamine in a test-tube, and add 5 cm^3 of dilute sodium hydroxide solution. Shake to form a fine oily suspension, and add 5 drops of benzoyl chloride. Fit a stopper to the tube and shake for a minute. Cool the tube and contents under the tap if necessary and remove the stopper periodically to release the pressure. Filter the residue of *N*-phenylbenzamide, using a small Hirsch funnel.

Transfer the residue to another test-tube and dissolve it in the smallest possible quantity of hot ethanol. Filter if necessary and allow the solution to cool. (If the crystals do not appear within 5 minutes, add a few drops of water, and 'scratch' the sides of the test-tube with a glass rod to 'seed'.) Filter the crystals, and dry them on some filter papers. M.p. 163 °C.

$$C_6H_5COCl + NaOH + C_6H_5NH_2 \longrightarrow$$
$$C_6H_5-CO-NH-C_6H_5 + NaCl + H_2O$$
$$N\text{-Phenylbenzamide}$$

7. **The carbylamine reaction.** Phenylamine, being a primary amine, undergoes the carbylamine reaction. For details see Section 4.11, experiment 2.

$$C_6H_5NH_2 + CHCl_3 + 3KOH \longrightarrow C_6H_5NC + 3KCl + 3H_2O$$
$$\text{Phenyl}$$
$$\text{isocyanide}$$

8. Place 2 cm^3 of water in a test-tube, and add 0.5 g of finely ground bleaching powder. Shake the mixture to form a suspension. To this mixture, add 1 drop of phenylamine. A violet coloration is produced. (This is a complex oxidation product of phenylamine, of unknown structure.)

9. Phenylamine, unlike aliphatic amines, forms a diazonium salt. (For details, see Section 21.1.)

10. Place 3 drops of phenylamine in a test-tube, and add *concentrated* hydrochloric acid dropwise until a clear solution is formed. Dilute to 5 cm^3 with water. Add 1 or 2 crystals of sodium nitrite, and warm gently. Under these conditions, phenylamine does not form a diazonium salt, but behaves like an aliphatic amine, yielding nitrogen.

11. Place 5 drops of benzaldehyde and 5 drops of phenylamine in a test-tube. Heat the mixture on a boiling water-bath for 15 minutes. Cool the tube under the tap. White, wax-like crystals of a Schiff's base are deposited while a layer of water rests on the surface.

$$C_6H_5CHO + C_6H_5NH_2 \longrightarrow C_6H_5CH=NC_6H_5 + H_2O$$

B. REACTIONS OF THE PHENYL, C_6H_5, GROUP

12. Place 5 drops of phenylamine in a test-tube, and add concentrated hydrochloric acid dropwise until the phenylamine dissolves. Add bromine water drop by drop until a white precipitate of 2, 4, 6-tribromophenylamine is formed.

   Contrast the ease of bromination of phenylamine with that of benzene (Section 18.1, experiment 1).

13. To 5 drops of phenylamine in a test-tube, add *concentrated* hydrochloric acid dropwise until it dissolves. Dilute with 5 drops of water, add 5 drops of hydrogen peroxide solution (5 volume), followed by 2 drops of freshly prepared iron(II) sulphate solution. A green solution is obtained from which the green dye, emeraldine, slowly crystallises.

20.3. Reactions of (Phenylmethyl)amine (Benzylamine)

A. REACTIONS OF THE AMINO, $-NH_2$, GROUP

1. To 2 drops of (phenylmethyl)amine in a test-tube, add 5 drops of water. Insert a piece of Universal Indicator paper (or red litmus paper) and shake. The paper turns blue. Contrast this with the behaviour of phenylamine (Section 20.2, experiment 1) and of aliphatic amines (Section 11.3, experiment 1).

2. Repeat experiment 2 in Section 20.2, using (phenylmethyl)amine instead of phenylamine. The precipitate of the sulphate dissolves in excess water.

3. Repeat experiment 3 in Section 20.2, using (phenylmethyl)amine instead of phenylamine.

$$C_6H_5CH_2NH_2 + HCl \longrightarrow (C_6H_5CH_2\overset{+}{N}H_3)Cl^-$$

4. Repeat experiments 4 and 5 in Section 20.2, using (phenylmethyl)amine. A white precipitate of the ethanoyl derivative is formed at once.

5. Repeat experiment 6 in Section 20.2, using (phenylmethyl)amine.

6. Repeat experiment 8 in Section 20.2, using (phenylmethyl)amine.

7. Repeat experiments 9 and 10 in Section 20.2, using (phenylmethyl)amine. It does not form a diazonium salt but reacts with nitrous acid, yielding nitrogen.

$$C_6H_5CH_2NH_2 + HNO_2 \longrightarrow C_6H_5CH_2OH + N_2 + H_2O$$

The yield of phenylmethanol is small.

B. REACTIONS OF THE PHENYL, C_6H_5, GROUP

8. Repeat experiment 12 in Section 20.2. The orange colour of bromine water is discharged and a white precipitate is formed.

9. Repeat experiment 13 in Section 20.2, using (phenylmethyl)amine. It is unable to undergo this reaction. The amino group is not attached to the benzene nucleus but is in the side chain.

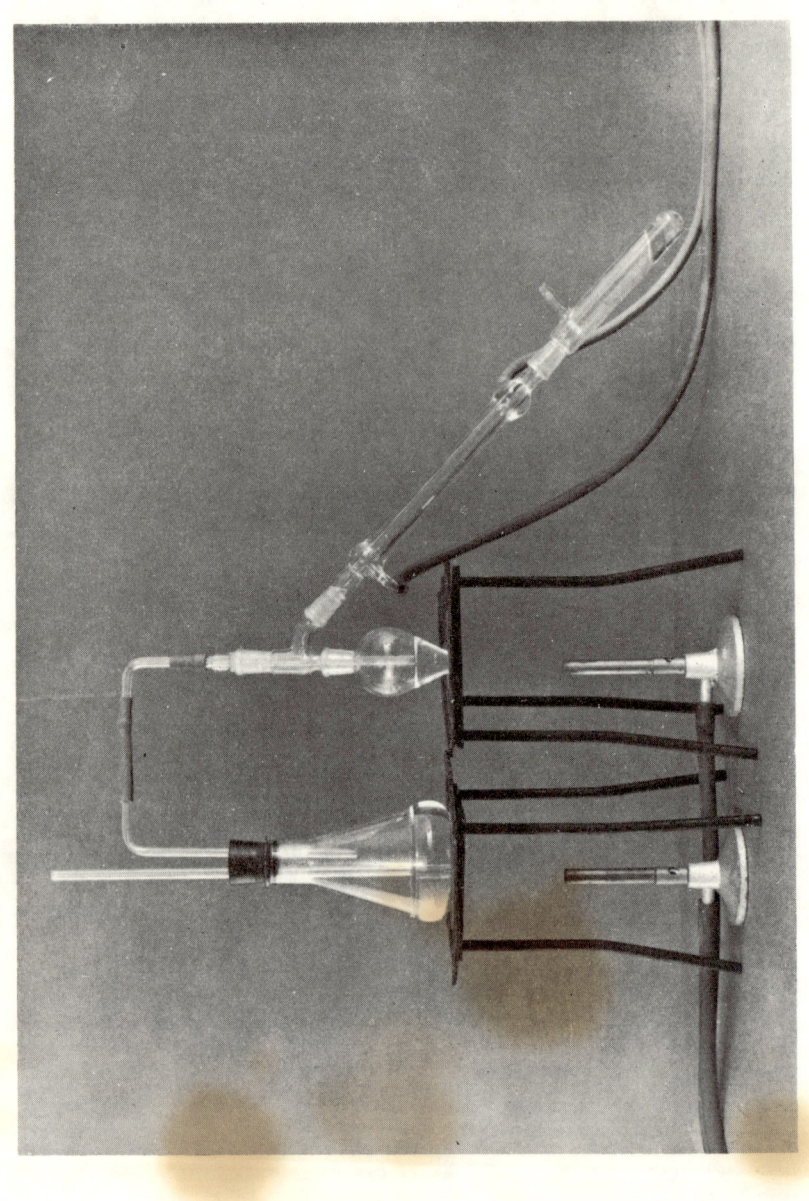

PLATE 5

Steam distillation. Preparations of aniline (Fig. 30, p. 108) and iodobenzene (p. 120).

20.4. Small-scale Preparation of *N*-Phenylethanamide (Acetanilide)

INTRODUCTION

Ethanoyl chloride and ethanoic anhydride can be used as ethanoylating agents. However, a mixture of ethanoic anhydride and ethanoic acid is often used, for the reaction is not violent and it has the added advantage over ethanoyl chloride of not generating hydrogen chloride fumes. *N*-Phenylethanamide is purified by recrystallisation from hot water.

REAGENTS

Glacial ethanoic acid (4 cm^3)
Ethanoic anhydride (4 cm^3)
Phenylamine (4 cm^3)

EQUATION

$$(CH_3CO)_2O + C_6H_5NH_2 \longrightarrow CH_3-CO-NH-C_6H_5 + CH_3COOH$$
$$N\text{-Phenylethanamide}$$

DETAILS

Place 4 cm^3 of ethanoic acid and 4 cm^3 of ethanoic anhydride in a flask. Cool the flask by immersing it in a beaker of cold water and add slowly 4 cm^3 of phenylamine with gentle swirling. Fit the flask with a reflux water condenser (cf. Figure 22) and boil the contents gently under reflux for half an hour.

Transfer the hot liquid to a 250 cm^3 beaker containing 100 cm^3 of cold water. Filter off the crystals of *N*-phenylethanamide at the pump, wash with cold distilled water, and dry in a steam oven.

The crystals may be further purified by recrystallisation from hot water.

PHYSICAL CONSTANTS

M.p. 113 °C; B.p. 304 °C.

21

DIAZONIUM SALTS

Structural Formula

$$\left[\bigcirc\!\!\!\!-\overset{+}{N}\!\equiv\!N \right] Cl^-$$

21.1. Test-tube Preparation of Benzenediazonium Chloride

Place 3 cm^3 of phenylamine in a boiling-tube. Add 10 cm^3 of water, then 8 cm^3 of concentrated hydrochloric acid. Cork the tube, and shake to dissolve the phenylammonium chloride. Remove the cork and insert the tube in a beaker containing a freezing mixture of ice and salt. The solution must be cooled to below 5°C. Make up a solution of 3 g of sodium nitrite in 8 cm^3 of water, and cool this solution to 5°C before adding it slowly to the amine solution, taking great care that the temperature of the solution does not rise above 10°C. The diazonium solution is used for the reactions without further purification.

$$C_6H_5NH_2 + HNO_2 + HCl \longrightarrow [C_6H_5N_2]^+Cl^- + 2H_2O$$
$$\text{Benzenediazonium}$$
$$\text{chloride}$$

21.2. Reactions of Benzenediazonium Chloride

A. REPLACEMENT REACTIONS. REPLACEMENT OF $-N_2^+Cl^-$ BY ANOTHER FUNCTIONAL GROUP

1. **Replacement by —OH group.** Transfer 2 cm^3 of the diazonium solution to a test-tube, and boil it gently. An oily liquid forms. Note the smell of phenol.

$$[C_6H_5N_2]^+Cl^- + H_2O \longrightarrow C_6H_5OH + N_2 + HCl$$

2. **Replacement by —Cl atom. Sandmeyer reaction.** In a test-tube, dissolve about 1 g of copper(I) chloride in a mixture of 1 cm^3 of concentrated hydrochloric acid and 2 cm^3 of water.

Place the test-tube in a beaker of warm water so that the solution is at 60° C. Add 3 cm³ of diazonium solution dropwise from a dropping pipette. Nitrogen is evolved, and chlorobenzene separates as an oil:

$$[C_6H_5N_2]^+Cl^- \xrightarrow{Cu_2Cl_2} C_6H_5Cl + N_2$$

3. **Replacement by —Cl atom. Gattermann reaction.** Add a few copper turnings to about 3 cm³ of the diazonium solution. Nitrogen is evolved slowly in the cold. Chlorobenzene separates as an oil. Note the odour of the chlorobenzene.

$$[C_6H_5N_2]^+Cl^- \xrightarrow{Cu} C_6H_5Cl + N_2$$

4. **Replacement by —I atom.** Transfer 2 cm³ of the diazonium solution to a test-tube. Make up a 1% solution of potassium iodide and cool it to below 5° C in a beaker of ice. Add 1 cm³ of the potassium iodide solution, dropwise, to the diazonium solution. Allow the mixture to stand for 5 minutes, and then gently boil. Oily drops of iodobenzene are formed:

$$[C_6H_5N_2]^+Cl^- + K^+I^- \longrightarrow C_6H_5I + N_2 + K^+Cl^-$$

The small-scale preparation of iodobenzene is described in Section 22.2.

B. COUPLING REACTIONS. AZO DYES

5. Transfer 2 cm³ of the diazonium solution to a test-tube. Add phenylamine, previously cooled to below 5° C, dropwise. A yellow precipitate of *N*-(phenylazo)phenylamine is formed:

6. Dissolve 2 crystals of phenol in 2 cm³ of dilute sodium hydroxide solution. Cool this solution to below 5° C and add the diazonium solution dropwise. A yellow precipitate of the dye, (4-hydroxyphenyl)azobenzene, is precipitated:

7. Repeat experiment 6, using naphthalen-2-ol instead of phenol. A red dye is formed:

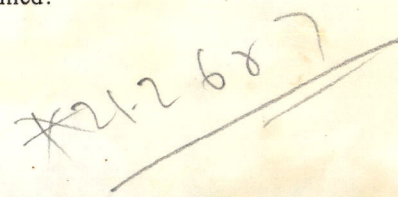

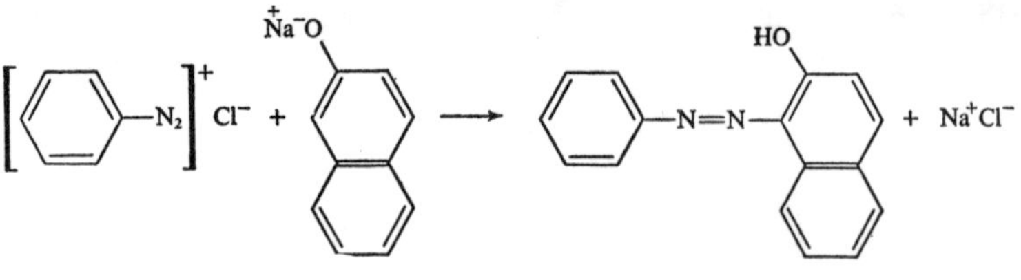

21.3. Preparation of Methyl Orange and Orange II

Dissolve 2 g of 4-aminobenzenesulphonic acid and 0.5 g of sodium carbonate in 20 cm^3 of water in a boiling tube. Cool the solution in a freezing mixture, and add 1 g of sodium nitrite dissolved in 2 cm^3 of water. Add 2 cm^3 of concentrated hydrochloric acid dropwise, keeping the temperature of the solution below 5° C. Divide the solution into two.

1. To one portion of solution, add 0.5 cm^3 of *N,N*-dimethylphenylamine dissolved in 0.5 cm^3 of ethanoic acid. The red form of **methyl orange** is obtained:

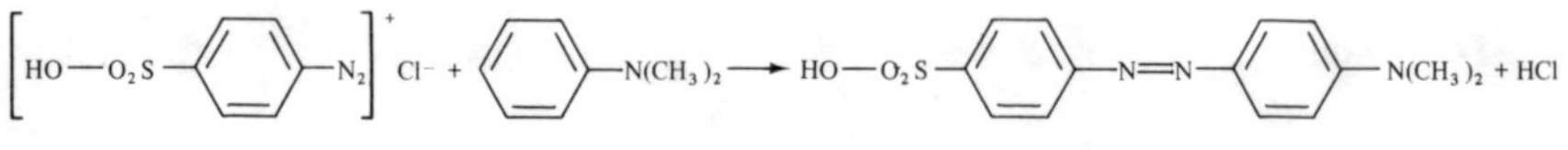

Methyl orange

If excess alkali is added, the yellow form is produced.

2. To the second portion of the solution, add 0.5 g of naphthalen-2-ol dissolved in 4 cm^3 of 2M sodium hydroxide solution. **Orange II** is precipitated.

Orange II

22

AROMATIC HALOGEN COMPOUNDS

22.1. Small-scale Preparation of Bromobenzene

INTRODUCTION

The hydrogen atoms in the aromatic nucleus can be **substituted** by halogen atoms if the reaction is carried out at room temperature with the halogen in the presence of a catalyst (halogen carrier). In this example, benzene is brominated, using bromine at room temperature. Bromobenzene is purified by distillation.

The mechanism of the reaction is thought to be ionic (cf. Section 22.6). In the bromination of benzene, iron(III) bromide, formed from iron and bromine, acts as the catalyst by withdrawing electrons from the bond between the bromine atoms:

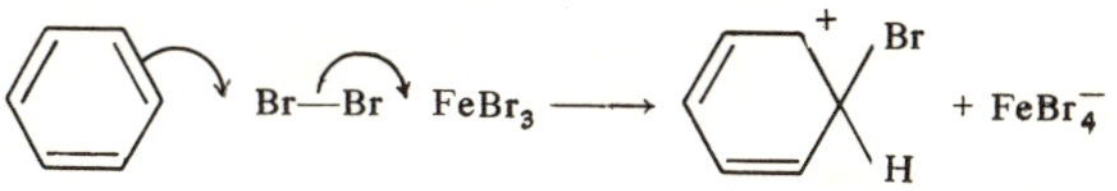

The charge on the carbonium ion is delocalised on the 2-, 4- and 6-positions. The carbonium ion then reacts with the anion:

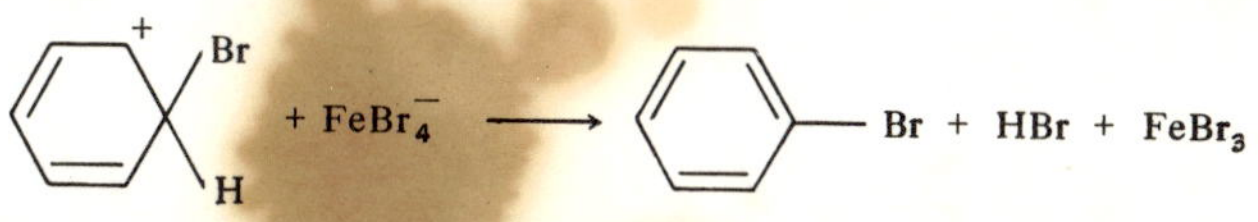

The catalyst is regenerated.

REAGENTS

Benzene (6 cm^3)
Bromine (3 cm^3)
Iron wire (0.2 g) *or* iron filings (0.2 g)
2M sodium hydroxide solution
Calcium chloride, anhydrous

EQUATION

$C_6H_6 + Br_2 \longrightarrow C_6H_5Br + HBr$

DETAILS

The experiment should be carried out in the fume cupboard, if possible.

Place 6 cm^3 of benzene and 0.2 g of clean iron wire (*or* 0.2 g iron filings) in the flask. Immerse the flask in a bath of cold water and set up the apparatus (Figure 31, Plate 6). Place 3 cm^3 of bromine in the dropping funnel **(CARE)**. Run the bromine slowly into the water-cooled flask. When all the bromine has been added, raise the temperature of the water-bath to 30° C and maintain at this temperature for about 20 minutes. Raise the temperature of the bath still further to 70° C. Maintain this temperature until the evolution of hydrogen

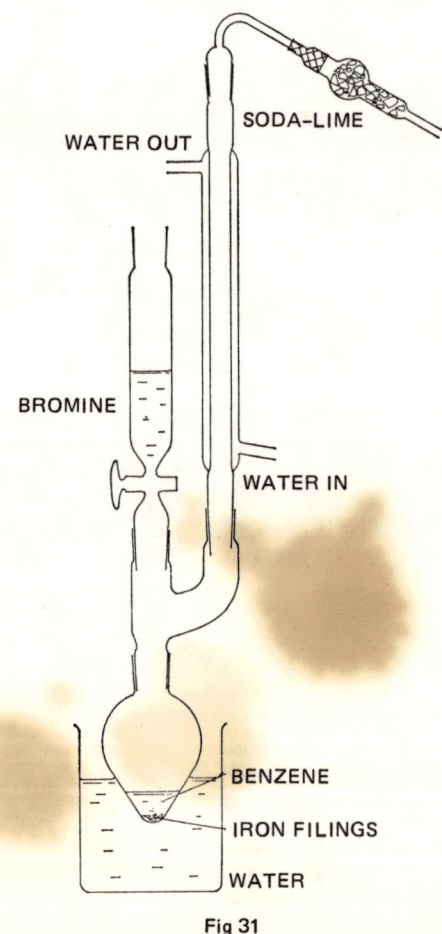

Fig 31

bromide ceases. The soda-lime tube should absorb most of the fumes of bromine and of hydrogen bromide. A further precaution may be necessary. A rubber tube should lead from the end of the soda-lime tube to the drain of a sink.

Remove the flask, cool under the tap, and transfer the contents either to the separating funnel or to a test-tube. Add an equal volume of dilute sodium hydroxide solution and shake. Allow the 2 layers to separate and remove and reject the upper aqueous layer. Test the crude bromobenzene with Universal Indicator paper (or blue litmus paper). If the reaction is acid, repeat the washing with another portion of sodium hydroxide solution. Wash twice with water, in each case rejecting the upper aqueous layer.

Transfer the liquid to a clean test-tube. Add 2 or 3 small pieces of anhydrous calcium chloride, cork, and allow to stand until the liquid is no longer turbid. Transfer the liquid to a clean, dry flask and distil, using an air condenser (cf. Figure 25, Plate 1). Collect the distillate between 152° C and 158° C.

PHYSICAL CONSTANTS

B.p. 156° C; density at 20° C: 1.49 g cm^{-3}

22.2. Small-scale Preparation of Iodobenzene

INTRODUCTION

It is difficult to iodinate benzene directly for the reaction between benzene and iodine is reversible:

$$C_6H_6 + I_2 \rightleftharpoons C_6H_5I + HI$$

Iodobenzene is usually prepared from benzenediazonium chloride, obtained from phenylamine. Potassium iodide reacts readily with diazonium compounds to form the aromatic iodo-compound.

Iodobenzene is purified from involatile inorganic impurities by steam distillation, for iodobenzene is almost insoluble in water. To obtain a good separation the distillate is shaken with several portions of ether, for the partition coefficient for iodobenzene between ether and water favours the ether layer. Final purification is by distillation.

REAGENTS

Phenylamine (2 cm^3)
Concentrated hydrochloric acid (6 cm^3)
Sodium nitrite (1.7 g)
Potassium iodide (5 g)
Diethyl ether
10% solution of sodium hydroxide
Calcium chloride, anhydrous

EQUATIONS

$$NaNO_2 + HCl \longrightarrow HNO_2 + NaCl$$

$$C_6H_5NH_2 + HNO_2 + HCl \longrightarrow [C_6H_5N_2]^+Cl^- + 2H_2O$$

Benzenediazonium
chloride

$$[C_6H_5N_2]^+Cl^- + KI \longrightarrow C_6H_5I + N_2 + KCl$$

1. PREPARATION OF BENZENEDIAZONIUM CHLORIDE SOLUTION

Place 2 cm^3 of phenylamine in a 50 cm^3 flask and add a mixture of 6 cm^3 of concentrated hydrochloric acid and 6 cm^3 of water. Swirl gently to dissolve the amine. Place a thermometer in the flask and cool the mixture in an ice-salt mixture.

Dissolve 1.7 g of sodium nitrite in 4 cm^3 of water in a test-tube, and cool in the freezing mixture. Introduce the mixture slowly into the flask. Stir the mixture with the thermometer and do not allow the temperature to rise above 10° C. The flask now contains a solution of benzenediazonium chloride.

2. PREPARATION OF IODOBENZENE

Dissolve 5 g of potassium iodide in 6 cm^3 of water in a test-tube, and cool in the freezing mixture. Add the solution to the benzenediazonium chloride solution, keeping the flask in the freezing mixture, and not allowing the temperature of the mixture to rise above 10° C. When all of the potassium iodide solution has been added, transfer the flask to a cold water-bath, and fit a reflux condenser (cf. Figure 22).

After 10 minutes, bring the water in the bath gently to the boil and maintain it at this temperature for about 15 minutes. Nitrogen is evolved and dark, oily drops of impure iodobenzene settle out.

Separate the iodobenzene by steam distillation, using the apparatus shown in Figure 30 and Plate 5.

Extract the iodobenzene from the distillate with three successive 4 cm^3 portions of ether, using the separating funnel. Combine the ethereal extracts and wash them first with 5 cm^3 of 10% sodium hydroxide solution and then with 5 cm^3 of water. In each case, reject the washings. Dry the ethereal solution of iodobenzene by allowing it to stand in contact with fused calcium chloride in a stoppered test-tube until the solution is quite clear.

Distil off the ether from a hot water-bath (cf. Figure 8). **Heat the water well away from the ethereal solution.** Remove the hot water-bath and distil the iodobenzene, using the condenser as an air condenser. Collect the fraction distilling between 185° C and 191° C.

PHYSICAL CONSTANTS

B.p. 188° C; density at 20° C: 1.83 g cm^{-3}

22.3. Reactions of Chlorobenzene and (Chloromethyl)benzene (Benzyl Chloride)

Structural Formulae

Chlorobenzene   (Chloromethyl)benzene

A. TO CONTRAST THE REACTIVITY OF A CHLORINE ATOM DIRECTLY ATTACHED TO THE NUCLEUS WITH THE REACTIVITY OF A CHLORINE ATOM IN A SIDE CHAIN

1. Place 5 drops of chlorobenzene and of (chloromethyl)benzene respectively in separate test-tubes. In another test-tube, for comparison, place 5 drops of 1-chlorobutane. To each test-tube, add 1 cm^3 of dilute sodium hydroxide solution. Shake and warm. Acidify with dilute nitric acid and add 1 cm^3 of silver nitrate solution.
   Compare the results with those obtained in Section 4.6.

B. TO SHOW THAT BOTH CHLOROCOMPOUNDS ARE EXHIBITING AROMATIC CHARACTERISTICS

2. Place 1 cm^3 of concentrated nitric acid in a test-tube, and then add 1 cm^3 of concentrated sulphuric acid. Shake the mixture and cool the test-tube under a stream of cold water. Divide the mixed acids into 2 portions. To one portion, add 5 drops of chlorobenzene. To the other, add 5 drops of (chloromethyl)-benzene. Cool under the tap and shake. Warm gently and note the almond odour of the 2- and 4-nitro derivatives of chlorobenzene and (chloromethyl)-benzene. For example:

2-nitrochlorobenzene

4-nitrochlorobenzene

22.4. Small-scale Praparation of Phenyl Magnesium Bromide Solution (a Grignard Reagent) and Benzoic Acid

INTRODUCTION

Grignard reagents are obtained by refluxing dry ethereal solutions of alkyl and aryl halides (usually the iodide or the bromide) with small magnesium turnings:

$$RX + Mg \longrightarrow R-Mg-X$$

A small crystal of iodine is usually required to initiate the reaction. The Grignard reagent is reasonably stable when dissolved in ether, and no attempt should be made to isolate it. It is this solution which is used for further reaction.

Grignard reagents undergo two series of reactions. First, by decomposition: for example, addition of water yields an alkane. Secondly, by addition of a group containing a double bond followed by decomposition of the intermediate. Thus, addition of methanal yields a primary alcohol, addition of a higher aldehyde yields a secondary alcohol, addition of a ketone yields a tertiary alcohol and addition of carbon dioxide yields a carboxylic acid. An example of the last reaction is given.

REAGENTS

Bromobenzene dried over anhydrous calcium chloride (5 cm^3)
Diethyl ether dried over sodium (15 cm^3)
Iodine crystals
Magnesium turnings (Grignard) (0.5 g)
Carbon dioxide (solid or Kipp's apparatus)
Concentrated hydrochloric acid
2M hydrochloric acid
2M sodium hydroxide solution
Sodium pellets
Calcium chloride, anhydrous

EQUATIONS

$$C_6H_5Br + Mg \longrightarrow C_6H_5-Mg-Br$$

$$C_6H_5-Mg-Br \xrightarrow{CO_2} C_6H_5 -\overset{\overset{\displaystyle O}{\|}}{C}-O-Mg-Br \xrightarrow{HCl} C_6H_5COOH + MgBrCl$$

DETAILS

(i) Preparation of phenyl magnesium bromide solution

All apparatus and materials used in the preparation of a Grignard reagent must be thoroughly dry since traces of moisture not only react with the reagent but also inhibit its formation. Make sure that the apparatus is clean and that it has been dried in an oven before the experiment.

Diethyl ether must stand over clean sodium wire or pellets and the bromobenzene over anhydrous calcium chloride in carefully stoppered tubes or flasks, if possible overnight, before the experiment is carried out.

Place 0.5 g of magnesium turnings in a flask and add one or two small crystals of iodine, followed by 10 cm^3 of dry ether. Stand the flask in a cold water-bath, add 2 cm^3 of dry bromobenzene, then fit a dry reflux condenser to the open end of which a calcium chloride drying tube is fitted.

Raise the temperature of the water-bath to 40-45° C, turn out the bunsen and allow the contents of the flask to reflux for 20-25 minutes. The disappearance of the colour of the iodine and the formation of a cloudiness in the reaction mixture are indications that the reaction is proceeding satisfactorily. Remove the warm water-bath and replace with a freezing mixture of ice and salt.

(ii) Preparation of benzoic acid

Arrange for the carbon dioxide, generated in the Kipp's apparatus, to be washed in water to remove traces of hydrochloric acid and to be dried by passing through concentrated sulphuric acid. A more satisfactory method is to place a few pieces of solid carbon dioxide in a conical flask and lead the carbon dioxide straight into the flask containing the solution, which should be immersed in ice.

Pass a gentle stream of dry carbon dioxide through the ethereal solution of phenyl magnesium bromide for 5-10 minutes. Decant the contents of the flask into a small beaker and place the latter in the freezing mixture. Dilute 3 cm^3 of concentrated hydrochloric acid by adding 3 cm^3 of water. Introduce the acid slowly, with stirring, into the beaker to liberate the benzoic acid.

Remove the beaker from the freezing mixture, add 15 cm^3 of ether and stir. Decant the liquid into a separating funnel and return the lower aqueous layer to the beaker. Repeat the ethereal extraction twice, using 5 cm^3 of ether each time.

Combine the ethereal extracts and shake with 10 cm^3 of dilute sodium hydroxide solution in a separating funnel. Remove the stopper from the funnel occasionally to release the pressure. Most of the benzoic acid enters the lower aqueous layer as the sodium salt. Transfer the aqueous layer to a beaker. (If a precipitate of magnesium hydroxide should appear, remove it by filtration through a Hirsch funnel.) Acidify the filtrate with dilute hydrochloric acid (testing the solution with Universal Indicator paper). A white precipitate of benzoic acid is obtained. Precipitation is hastened by cooling in the freezing mixture and scratching with a glass rod. Filter off the precipitate; wash *in situ* with distilled water. Dry the solid and take its melting point. If time, purify by recrystallisation from hot water. Dry the crystals in the oven at about 100° C and redetermine the melting point.

PHYSICAL CONSTANT

M.p. 121° C.

22.5. Small-scale Preparation of D.D.T.

Place 1 g of the hydrate of trichloroethanal (chloral hydrate) and 1.5 cm³ of chlorobenzene in a test-tube. Warm in a water-bath until the solid has dissolved. Add 10 cm³ of concentrated sulphuric acid (which absorbs water and displaces the equilibrium to the right). Stopper well and shake the mixture for about an hour. Pour the mixture into 20 cm³ of water in a small beaker. Filter the precipitate of D.D.T.

Transfer the solid to a beaker and shake with 5 cm³ of a 2% solution of sodium carbonate. Filter. Wash until washings are neutral.

Transfer the precipitate to a watch-glass and dry in an oven or over a water-bath. M.p. 107–108° C.

22.6. Small-scale Preparation of Hexachlorocyclohexane (Benzene Hexachloride)

An addition reaction between benzene and a halogen takes place in the presence of ultra-violet light. The ultra-violet light causes the decomposition of the chlorine molecule:

$$Cl_2 \xrightarrow{\text{u/v light}} Cl\cdot + Cl\cdot$$

The chlorine atoms add on to the benzene nucleus (cf. mechanism in Section 22.1).

Hexachlorocyclohexane is purified by recrystallisation from benzene. It exhibits geometric isomerism, the γ-isomer acting as an insecticide, and is sold under the name of 'Gammexane'.

REAGENTS

Benzene (15 cm³)
Potassium permanganate, solid
Concentrated hydrochloric acid
10% solution of sodium hydroxide

EQUATION

$$C_6H_6 + 3Cl_2 \xrightarrow{\text{u/v light}} C_6H_6Cl_6$$

DETAILS

Chlorine (generated by the action of concentrated hydrochloric acid on solid potassium permanganate) is dried by passage through concentrated sulphuric acid. It is passed through benzene (10 cm^3) at a slow rate for about 30 minutes, the benzene being warmed to about 45° C on a water-bath (Figure 32) and irradiated by ultra-violet radiation.

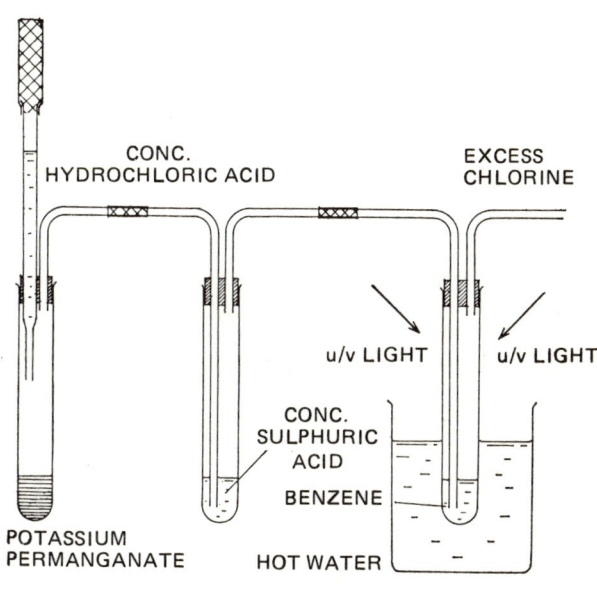

Fig 32

If possible, the chlorine escaping should be washed in a 10% solution of sodium hydroxide and passed into a vent of a fume cupboard.

The resulting benzene solution is gently evaporated on a water-bath **(no flame)** until crystals of hexachlorocyclohexane are formed. The solid residue is filtered, dried, and recrystallised from benzene.

PHYSICAL CONSTANTS

M.p. α-isomer 157° C (*ca.* 70%)
β-isomer 200° C (*ca.* 5%)
γ-isomer 111° C (*ca.* 10%)
δ-isomer 132° C (*ca.* 15%)

23

AROMATIC SULPHONIC ACIDS

23.1. Small-scale Preparation of Benzenesulphonic Acid and Sodium Benzenesulphonate

INTRODUCTION

The sulphonation of aromatic compounds is often carried out using sulphuric acid. The conditions of the reaction depend on the structure of the compound to be sulphonated.

Benzene is sulphonated with either concentrated or fuming sulphuric acid.

REAGENTS

Benzene (10 cm^3)
Concentrated sulphuric acid (10 cm^3)
Calcium carbonate, powdered (10 g)
Saturated sodium carbonate solution

EQUATIONS

$$C_6H_6 + H_2SO_4 \longrightarrow C_6H_5SO_3H + H_2O$$

$$2C_6H_5SO_3H + CaCO_3 \longrightarrow (C_6H_5SO_3)_2Ca + CO_2 + H_2O$$

$$(C_6H_5SO_3)_2Ca + Na_2CO_3 \longrightarrow 2C_6H_5SO_3Na + CaCO_3$$

DETAILS

Place 10 cm^3 of concentrated sulphuric acid in the flask and add 10 cm^3 of benzene. Reflux the mixture until two liquid layers no longer separate (about 6 hours) (cf. Figure 22). Allow the liquid to cool.

Pour the liquid into 100 cm^3 of water in a beaker and bring gently to the boil. Stir in 10 g of powdered calcium carbonate, and filter the hot solution at the pump. Reject the residue of calcium sulphate. Thus excess sulphuric acid is removed.

Concentrate the solution to about half bulk by evaporation. Add saturated sodium carbonate solution until there is no further precipitation of calcium carbonate. Filter at the pump, rejecting the residue of calcium carbonate. Concentrate the filtrate by evaporation until a test portion deposits crystals on cooling. Allow the solution to cool and to crystallise. Filter the mixture, using a Buchner funnel, and dry the residue between pieces of filter paper.

The sodium benzenesulphonate could be retained for the preparation of phenol (Section 24.1).

PHYSICAL CONSTANT

M.p. of benzenesulphonic acid, 65° C.

23.2. Preparation of a Detergent

If an alkylbenzene (for example Dobane JN) is sulphonated and then neutralised with sodium hydroxide, a detergent is formed (Section 28.4).

23.3. Reactions of Sodium Benzenesulphonate

Preparation of phenol. For details, see Section 24.1.

24

PHENOLS

24.1. Small-scale Preparation of Phenol

Structural Formula

INTRODUCTION

Phenol can be prepared by heating a mixture of sodium benzenesulphonate and sodium hydroxide. Sodium phenate is formed, but free phenol is liberated on addition of mineral acid.

Phenol is extracted from the mixture, using small portions of ether, for the partition coefficient for phenol between ether and water favours the ether layer.

Final purification of phenol is by distillation.

REAGENTS

Sodium benzenesulphonate (6 g)
Sodium hydroxide pellets (10 g)
Concentrated hydrochloric acid
Diethyl ether (15 cm^3)
Sodium sulphate, anhydrous

EQUATIONS

$$C_6H_5SO_3Na + 2NaOH \longrightarrow C_6H_5ONa + Na_2SO_3 + H_2O$$

$$C_6H_5ONa + HCl \longrightarrow C_6H_5OH + NaCl$$

$$(Na_2SO_3 + 2HCl \longrightarrow 2NaCl + H_2O + SO_2)$$

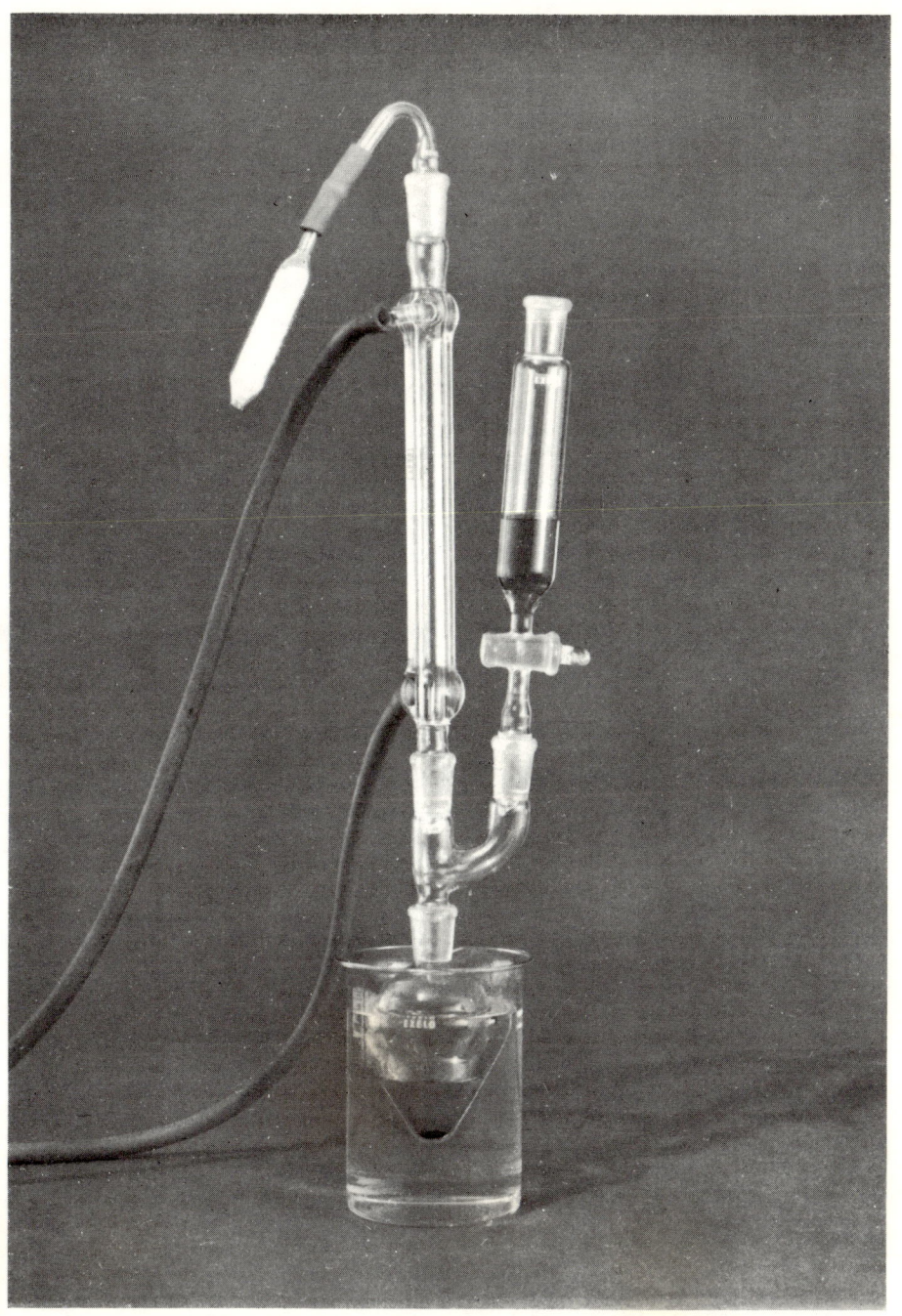

PLATE 6

Preparations of bromobenzene (Fig. 31, p. 118) and phenylethanone
(Fig. 34, p. 137)

DETAILS

Fit a semi-micro test-tube to a 0–360° C thermometer, using a short length of rubber tubing (Figure 33). This will protect the bulb of the thermometer when it is used as a stirrer.

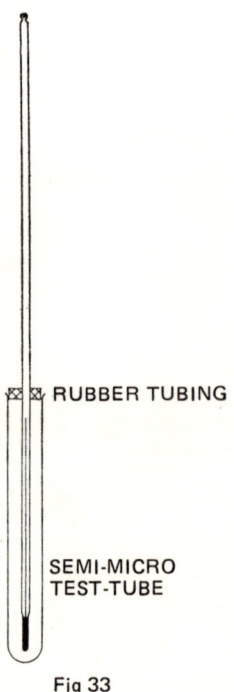

RUBBER TUBING

SEMI-MICRO
TEST-TUBE

Fig 33

Place 10 g of sodium hydroxide pellets and 2 cm³ of water in a nickel crucible. Heat gradually to 250° C, stirring with the thermometer. Stir 6 g of powdered sodium benzenesulphonate into the molten alkali. Maintain the mixture at this temperature for 1 hour, stirring occasionally. Remove the thermometer and allow the melt to cool and to solidify.

Add a little water to the crucible, warm, and pour the solution into a 250 cm³ beaker. Repeat this procedure to remove all the solid from the crucible, using about 30 cm³ of water in all. Add concentrated hydrochloric acid slowly to the solution, stirring until it is just acid. This will liberate phenol as dark oily drops.

Extract the phenol three times with ether, using 5 cm³ portions on each occasion. Combine the ethereal extracts. Dry the solution by allowing it to stand over 1 g of anhydrous sodium sulphate for 30 minutes in a stoppered test-tube.

Transfer the extract to a clean, dry flask. Distil off the ether from a water-bath (cf. Figure 8). **Do not use a flame.** The water must be previously heated to 60° C. Clean and dry the condenser and receiver. Distil off the phenol, using the condenser as an air condenser. Collect the fraction distilling in the range 179–183° C.

PHYSICAL CONSTANTS

M.p. 42° C; B.p. 181° C.

24.2 Reactions of Phenol

A. REACTIONS DIFFERENT FROM THOSE OF ETHANOL
(cf. SECTION 5.2)

1. Dissolve 0.5 g of phenol in about 5 cm^3 of water in a test-tube. Add 1 drop of Universal Indicator solution (or blue litmus solution). A red colour shows that phenol is an acid.

$$C_6H_5OH \rightleftharpoons C_6H_5O^- + H^+$$

2. To about 0.5 g of phenol in a test-tube, add about 5 cm^3 of water. Shake. Phenol does not dissolve readily in water, and 2 layers form when the test-tube is allowed to stand. Now add dilute sodium hydroxide solution dropwise. The phenol dissolves. This is due to the formation of the salt, sodium phenate, which is soluble in water:

$$C_6H_5OH + Na^+OH^- \longrightarrow C_6H_5O^-Na^+ + H_2O$$

Phenol		Sodium phenate

$$Acid + Base \longrightarrow Salt + Water$$

3. Make up a neutral solution of iron(III) chloride (Section 8.2, experiment 1). Place 5 drops of this solution in a test-tube, and add 1 crystal of phenol (or 1 drop of an aqueous solution of phenol). There is a violet coloration, characteristic of all compounds containing the enol group (Section 9.2, experiment 2).

4. To a few crystals of phenol in a test-tube, add 1 cm^3 of water. Shake and warm the solution. Allow to cool and add bromine water dropwise, until a precipitate of 2,4,6-tribromophenol is obtained:

5. **The phthalein test.** Mix 0.1 g of phenol and 0.1 g of benzene-1,2-dicarboxylic anhydride together in a test-tube. Add 1 drop of concentrated sulphuric acid. Warm the mixture until it is molten. Continue heating for about 3 minutes. Cool the mixture and add dilute sodium hydroxide solution to the solid mass. A red solution is formed. Add dilute hydrochloric acid to the red solution. When the end-point is reached, the solution turns from red to colourless. Excess alkali turns the solution red again. The substance formed is phenolphthalein.

6. **Liebermann's test.** Place 0.1 g of phenol in a test-tube. Add one small crystal of sodium nitrite and then 8 drops of concentrated sulphuric acid. Shake gently and a green or blue colour develops. Pour the mixture into a test-tube containing about 2 cm^3 of water. A red colour is formed. On adding excess dilute sodium hydroxide solution, the green or blue colour returns.

B. REACTIONS SIMILAR TO THOSE OF ETHANOL (cf. SECTION 5.2)

7. Phenol reacts with ethanoyl chloride to form phenyl ethanoate. To a few crystals of phenol, add ethanoyl chloride dropwise (**CARE**):

$$CH_3COCl + C_6H_5OH \longrightarrow CH_3COOC_6H_5 + HCl$$

8. Phenol reacts with ethanoic anhydride to form phenyl ethanoate (Section 9.6, experiment 3).

9. **Schotten-Baumann reaction.** Dissolve a few crystals of phenol in 2 cm^3 of dilute sodium hydroxide solution. Add benzoyl chloride drop by drop and shake. A white precipitate of phenyl benzoate is formed:

$$C_6H_5COCl + NaOH + C_6H_5OH \longrightarrow C_6H_5COOC_6H_5 + NaCl + H_2O$$
$$\text{Phenyl benzoate}$$

The ester can be purified by filtering, washing with water, and redissolving in the minimum of warm ethanol. Allow this solution to cool, and crystals of the ester are deposited which can be filtered, washed, and dried. M.p. 69° C.

25

AROMATIC ALCOHOLS

25.1. Reactions of Phenylmethanol (Benzyl Alcohol)

The reactions of phenylmethanol are similar to those of aliphatic alcohols (Section 5.2). It is important to realise that aromatic alcohols are not phenols. Phenylmethanol should be freshly distilled.

A. SOME REACTIONS SIMILAR TO THOSE OF ETHANOL (cf. SECTION 5.2)

1. To 5 drops of phenylmethanol, add 10 drops of dilute sulphuric acid and 2 drops of potassium dichromate solution. The solution turns from orange to green on slight warming, due to the reduction of potassium dichromate to chromium(III) sulphate, and phenylmethanol is oxidised to benzaldehyde.

2. To 5 drops of phenylmethanol in a test-tube, add 10 drops of dilute sulphuric acid and 2 drops of a 1% solution of potassium permanganate solution and gently warm. The solution turns from purple to colourless as potassium permanganate is reduced to manganese(II) sulphate and the phenylmethanol is oxidised to benzaldehyde.

3. Warm a mixture of 5 drops of phenylmethanol and 5 drops of ethanoic acid with 1 drop of concentrated sulphuric acid. Note the smell of the ester, (phenylmethyl) ethanoate.

$$CH_3COOH + C_6H_5CH_2OH \xrightarrow{H^+} CH_3COOCH_2C_6H_5 + H_2O$$

4. Place 5 drops of phenylmethanol in a test-tube, and add 1 drop of ethanoyl chloride **(CARE)**. Add about 5 cm^3 of water. The ester separates as an oil and has the characteristic smell of many esters.

$$CH_3COCl + C_6H_5CH_2OH \longrightarrow CH_3COOCH_2C_6H_5 + HCl$$

B. SOME REACTIONS THAT ARE DIFFERENT FROM THOSE OF PHENOL (cf. SECTION 24.2)

5. Repeat the experiments 1, 2, 3, 5 and 6 in Section 24.2. These show that the compound is not a phenol.

26

AROMATIC ALDEHYDES AND KETONES

26.1. Small-scale Preparation of Benzaldehyde

INTRODUCTION

Acidified sodium (or potassium) dichromate solution oxidises phenylmethanol to benzaldehyde and then to benzoic acid. In order to obtain a good yield of benzaldehyde, it is important that the oxidising agent is not in excess.

REAGENTS

Phenylmethanol (6 cm^3)
Sodium dichromate (5 g)
Concentrated sulphuric acid (4 cm^3)
Calcium chloride, anhydrous

EQUATION

$$Na_2Cr_2O_7 + 4H_2SO_4 + 3C_6H_5CH_2OH \longrightarrow Na_2SO_4 + Cr_2(SO_4)_3$$
$$+ 7H_2O + 3C_6H_5CHO$$

DETAILS

Place 10 cm^3 of water in a flask and add slowly 4 cm^3 of concentrated sulphuric acid, swirling gently and cooling under the tap. Immerse the flask in a beaker of cold water and fit it with a reflux condenser as shown in Figure 10.

Dissolve 5 g of sodium dichromate in 5 cm^3 of water contained in a small beaker. Add 6 cm^3 of phenylmethanol and stir with a glass rod. Add the mixture in 1 cm^3 portions, using a dropping pipette, to the acid in the flask. Swirl the contents of the flask gently after the addition of each portion, keeping the flask immersed in cold water.

When all the mixture has been transferred to the flask, bring the water in the beaker slowly to the boil and allow the contents of the flask to reflux for 10 minutes to complete the reaction.

Allow the apparatus to cool. Wash the condenser with warm water and arrange the apparatus for distillation (Figure 25), placing anti-bumping granules in the flask. Distil the mixture over a gauze, using a small flame. Collect 15-20 cm^3 of distillate which consists of a mixture of benzaldehyde and water.

Transfer the distillate to a separating funnel and run the lower layer of benzaldehyde into a clean, dry 100 cm^3 beaker. Extract benzaldehyde from the aqueous layer by shaking with two separate 5 cm^3 portions of ether and transfer the ethereal extracts to the beaker. If it is necessary, and water is present, transfer the mixture to a clean, dry separating funnel and discard any lower aqueous layer.

Run the ethereal solution into a boiling tube, and add some small pieces of anhydrous calcium chloride. Stopper the tube and shake it for a few minutes.

Decant the solution into a clean, dry flask and distil off the ether from a hot water-bath (the water must be previously heated to about 70° C) (Figure 8). **DO NOT USE A FLAME**.

Clean and dry the condenser and receiver and distil off the benzaldehyde, collecting the fraction distilling in the range 178-181° C.

PHYSICAL CONSTANTS

B.p. 179° C; density at 15° C: 1.05 g cm^{-3}

26.2. Reactions of Benzaldehyde

A. REACTIONS SIMILAR TO THOSE OF METHANAL AND ETHANAL

1. **The silver mirror test** (cf. Section 7.6, experiment 1). As benzaldehyde is sparingly soluble in water it does not readily reduce an ammoniacal solution of silver nitrate.

2. **Schiff's reagent** (cf. Section 7.6, experiment 3). Note that benzaldehyde restores the pink colour slowly.

3. Unlike ethanal, benzaldehyde does not reduce **Fehling's solution** readily (Section 7.6, experiment 2).

4. **Action of oxidising agents.** Benzaldehyde decolorises potassium permanganate solution acidified with dilute sulphuric acid. The coloured permanganate ions are reduced to manganese(II) ions (cf. Section 7.6, experiment 4).

5. Benzaldehyde reduces potassium dichromate solution acidified with dilute sulphuric acid to green chromium(III) ions, while the aldehyde is oxidised to the acid (cf. Section 7.6, experiment 5).

6. **Addition reactions.** Benzaldehyde undergoes an addition reaction with sodium hydrogensulphite (cf. Section 7.6, experiment 6).

$$C_6H_5 - \overset{\overset{\displaystyle H}{|}}{C} = O + NaHSO_3 \longrightarrow C_6H_5 - \overset{\overset{\displaystyle H}{|}}{\underset{\underset{\displaystyle SO_3^-Na^+}{|}}{C}} - OH$$

Benzaldehyde
hydrogensulphite

Condensation reactions

7. Benzaldehyde undergoes condensation reactions. For example, it reacts with 2,4-dinitrophenylhydrazine to form a yellow precipitate of benzaldehyde 2,4-dinitrophenylhydrazone, m.p. $273°$ C (cf. Section 7.6, experiment 8).

8. Repeat experiment 9 in Section 7.6, using benzaldehyde in place of ethanal (M.p. of benzaldehyde semicarbazone, $214°$ C.)

B. REACTIONS SIMILAR TO THOSE OF METHANAL ONLY. THESE REACTIONS ARE UNLIKE THOSE OF ETHANAL

9. **Reaction with alkali. Cannizzaro reaction**. Mix together 5 cm^3 of benzaldehyde, 10 cm^3 of diisopropyl ether and 5 cm^3 of a saturated solution of potassium hydroxide in a boiling tube. Stopper the tube, shake for at least 10 minutes and allow to stand for several hours (overnight if possible).

$$2C_6H_5CHO + KOH \longrightarrow C_6H_5COO^-K^+ + C_6H_5CH_2OH$$

Pour the mixture into a beaker containing about 20 cm^3 of water, which will dissolve the potassium benzoate formed.

Separate the mixture, using a separating funnel. Extract the aqueous layer with two or three small portions of diisopropyl ether.

Add dilute hydrochloric acid to the aqueous layer to precipitate the benzoic acid. Filter the acid and dissolve it in the minimum of boiling water. Allow to cool and filter the needle-shaped crystals. M.p. $121°$ C.

$$C_6H_5COOK + HCl \longrightarrow C_6H_5COOH + KCl$$

Benzoic acid

Pour the ethereal extract into a small conical flask and add some solid anhydrous potassium carbonate to dry it. Allow to stand for 30 minutes and then fractionate the dry extract. **(CARE–ETHER.)** First use a water-bath, using water previously heated (cf. Figure 8), until the ether has been distilled. Then take away the water-bath and use a bunsen flame to distil phenylmethanol. B.p. $204–207°$ C.

Unlike ethanal, benzaldehyde does not form a resin with strong solutions of alkali.

26.3. Small-scale Preparation of Phenylethanone (Acetophenone)

INTRODUCTION

Phenylethanone is prepared from benzene and ethanoyl chloride using a Friedel-Crafts reaction. Aluminium chloride acts as the catalyst.

$$CH_3COCl + AlCl_3 \longrightarrow CH_3CO^+ + AlCl_4^-$$
$$C_6H_6 + CH_3CO^+ \longrightarrow C_6H_5COCH_3 + H^+$$
$$AlCl_4^- + H^+ \longrightarrow AlCl_3 + HCl$$

The ketone is purified by extraction with benzene, for the partition coefficient for phenylethanone between benzene and water favours the organic layer. Final purification is by distillation.

REAGENTS

Benzene (9 cm^3)
Ethanoyl chloride (4 cm^3)
Aluminium chloride, anhydrous (6 g)
10% solution of sodium hydroxide

EQUATION

$$C_6H_6 + CH_3COCl \xrightarrow[\text{catalyst}]{\text{AlCl}_3 \text{ as}} C_6H_5COCH_3 + HCl$$
$$\text{Phenylethanone}$$

DETAILS

Place 6 g of fresh, anhydrous aluminium chloride in a flask. Add 4 cm^3 of dry benzene and set up the apparatus in a fume cupboard (Figure 34, Plate 6). Place 4 cm^3 of ethanoyl chloride in the dropping funnel and immerse the flask in a bath of cold water. Add the ethanoyl chloride slowly from the tap funnel, swirling gently after each addition. When all of the ethanoyl chloride has been added, raise the temperature of the water-bath to 50-60° C and maintain the contents of the flask at this temperature, under reflux, for half an hour.

Transfer the contents of the flask to a beaker containing 30 cm^3 of distilled water. Stir and allow the phenylethanone to separate as a dark oil. Transfer the liquid to a separating funnel, add 5 cm^3 of benzene and shake. The phenylethanone dissolves in the benzene layer. Allow two layers to separate, and then remove and reject the lower aqueous layer.

Wash the benzene layer with 5 cm^3 of dilute sodium hydroxide solution and then with 5 cm^3 of water, in each case rejecting the lower aqueous layer. Dry the liquid by allowing it to stand over anhydrous calcium chloride in a stoppered test-tube. Transfer the dry solution to a clean, dry flask.

Set up the apparatus as shown in Figure 8. Distil off the benzene on a water-bath.

Empty the condenser of water and use it as an air condenser. Distil off the

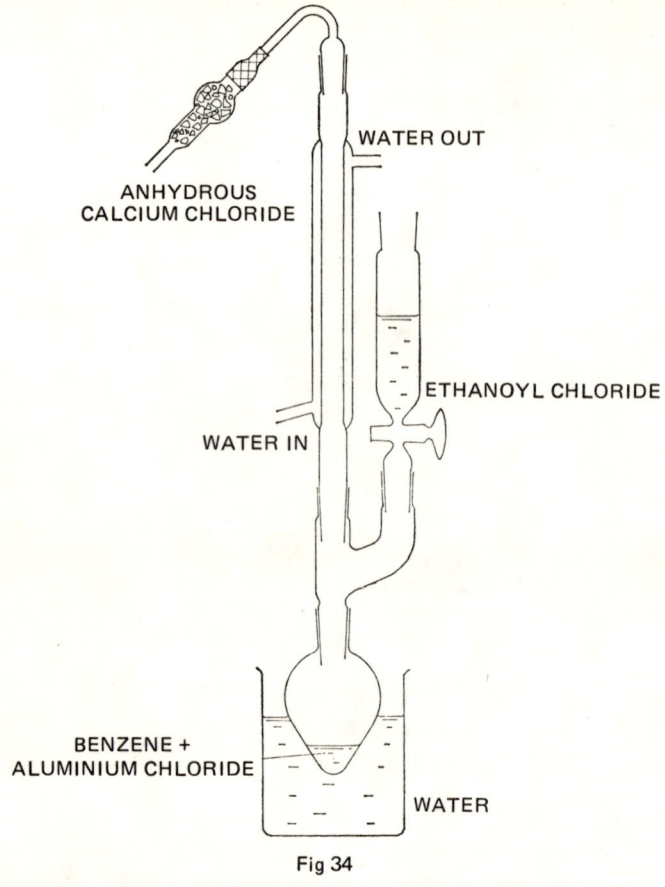

WATER OUT

ANHYDROUS
CALCIUM CHLORIDE

ETHANOYL CHLORIDE

WATER IN

BENZENE +
ALUMINIUM CHLORIDE

WATER

Fig 34

ketone using a bunsen flame instead of a water-bath. Collect the fraction distilling between 195° C and 203° C.

PHYSICAL CONSTANTS

M.p. 20° C; B.p. 202° C; density at 20° C: 1.03 g cm^{-3}

26.4. Reactions of Phenylethanone

A. REACTIONS SIMILAR TO THOSE OF PROPANONE (cf. SECTION 7.8)

1. Phenylethanone, like aliphatic ketones, is not a strong reducing agent. It does not undergo the **silver mirror test** (Section 7.6, experiment 1), or **Fehling's**

test (Section 7.6, experiment 2).

It does not restore the colour to **Schiff's reagent** (Section 7.6, experiment 3).

2. Phenylethanone, like propanone, undergoes the **iodoform reaction.** This shows that the molecule contains the group CH_3CO- (For details see Section 7.6, experiment 13.)

3. Phenylethanone, like propanone, reacts with 2,4-dinitrophenylhydrazine. M.p. of the 2,4-dinitrophenylhydrazone, 250° C. (For details see Section 7.6, experiment 8.)

   This condensation reaction is typical of all compounds containing a reactive $>C=O$ **group.**

4. Repeat experiment 9 in section 7.6, using phenylethanone instead of ethanal (M.p. of phenylethanone semicarbazone, 162° C.)

   B. REACTIONS DIFFERENT FROM THOSE OF PROPANONE (cf. SECTION 7.8)

5. Phenylethanone readily reduces acidified potassium permanganate solution, and is itself oxidised to benzoic acid.

   Contrast this reaction with that of propanone.

27

AROMATIC ACIDS AND THEIR DERIVATIVES

27.1. Preparations of Benzoic Acid

1. From benzaldehyde. Cannizzaro reaction (Section 26.2, experiment 9).
2. From bromobenzene (Section 22.4).

27.2. Properties of Benzoic Acid

1. Heat about 0.5 g of benzoic acid in a test-tube. Note the sublimate of long needle-shaped crystals on the side of the test-tube.
2. Mix 5 drops of ethanol with 0.5 g of benzoic acid in a test-tube and add 1 drop of concentrated sulphuric acid. Warm the mixture. Note the pleasant smell of ethyl benzoate.

$$C_6H_5COOH + C_2H_5OH \xrightarrow{\;H^+\;} C_6H_5COOC_2H_5 + H_2O$$

27.3. Reduction of a Carboxylic Acid by Lithium Aluminium Hydride

INTRODUCTION

Lithium aluminium hydride is used to reduce, amongst others, the following functional groups:

Carboxyl and aldehyde to primary alcohol

Carbonyl to secondary alcohol

Cyanide, amide and nitro to amino.

Its powerful nature is exemplified by its ability to reduce carboxylic acids to primary alcohols, and this is why an example is given here. Furthermore, it is a specific reagent; for example, it does not reduce unsaturated carbon–carbon bonds (as in alkenes and alkynes).

The acid chosen for this reaction is 2-chlorobenzoic acid as the product, 2-chlorophenylmethanol, is a solid.

REAGENTS

Lithium aluminium hydride (0.5 g)
2-Chlorobenzoic acid (1.5 g)
Diethyl ether, dried over sodium (30 cm^3)
Ethyl ethanoate (5 cm^3)
M sulphuric acid (20 cm^3)
Sodium sulphate, anhydrous

DETAILS

Lithium aluminium hydride is a dangerous chemical. It reacts violently with water and only dry solvents and dry apparatus must be used. Experiments should be done in a fume cupboard with a satisfactory exhaust for the hydrogen formed during reaction to be led away. There should be no naked flames nearby.

Place 30 cm^3 of diethyl ether, previously dried over sodium, in a round-bottom flask, which has been previously carefully dried. Weigh out 0.5 g of lithium aluminium hydride on a watch-glass and add it, in **very small** quantities, to the ether. If there is any effervescence, it means that the ether is not dry.

Add, in **very small** quantities at a time, 1.5 g of 2-chlorobenzoic acid to the solution of lithium aluminium hydride in ether. After all the acid has been added, reflux the mixture, using a beaker of hot water, for about 30 minutes.

Then add, dropwise, 5 cm^3 of ethyl ethanoate which will be reduced by the excess lithium aluminium hydride and thus decompose it. Allow the mixture to reflux for a further 10 minutes.

Cool the mixture and then add 20 cm^3 of M sulphuric acid. 2-Chlorophenyl-methanol is liberated from the complex aluminium compound formed and dissolves in the ether layer.

Place the mixture in a separating funnel and run the ether layer into a conical flask. Add some anhydrous sodium sulphate, fit a stopper to the flask and swirl the mixture for about 5 minutes.

Decant the solution into a flask and distil off the ether (Figure 8), using a beaker of hot water.

Detach the flask and place it in a beaker of ice. Filter off the crystals of the alcohol and dry them between filter papers. Take the melting point of the crystals (Section 31.1). The melting point before further purification will be about 70° C.

If time permits, recrystallise the crystals from a dilute aqueous solution of ethanol.

PHYSICAL CONSTANTS

M.p. 74° C; B.p. 230° C.

27.4. Preparation of Ethyl Benzoate

As in the preparation of ethyl ethanoate (Section 9.1), this is an example of an **esterification**:

$$\text{Alcohol} + \text{Acid} \rightleftharpoons \text{Ester} + \text{Water}$$

It is a reversible reaction. In order to displace the equilibrium to the right, water is absorbed by addition of concentrated sulphuric acid. Hydrogen ions catalyse the reaction (Section 9.1).

The ester is obtained pure by first distilling off excess alcohol, and then adding alkali, thus forming a salt of benzoic acid, which is non-volatile. Ethyl benzoate is finally purified by distillation.

REAGENTS

Benzoic acid (4 g)
Ethanol (15 cm^3)
Concentrated sulphuric acid (2 cm^3)
Diethyl ether
10% solution of sodium carbonate

EQUATION

$$C_6H_5COOH + C_2H_5OH \xrightarrow{\text{H}^+} C_6H_5COOC_2H_5 + H_2O$$

DETAILS

Place 15 cm^3 of ethanol in the flask. Add slowly, with gentle swirling and cooling under the tap, 2 cm^3 of concentrated sulphuric acid. Add 4 g of benzoic acid, and reflux the mixture for 1 hour over a gauze or a sand-bath using a water condenser (cf. Figure 22).

Rearrange the apparatus for distillation (cf. Figure 23 and Plate 4) and remove excess ethanol.

Add a 10% solution of sodium carbonate to the residue in the flask, with shaking, until the liquid is alkaline (testing it with Universal Indicator paper). The excess benzoic acid has been converted into sodium benzoate which, being an ionic compound, is insoluble in ether.

Transfer the solution to a separating funnel, add 10 cm^3 of ether and shake. Remove the stopper from the funnel occasionally to relieve the pressure. Separate and run the ethereal solution into a clean, dry flask. Extract the solution a second time with 10 cm^3 of ether, and combine the two ethereal extracts in the flask.

Arrange for a second distillation. Distil off the ether using a hot water-bath (cf. Figure 8). **DO NOT USE A FLAME.**

Then, using a gauze and a flame, distil off the ethyl benzoate. Collect the fraction boiling between 209° C and 213° C.

PHYSICAL CONSTANTS

B.p. 213° C; density at 20° C: 1.05 g cm^{-3}

27.5. Reactions of Ethyl Benzoate

1. **Saponification.** Place 2 cm^3 of ethyl benzoate and 20 cm^3 of sodium hydroxide solution (made up by dissolving 5 g of sodium hydroxide in 20 cm^3 of
water) in a flask, and reflux the mixture for 30 minutes (cf. Figure 22).

$$C_6H_5COOC_2H_5 + NaOH \longrightarrow C_6H_5COONa + C_2H_5OH$$

Distil the mixture (cf. Figure 23 and Plate 4) and collect 4-5 cm^3 of
distillate. Carry out some tests for ethanol (Section 5.2, experiments 2, 5, 6,
and 8).

Transfer the liquid remaining in the flask to a small beaker and add dilute
sulphuric acid until a precipitate is formed:

$$2C_6H_5COONa + H_2SO_4 \longrightarrow 2C_6H_5COOH\downarrow + Na_2SO_4$$

Filter the crystals, using a Hirsch funnel (Figure 13(a)). Dissolve the crystals in the minimum of hot water in a test-tube (filtering off any residue if
necessary). Allow the solution to cool and filter the crystals of benzoic acid
and dry them on filter paper. Determine their melting-point (Section 31.1).

27.6. Reactions of Benzoyl Chloride

1. Place 5 drops of benzoyl chloride in a test-tube, and add 5 drops of water.
Note that hydrolysis is much slower than with ethanoyl chloride, and that
hydrogen chloride is not evolved so rapidly.

$$C_6H_5COCl + H_2O \longrightarrow C_6H_5COOH + HCl$$

2. **Schotten-Baumann reaction.** Benzoyl chloride is a **benzoylating agent**, and
will **benzoylate** phenylamine to *N*-phenylbenzamide (Section 20.2, experiment 6) and phenol to phenyl benzoate (Section 24.2, experiment 9).

27.7. Reactions of 2-Hydroxybenzoic Acid (Salicylic Acid)

A. 2-HYDROXYBENZOIC ACID UNDERGOES THE REACTIONS OF A CARBOXYLIC ACID AND A PHENOL

1. Shake a small amount of 2-hydroxybenzoic acid with some water in a test-
tube. Add 2 drops of Universal Indicator solution (or blue litmus solution).

2. Shake a small amount of 2-hydroxybenzoic acid with some water in a test-tube. Add dilute sodium hydroxide solution drop by drop until nothing more appears to happen:

$$+ \; 2NaOH \; \longrightarrow \qquad + \; 2H_2O$$

B. REACTIONS OF 2-HYDROXYBENZOIC ACID ACTING AS AN AROMATIC CARBOXYLIC ACID

3. Place about 0.1 g of 2-hydroxybenzoic acid in a test-tube, and heat gently. Unlike benzoic acid, it decomposes when heated under these conditions. Note the smell of phenol.

$$\longrightarrow \qquad + \; CO_2$$

Decarboxylation of the acid has occurred.

4. Mix about 0.5 g of 2-hydroxybenzoic acid and about 1 g of soda-lime in a test-tube. Warm. Note the smell of phenol.

$$+ \; 2NaOH \; \longrightarrow \qquad + \; 2H_2O$$

$$+ \; NaOH \; \longrightarrow \qquad + \; Na_2CO_3$$

(Much of the phenol is trapped as sodium phenate, but this can be liberated by adding excess dilute sulphuric acid.)

5. To a mixture of 5 drops of methanol and about 0.5 g of 2-hydroxybenzoic acid in a test-tube, add 1 drop of concentrated sulphuric acid. Warm the mixture and note the smell of the methyl ester (Oil of Wintergreen).

C. REACTIONS OF 2-HYDROXYBENZOIC ACID ACTING AS A PHENOL

6. Mix together 0.5 g of the acid and 1 cm³ of pyridine in a test-tube. Cool the mixture in ice. Add 8 drops of ethanoyl chloride. Shake the mixture well before adding each drop.

   Warm the mixture in a test-tube in a beaker of hot water for about 3 minutes. Pour the mixture into about 20 cm³ of cold water in a beaker. White crystals of 2-carboxyphenyl ethanoate (aspirin) are deposited. Dissolve the crystals in a minimum of hot benzene, and allow the solution to cool. The crystals can be filtered, washed, and dried. M.p. 133–135° C.

   Note that the crystals are not very soluble in water. To a few crystals, add a solution of a calcium compound (e.g. lime water) and warm. Note that the crystals dissolve, forming the soluble calcium salt (soluble aspirin, e.g. Disprin).

7. Place a few crystals of 2-hydroxybenzoic acid in water and shake. Add 5 drops of a neutral iron(III) chloride solution (Section 8.2, experiment 1). A violet coloration is formed, showing that the acid contains the enol group (cf. Section 24.2, experiment 3).

8. Dissolve a few crystals of 2-hydroxybenzoic acid in 1 cm³ of water, and add bromine water dropwise until there is a slight excess of bromine. A white precipitate of 2,4,6-tribromophenol is obtained. Filter, wash the residue with water, and find the m.p. of the dry product, 95° C. Note the ease with which bromine displaced a carboxyl group when the latter is in the 2-position with respect to a hydroxyl group.

28

THE MANUFACTURE OF CHEMICALS FROM OIL

28.1. Cracking of Oil to form Alkenes

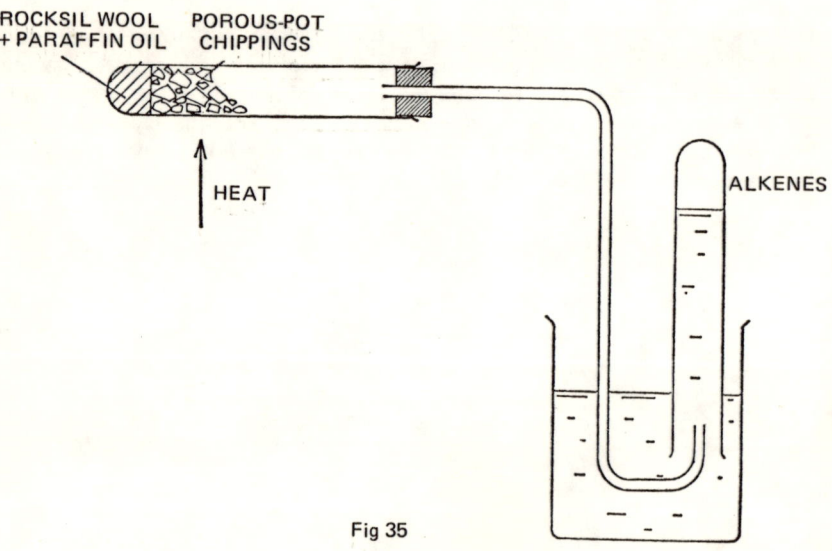

Fig 35

Pour some paraffin oil into a test-tube to a depth of about 2 cm. Push down some Rocksil wool to soak up the liquid; there should be enough wool to occupy about 2 cm at the bottom of the tube. Fill about 7 cm of the tube with porous pot chippings. Set up the tube horizontally and fit with a delivery tube (Figure 35). Heat the middle of the tube and collect the gases over water in test-tubes. Cork the test-tubes when they are full of gas.

28.2. Reactions of the Products

1. Ignite the gas and then test the products with lime water.

2. Test the gas by shaking it with 5 drops of bromine dissolved in tetrachloromethane, to show whether unsaturated hydrocarbons (e.g. alkenes) have been formed.

3. Shake the gas with 3 drops of dilute sulphuric acid and 1 drop of dilute potassium permanganate solution.

28.3. Preparation of a Detergent from an Alcohol

To 5 g of dodecan-1-ol in a small flask, add 2 cm³ of chlorosulphonic acid (CARE), dropwise and with stirring, keeping the temperature below 35° C. Stir the mixture for a further 10 minutes. Divide the mixture into 2 parts.

$$ROH + Cl-SO_2-OH \longrightarrow RO-SO_2-OH + HCl$$

PART I. TO PREPARE A SOLID DETERGENT

To one part of the dodecyl sulphate, add a dilute solution of sodium hydroxide until the mixture is neutral. Evaporate the mixture over a water-bath and filter the solid detergent. The solid can be recrystallised from ethanol.

$$RO-SO_2-OH + NaOH \longrightarrow RO-SO_2-O^-Na^+ + H_2O$$

PART II. TO PREPARE A LIQUID DETERGENT

To the second part of the dodecyl sulphate, add a 10% solution of triethanolamine in water until the mixture is neutral.

28.4. Preparation of a Detergent from an Aromatic Hydrocarbon

Place 10 g of an alkylbenzene, for example Dobane JN, in a flask, and add 17 g of concentrated sulphuric acid very slowly by means of a tap funnel. The addition should take about 60 minutes and the temperature should not rise above 40° C.

Warm the mixture for an hour at a temperature of 45–50° C. Cool the mixture and add 12 g of sodium hydroxide dissolved in 20 cm³ of water. A solution of the detergent, a sodium alkyl benzenesulphonate, and sodium sulphate are formed. On evaporation, solid detergent is formed which can be filtered.

$$R-\text{C}_6\text{H}_4-SO_3H + NaOH \longrightarrow R-\text{C}_6\text{H}_4-SO_3^-Na^+ + H_2O$$

The addition of acid must be slow, the temperature carefully controlled, and stirring must be effective. 'Hot-spots' are liable to develop and decomposition occurs. There may be, therefore, discoloration of the detergent.

28.5. Preparation of a Selective Weed Killer

To 5 g of sodium hydroxide in 25 cm³ of water, in an evaporating basin, add 8 g of 2,4-dichlorophenol and 5 g of monochloroethanoic acid. Evaporate the mixture to dryness on a water-bath. If an oil separates, add a little more concentrated sodium hydroxide solution:

$$Cl-CH_2-COOH + NaOH \longrightarrow Cl-CH_2-COONa + H_2O$$

$$Cl-C_6H_3(Cl)-ONa + ClCH_2COONa \longrightarrow Cl-C_6H_3(Cl)-OCH_2COONa + NaCl$$

Dissolve the residue in about 150 cm³ of hot water in a 400 cm³ beaker and acidify with concentrated hydrochloric acid. On cooling and stirring, crystals of 2,4-dichlorophenoxyethanoic acid are produced, which can be filtered at the pump and recrystallised from benzene (to which a little petroleum ether may be added if the crystals do not separate).

$$Cl-C_6H_3(Cl)-OCH_2COONa + HCl \longrightarrow Cl-C_6H_3(Cl)-OCH_2COOH + NaCl$$

A 0.5% aqueous solution (to which sodium carbonate is added to neutralise the free acid) can be made up. Some detergent (e.g. Teepol), as a wetting agent, and carbamide (urea), as a fertiliser, are added. Strips of grass can be marked out with tape and sprayed. At least one strip should not be sprayed so that it can act as a control. The grass is unharmed but the weeds begin to wither after 4–5 days and will be destroyed after several weeks.

29

CHEMICALS FROM COAL

29.1. Destructive Distillation of Coal

Heat about 2 g of powdered coal in a hard glass boiling-tube. Collect the tar and ammoniacal liquor in a small conical flask, surrounded with ice, and collect the coal gas in test-tubes by displacement of water (Figure 36).

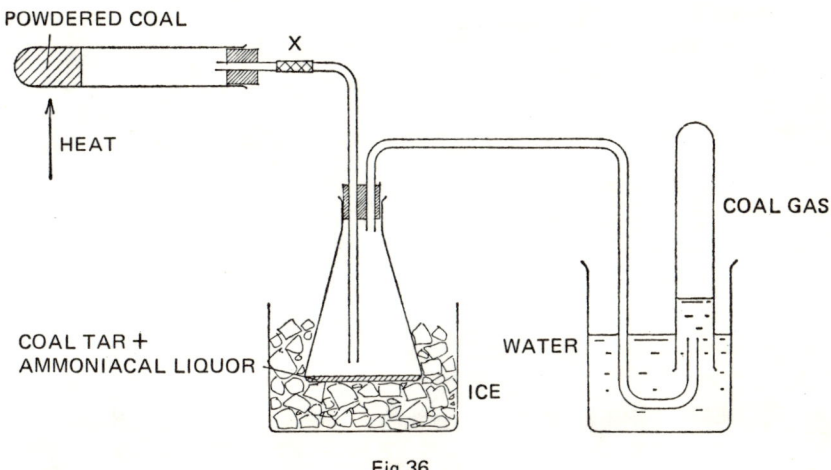

POWDERED COAL

X

HEAT

COAL GAS

COAL TAR +
AMMONIACAL LIQUOR

WATER

ICE

Fig 36

29.2. Reactions of the Ammoniacal Liquor

1. Transfer a few drops of the liquor to a test-tube and add dilute sodium hydroxide solution. Warm and test for ammonia with moist Universal Indicator paper (or red litmus paper).

2. Smell the tar formed and note the smell of phenol.

29.3. Reactions of Coal Gas

1. Burn the coal gas at the end of the tube. Note that it burns with an almost colourless flame. Detach the tube at X (Figure 36) and light the gas. Note

that the coal gas burns with a very smoky flame as the gas now contains aromatics.

2. Extinguish the flame and place moist lead(II) ethanoate paper at the end of the tube and note that it turns black owing to the presence of hydrogen sulphide.

29.4. The Residue

1. Examine the solid residue and note the amorphous character of the coke.

2. PRODUCTION OF WATER GAS ('WET-ROCKSIL' METHOD)

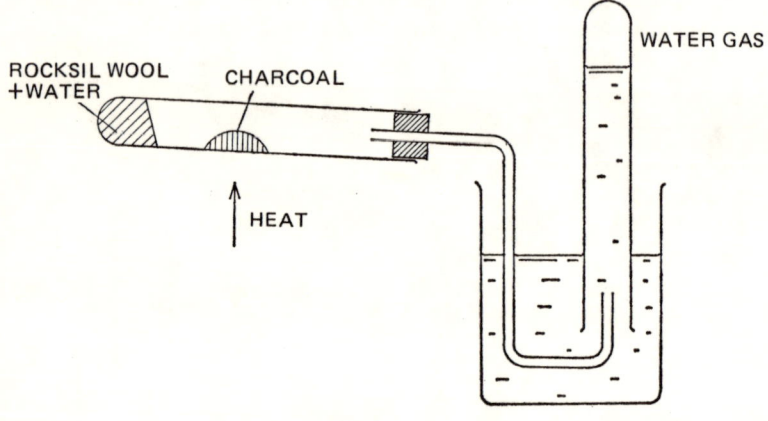

Fig 37

Place about 2 cm^3 of water in a test-tube and push down a plug of Rocksil wool to the bottom of the test-tube, so that the water is soaked up. Place some small pieces of coke or wood charcoal half-way along the tube and set up the apparatus as shown in Figure 37. Heat the coke or charcoal strongly and collect the water gas in test-tubes.

$$C + H_2O \longrightarrow CO + H_2$$

Test the gas by igniting it. After ignition, add lime water to the test-tube and shake. The lime water will turn milky, indicating carbon dioxide. This should be due to the combustion of carbon monoxide:

$$2CO + O_2 \longrightarrow 2CO_2$$

However, there may be carbon dioxide present in the original gas, due to the combustion of the coke or charcoal. A test-tube of the original gas must, therefore, be tested with lime water.

30

PLASTICS

30.1. Preparation of Some Thermosoftening Plastics

1. PREPARATION OF METHYL 2-METHYLPROPENOATE (METHYL METHACRYLATE) AND ITS POLYMERISATION

Distil about 1 g of Perspex chippings from a test-tube into a cold test-tube. The liquid distillate is the monomer, methyl 2-methylpropenoate. If the liquid is discoloured, it may be advisable to redistil under reduced pressure.

To the liquid in a test-tube, add about 0.1 g of di(dodecanoyl) peroxide, stopper the tube, and shake the mixture until the solid has dissolved. Place the stoppered tube in a beaker of water and gently bring it to the boil (**CARE!**—the stopper may fly off with considerable force.) The liquid sets after about 15–30 minutes, to a hard mass, Perspex.

$$n \begin{pmatrix} H & CH_3 \\ | & | \\ C=C \\ | & | \\ H & COOCH_3 \end{pmatrix} \longrightarrow \begin{pmatrix} H & CH_3 \\ | & | \\ -C-C- \\ | & | \\ H & COOCH_3 \end{pmatrix}_n$$

2. PREPARATION OF POLY(PHENYLETHENE) (POLYSTYRENE)

Place 5 cm^3 of phenylethene with 0.1 g of di(dodecanoyl) peroxide in a test-tube. Mix thoroughly and place the test-tube in a beaker of boiling water until a solid is formed. The polymer is soluble in benzene and can be precipitated from its solution by adding ethanol:

$$n \begin{pmatrix} & & H \\ & & | \\ & C=C \\ & | & | \\ & H & H \end{pmatrix} \longrightarrow \begin{pmatrix} & & H \\ & & | \\ & -C-C- \\ & | & | \\ & H & H \end{pmatrix}_n$$

3. PREPARATION OF NYLON 66

Place about 5 cm^3 of a 5% solution of hexanedioyl chloride in tetrachlorome-thane in a 25 cm^3 beaker. Add slowly from a tap-funnel an equal volume of a 5% aqueous solution of 1,6-diaminohexane, to which 5 drops of dilute (2M) ammonia solution have been added. The aqueous layer should rest on the tetra-chloromethane layer, and no attempt should be made to mix the two. Warm the beaker and contents to about 50° C in a water-bath, in order to ensure that the product is not too brittle. Remove the beaker carefully from the water-bath, and draw a thread of nylon from the liquid interface by means of a small (4–8 mm) wire loop. A glass rod also may be used for this purpose, with the advantage that rotation of the rod ensures that the nylon fibre is wrapped round it as the fibre is drawn from the interface.

$$H_2N-(CH_2)_6-N{\overset{H}{\underset{|}{}}}H \; + \; Cl{-}\overset{O}{\overset{\|}{C}}-(CH_2)_4-\overset{O}{\overset{\|}{C}}-Cl \longrightarrow$$

1, 6-Diaminohexane   Hexanedioyl chloride

$$HCl \; + \; H_2N-(CH_2)_6-\overset{H}{\underset{|}{N}}-\overset{O}{\overset{\|}{C}}-(CH_2)_4-\overset{O}{\overset{\|}{C}}-\overset{H}{\underset{|}{N}}-\dots$$

Nylon 66

The repetition of the peptide linkage $-\overset{O}{\overset{\|}{C}}-\overset{H}{\underset{|}{N}}-$ in the nylon molecular chain should be compared with that which occurs in the structure of proteins. This nylon is designated 66 since the molecules of both of the reactants from which it is made contain a chain of six carbon atoms. In the commercial process hexane-dioic acid is used.

4. PREPARATION OF NYLON 610

The same method of preparation is employed as for Nylon 66, decanedioyl chloride being used in place of hexanedioyl chloride.

$$H_2N-(CH_2)_6-N{\overset{H}{\underset{|}{}}}H \; + \; Cl{-}\overset{O}{\overset{\|}{C}}-(CH_2)_8-\overset{O}{\overset{\|}{C}}-Cl \longrightarrow$$

1, 6-Diaminohexane   Decanedioyl chloride

$$HCl \; + \; H_2N-(CH_2)_6-\overset{H}{\underset{|}{N}}-\overset{O}{\overset{\|}{C}}-(CH_2)_8-\overset{O}{\overset{\|}{C}}-\overset{H}{\underset{|}{N}}-\dots$$

Nylon 610

The decanedioyl chloride molecule contains a chain of ten carbon atoms, while that of the amine has six. The product is therefore designated Nylon 610.

5. DRAWING A NYLON FIBRE

Warm carefully, over a small bunsen flame, about 1 g of Nylon 6 pellets in a test-tube. Draw a fibre from the melt, using a thin wire. The fibre has high strength and elasticity. These properties may be tested by hand-stretching the fibre. Examine the fibres through a polaroid.

Nylon 6 is manufactured from cyclohexane via cyclohexanone. The latter is reacted with hydroxylamine sulphate to give the oxime which undergoes catalytic rearrangement to form 6-hexanelactam which polymerises to yield Nylon 6.

Nylon 6 is similar in appearance to Nylon 66, but it is softer and has a lower melting-point.

5. PREPARATION OF A GLYPTAL RESIN

To 3 g of benzene-1,2-dicarboxylic anhydride in a test-tube, add 2 g of propane-1,2,3-triol. Heat to about 160° C, using a thermometer to stir. As steam is evolved, raise the temperature slowly to 250° C. The mixture swells to form a brittle mass. Cool and crush the mass to powder.

A three-dimensional polymer may also be formed.

This experiment should be performed in a fume cupboard.

30.2. Preparation of Thermosetting Plastics

1. PREPARATION OF A PHENOL-METHANAL PLASTIC (BAKELITE TYPE)

Place 2 cm³ of formalin in a test-tube and add 1 g of phenol. Add 2 drops of a concentrated solution of sodium hydroxide and warm the mixture over a small bunsen flame until a resin is formed. It is red and viscous.

Final polymerisation is effected by curing, i.e. by heating the resin for about 4–6 hours at about 50° C in an oven. A hard pink mass is obtained.

2. PREPARATION OF A CARBAMIDE-METHANAL RESIN

Place about 0.5 g of carbamide in a test-tube, and add about 1 cm^3 of concentrated hydrochloric acid and 5 cm^3 of water. Add 10 drops of formalin and shake the mixture. Allow the mixture to stand and a white powder is deposited. This is a thermosetting plastic.

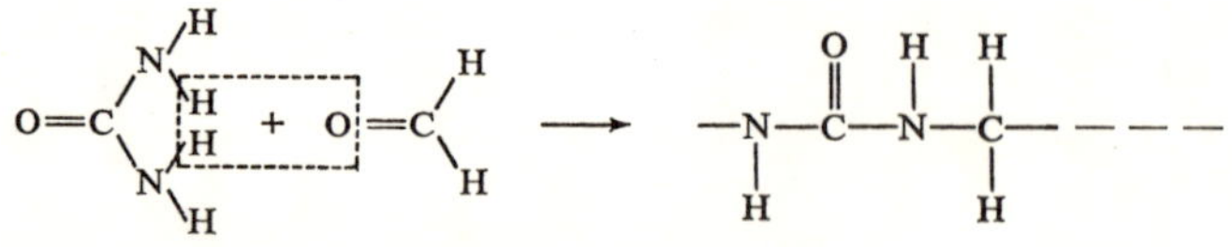

3. PREPARATION OF A MELAMINE-METHANAL RESIN

To 10 cm^3 of formalin in a beaker add dropwise M sodium hydroxide solution until the pH is about 7.5 (using narrow-range Universal Indicator papers to test the pH).

Divide the solution into two equal parts in separate test-tubes. To each solution add 2.5 g of melamine, and heat them in a beaker containing water at 80° C in a fume cupboard. Stir the contents of each tube with a 0–110° C thermometer. After about 10 minutes the melamine dissolves in the formalin to give a clear syrup consisting of methylol melamines.

Remove one of the tubes from the water-bath, cool, and add dropwise dilute hydrochloric acid until the pH is about 6. Methylol melamines crystallise out on standing but redissolve on heating.

Acidify the contents of the second tube in a similar manner, but heat the solution, in the fume cupboard, over a small bunsen flame until a gel of melamine

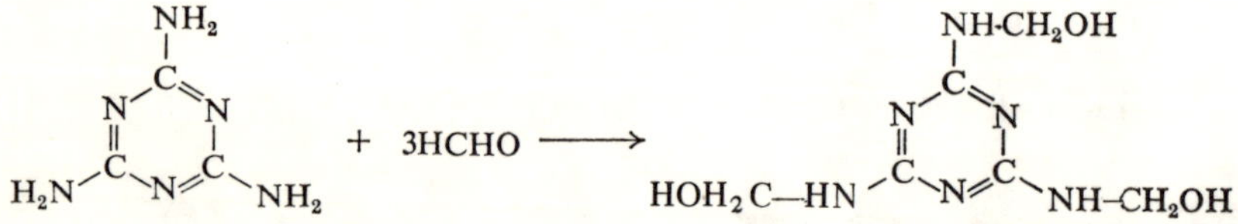

Trimethylol melamine

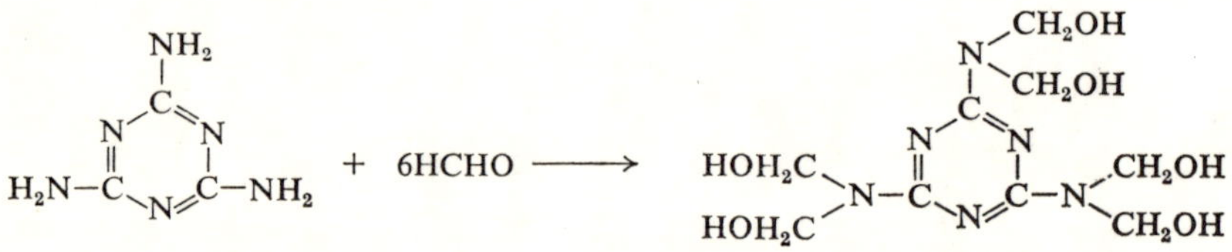

Hexamethylol melamine

resin is obtained. The acid increases the rate of polymerisation. At this stage, the resin is partially soluble and consists of linear branched molecules.

(a) **Ether linkage**

$$R-NH-CH_2OH + HOCH_2-NH-R \longrightarrow R-NH-CH_2OCH_2-NH-R$$
$$+ H_2O$$

Trimethylol
melamine

'R' represents the melamine residue.

(b) **Methylene linkage**

$$R-NH-CH_2OH + H-NH-R \longrightarrow R-NH-CH_2NH-R + H_2O$$

Trimethylol
melamine

(c) **Azomethine linkage**

$$R-NH-CH_2OH \longrightarrow R-N=CH_2 + H_2O$$

Trimethylol
melamine

Transfer the gel to a watch-glass, and heat it in an oven at about 150° C for 5–10 minutes. The produce is a brittle mass. This process is known as curing.

4. PREPARATION OF AN EPIKOTE RESIN

Pour 20 cm^3 of Epikote 815 into a small beaker or tin and add 3 cm^3 of bis-(2-aminoethyl)amine. Stir vigorously and allow the mixture to stand. After about 30–60 minutes considerable heat is evolved and a very hard mass is formed of a thermosetting Epikote resin.

The amine has a harmful vapour, and contact with skin, eyes, and clothing should be avoided. **Gloves and goggles should be worn and the experiment done in a fume cupboard.**

30.3. Preparation of a Polyurethane Foam Polymer

To about 5 cm^3 of a triol in a small tin or old beaker, add 10 cm^3 of a diiso-cyanate. Mix the two liquids together with a knife for about 15 seconds. Clean the knife at once. The foam is expanded by the carbon dioxide produced during the reaction, because some water, added to the triol by the manufacturer, reacts with the diisocyanate:

$$OCNRNCO + 2H_2O \longrightarrow H_2NRNH_2 + 2CO_2$$

The diisocyanate is dangerous to eyes and skin. Gloves and goggles should be worn. Any areas splashed MUST BE WASHED WITH WARM WATER AND THEN SOAP AND WATER.

A triol such as Carodol GXR13 and a diisocyanate such as Caradate 30 are suitable.

30.4. Preparation of a Synthetic Rubber ('Thiokol')

Dissolve 2 g of sodium hydroxide in 50 cm^3 of boiling water in a beaker. To the boiling solution, add carefully 5 g of flowers of sulphur. When most of the sulphur has dissolved, filter and collect the clear yellow-brown solution in a beaker.

Add 10 cm^3 of 1,2-dichloroethane with continuous stirring at 70-80° C. Spongy lumps of rubber are formed.

Decant the liquid and wash the solid thoroughly with water. Squeeze out surplus water and test the solid for its rubber properties.

30.5. Preparation and Properties of a Silicone

Allow the VAPOUR of dichlorodimethylsilane (CARE) to pass through a glass tube or burette using a filter pump. Also allow a filter paper to come into contact with the vapour.

Although the glass and paper may appear to be dry, there is a considerable number of layers of water molecules adsorbed on to the surface. These react with the dichlorodimethylsilane vapour to form diols, which then polymerise to yield a silicone.

$$\text{HO}-\underset{\overset{|}{CH_3}}{\overset{\overset{CH_3}{|}}{Si}}-\left[\,O-\underset{\overset{|}{CH_3}}{\overset{\overset{CH_3}{|}}{Si}}-\right]_n O-\underset{\overset{|}{CH_3}}{\overset{\overset{CH_3}{|}}{Si}}-\text{OH}$$

Fill the treated glass tube (or burette) with water and examine the meniscus. Compare the meniscus with that of an untreated tube.

Allow water to trickle down the tube which is held at a slight angle to the horizontal. Note that the water forms globules readily.

Allow the treated filter paper to come into contact with water, and contrast its water-repelling properties with the properties of an untreated filter paper.

31

THE DETERMINATION OF MELTING-POINTS AND OF BOILING-POINTS

31.1. Determination of the Melting-point of a Solid

A pure solid has a sharp melting-point provided that it does not decompose at or below the melting-point.

The apparatus employed in the determination of melting-points is illustrated in Figure 38.

The melting-point tube is made by heating thin-walled capillary tubing and drawing it out. Each melting-point tube should be about 8–10 cm long and 1.0–1.5 mm in diameter.

The dry powdered solid is introduced into this tube to a depth of about 1 cm. The solid can be introduced readily by scooping a little of the powdered solid into the open end of the tube, then allowing it to fall, sealed end downwards, about 50 cm on to the bench top, guided by a wider glass tube as illustrated in Figure 39, or by vibrating the melting-point tube with a file. The melting-point tube is attached to the thermometer by an elastic band. The band must not be allowed to come into contact with the medicinal paraffin or any other liquid which may be employed in the bath.

The melting-point bath is heated with a small flame and the bath liquid is stirred gently and continuously. The rate of rise of temperature should be no greater than 3–5° C per minute. After a first melting-point determination has been made, the bath may be allowed to cool until the compound solidifies and a second determination may be effected. Alternatively a fresh sample may be used. Owing to the probability of supercooling, use is not made of the temperature of solidification.

MIXED MELTING-POINTS

It sometimes happens that several compounds in the same class, or derivatives of these compounds, have melting-points differing by only 1 or 2 degrees. This makes positive identification of the compound more difficult. In such cases, the original substance is mixed intimately with a pure substance with which it is thought to be identical. The melting-point of the mixture is determined. If the melting-point of the mixture is the same as that of the original substance then the latter and the pure substance are identical.

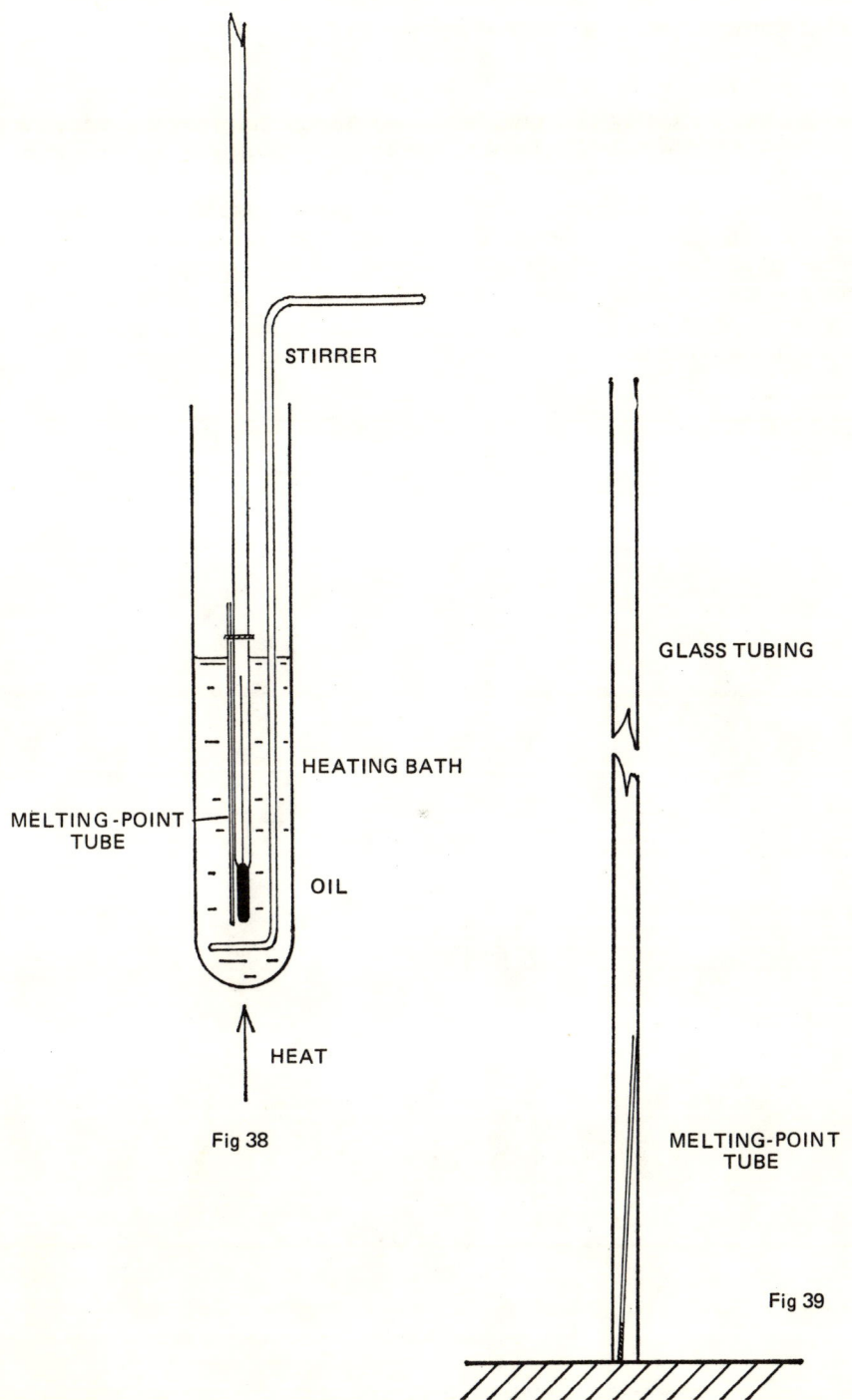

STIRRER

HEATING BATH

GLASS TUBING

MELTING-POINT
TUBE

OIL

MELTING-POINT
TUBE

HEAT

Fig 38

Fig 39

31.2. Determination of the Boiling-point of a Liquid

At a given pressure, the boiling-point of a pure liquid has a constant value. (This applies also to azeotropic mixtures of liquids.) Provided that there is an adequate supply of a liquid, its boiling-point at atmospheric pressure may be determined, using the apparatus as shown in Figure 25.

The bulb of the thermometer is adjusted to a position just below the outlet of the distilling flask. The thermometer should not be immersed in the boiling liquid owing to the possibility of superheating. If the liquid to be distilled is flammable (for example, ether, benzene) heating should be carried out with the aid of a heating bath containing a suitable liquid, previously heated well away from the apparatus for safety (see, for example, Figure 8).

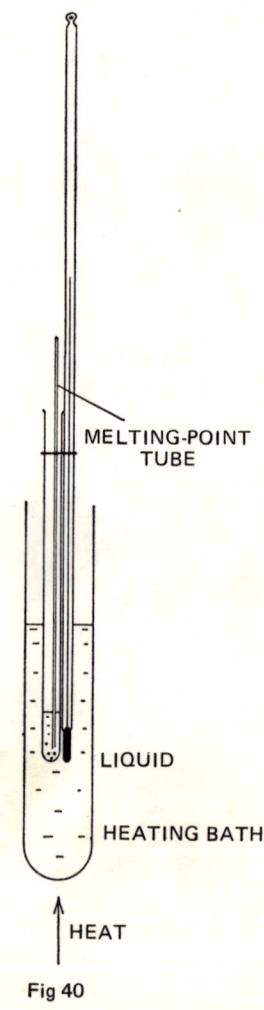

MELTING-POINT
TUBE

LIQUID

HEATING BATH

HEAT

Fig 40

If only a small quantity of a liquid is available, its boiling-point may be determined by the **Siwoloboff method** (Figure 40). The open end of a melting-point tube is immersed in a few drops of the liquid contained in a thin-walled tube having a diameter of about 4 mm. The wider tube is secured to a thermometer by means of an elastic band and is heated slowly in either a water-bath or an oil-bath. At first, bubbles of vapour escape intermittently from the open end of the melting-point tube. Near the boiling-point, the vapour escapes in a continuous stream of bubbles. At this stage, the apparatus is allowed to cool and the temperature at which the liquid recedes into the melting-point tube is taken as the boiling-point.

32

CHROMATOGRAPHY

32.1. Introduction

Most of the routine methods of separation and purification have been used in the preparation of organic compounds described in previous chapters of this book. These methods include the normal criteria of purity (melting-point, mixed melting-point, and boiling-point) and methods of separation and purification such as filtration and recrystallisation, extraction by partition between two immiscible solvents, distillation, steam distillation, drying, etc. However, separation and purification of substances by chromatography is becoming increasingly important. This is because very complex mixtures are readily separated, both on a small scale as in paper, thin-layer, and gas chromatography, and on a larger scale as in column, ion-exchange, and in preparative gas chromatography.

The following methods are described:

1. Column chromatography
2. Thin-layer chromatography
3. Ion-exchange chromatography
4. Paper chromatography
5. Gas chromatography

32.2. Column Chromatography

Column chromatography upon substances such as activated alumina, silica, or charcoal is a technique regularly adopted today both for the separation of mixtures of neutral substances with fairly similar chemical and physical properties and for the final purification of organic compounds from impurities not easily removed by simple crystallisation. Strongly acidic or basic compounds and salts are best separated by the use of ion-exchange columns (Section 32.4).

The procedures given below illustrate the methods that should be used with activated alumina as the adsorbent but do not differ in principle from those to be employed with other adsorbents.

A mixture of solids can be separated from solution by allowing the solution to pass through any insoluble solid which can selectively adsorb one or more of the solid components. As activated alumina is a strongly polar and basic substance, it adsorbs irreversibly organic acids and some phenols, but will adsorb

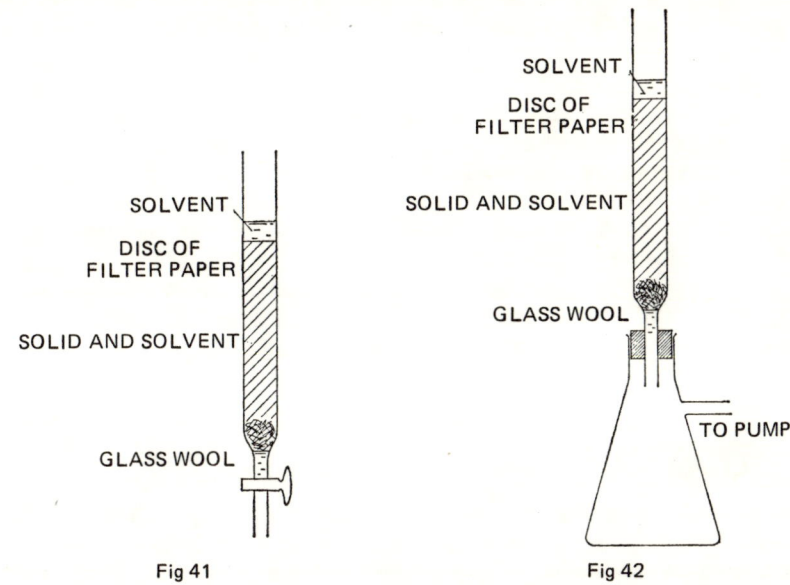

SOLVENT

DISC OF
FILTER PAPER

SOLID AND SOLVENT

GLASS WOOL

TO PUMP

SOLVENT

DISC OF
FILTER PAPER

SOLID AND SOLVENT

GLASS WOOL

Fig 41   Fig 42

reversibly other polar organic compounds, such as alcohols, ketones, and amines. The components are then washed off the column with a pure solvent or mixture of solvents. First to be removed will be the least polar compound, and then the other components of the mixture in regular order. This procedure is termed **elution**.

The physical process of elution comprises in part the equilibrated solution of substances adsorbed on the alumina surface and in part the displacement of adsorbed polar substances by polar solvents, the latter process being the more important for firmly held compounds.

To ensure efficient separation of organic substances on an alumina column, graded elution is used, i.e. the solvent should be changed in a regular manner, starting with a non-polar solvent and gradually replacing it by a more polar one. The usual sequence of suitable volatile solvents is (i) petroleum ether (b.p. 60-80° C), (ii) benzene, (iii) diethyl ether, (iv) ethyl ethanoate, (v) methanol, though trichloromethane can often be used with advantage to replace this or ethyl ethanoate. Mixed solvents, e.g. petroleum ether-benzene, can be used to achieve still more graduation when closely similar substances, such as isomers, have to be separated.

PREPARATION OF A COLUMN

Use a glass column of about 30 cm length and 10-20 mm diameter. A plug of glass wool is placed in the narrow neck at the bottom of the tube (Figure 41).

(A burette is sometimes convenient to use.)

Fill the glass column half-full of a pure liquid (e.g. dry benzene, petroleum ether, ether or water), and pour a slurry of the solid and the pure liquid into the column. The solid will sink to the bottom, forming a uniform column if the tube is tapped vigorously. (Tap the column with a piece of glass tubing round which there is some thick rubber tubing.) Uneven packing leads to cracks and channels. Excess solvent is run out of the column.

The solid should occupy about three-quarters of the column and should always be covered by solvent. A small amount of sand or a disc of filter paper is placed on top of the solid column to prevent disturbance of the column when the solution is added.

The solution of the mixture to be separated is added via a tap funnel or by a pipette. In each case, it is essential not to disturb the top of the column and to add the solution evenly over the whole area of the column. If the separation is slow, suction can be applied at the bottom of the column (Figure 42). The solvent should percolate through at about 10 cm³ per minute.

SEPARATION OF DYES

Prepare a column of alumina, using water as the liquid. Place 3 cm³ of a 0.1% aqueous solution, containing equal parts by weight of malachite green and methylene blue, on the column. Elute with distilled water to wash through the malachite green. Then elute with ethanol to wash through the methylene blue.

EXTRACTION OF CAROTENES, CHLOROPHYLLS, AND XANTHOPHYLLS FROM LEAVES

Soak about 10 g of finely crushed grass, leaves, or plant stems in 50 cm³ of methanol for about 24 hours. Filter, and wash the residue with another 25 cm³ of methanol.

Shake the combined filtrates with 25 cm³ of petroleum ether (b.p. 80–100° C) and add 50 cm³ of water. Pour the mixture into a separating funnel, and then discard the lower water-alcohol layer.

Prepare a column of alumina (80–200 mesh) using a slurry of alumina in benzene, and pour the extract into the column. Develop the column with benzene, until the first band of carotenes (yellow-orange) passes through into a test-tube.

Now develop the column with a second solvent (60 parts of butan-1-ol, 20 parts ethanol, 20 parts water) to separate the xanthophylls (pink-brown colour) from the chlorophylls (green).

PURIFICATION OF ANTHRACENE

Prepare a column of alumina using hexane (or petroleum ether, b.p. 80–100° C) as the liquid.

Dissolve about 0.5 g of crude anthracene in 50 cm³ of hexane and pass the solution through the column. Examine the column under ultra-violet light. Develop the chromatogram with 50–100 cm³ of hexane.

At the top of the column, there is a deep-blue, fluorescent zone, due to carbazole. Further down, there is a yellow, non-fluorescent zone, due to naphthalene. The anthracene is eluted but can be seen at the bottom of the column as a blue fluorescent zone under ultra-violet light.

32.3. Thin-layer Chromatography

Thin-layer chromatography uses principles of adsorption similar to column chromatography. However, it is on a much smaller scale and as such it is generally used as an analytical rather than a purification technique.

A solution of the sample to be analysed is placed as a spot on the surface of a solid adsorbent (such as silica gel or alumina) which has been spread as a thin layer on a glass plate. When the solvent, in which the solute is to be analysed, has evaporated, the plate is placed in a tall beaker so that the lower end of the plate is just below the surface of the solvent. The solvent is drawn up by capillary action. As the solvent front travels past the spot, the components in the sample will move with the solvent at different rates. These rates will depend on the nature of the solutes, solvent, and the adsorbent, in exactly the same way as for column chromatography.

R_F VALUES

The distance which each substance travels on the paper, relative to the distance the solvent front travels, can be measured. The measurement is known as the R_F value. The distance which the solvent has travelled is calibrated from 0 to 1, and the distance that the solutes travel is measured accordingly. Thus in Figure 43, solute X has an R_F value of 0.25, and solute Y has an R_F value of 0.70. The mixture was placed on the plate at A.

The R_F values characterise the substances, but they depend on the conditions of the experiment; particularly important are the nature of the solvent and the temperature. R_F values must be measured under controlled conditions and must be compared only with R_F values obtained by other workers under the same conditions.

PREPARATION OF THIN-LAYER PLATES

To prepare thin-layer plates, care must be taken to ensure that the adsorbent is distributed evenly. In these experiments this is not done as the apparatus needed is expensive. However, the following experiments will illustrate the usefulness of the method.

Make a slurry of silica gel (35 g) (Appendix III) in trichloromethane (100 cm^3) in a stoppered flask. Pour the slurry into a tall beaker (or gas jar).

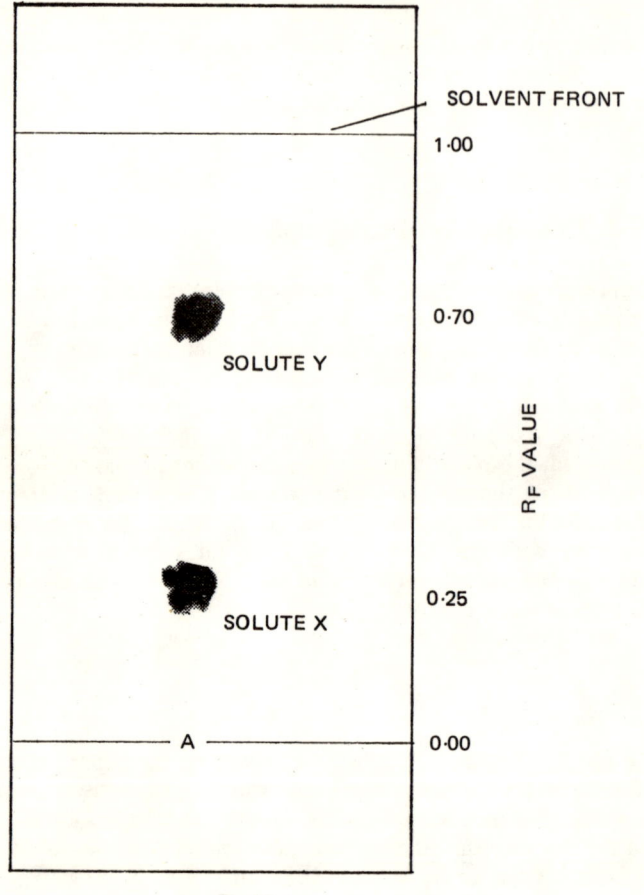

Fig 43

Dip two microscope glass slides (15 x 2 cm) back to back in the slurry (making sure that it is well shaken). Withdraw them at a steady rate. Separate them and hold them horizontally, waving them gently to aid the evaporation of trichloromethane. Wipe clean the rear surface and edges of the slide (Figure 44).

APPLICATION OF THE SAMPLE

Gently scratch with a needle or a razor-blade lines about 2 mm long parallel to the base of the slide, about 2 cm from the bottom. Enough space should be left between the scratches to allow application of drops of each solution of sample to be analysed and each standard solution.

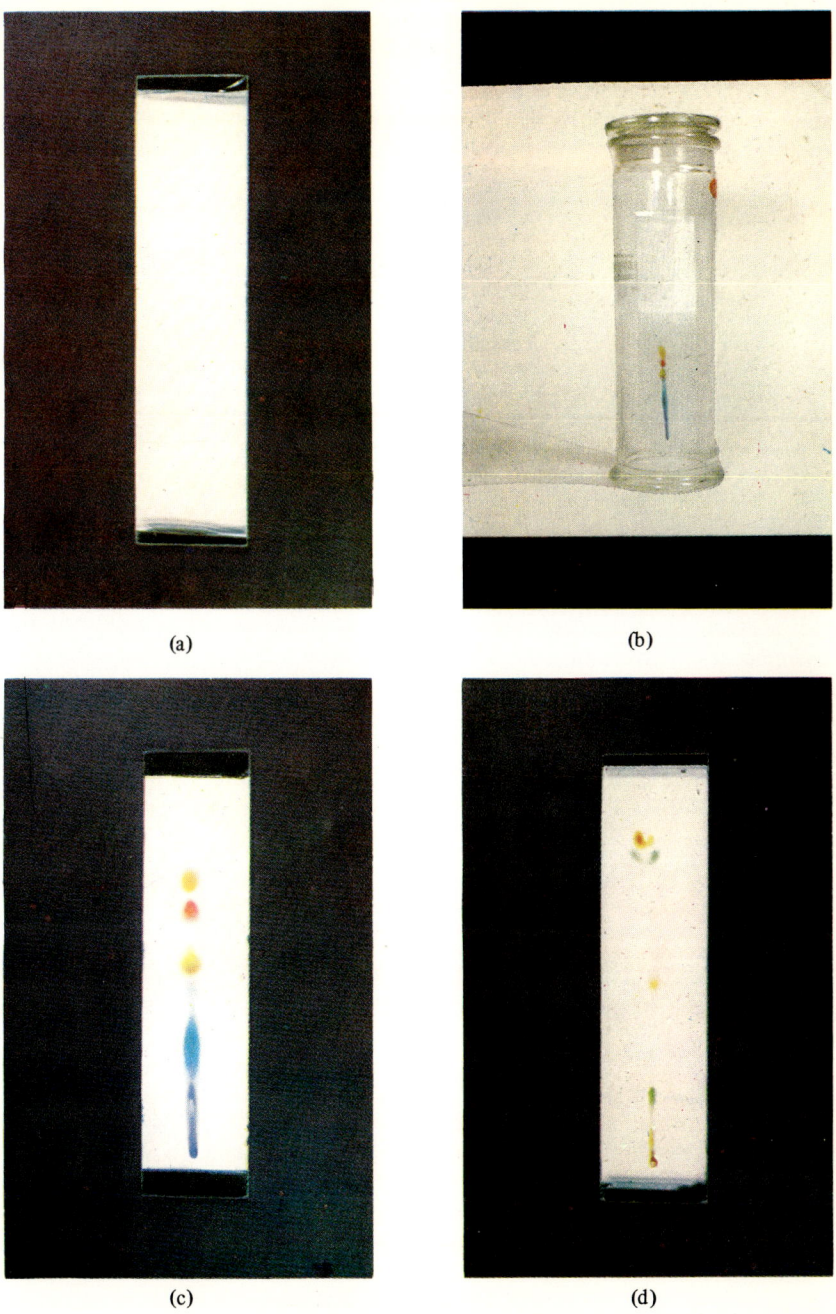

Fig 44. Thin-layer Chromatography

(a) Thin-layer plate
(b) Development of a thin-layer plate
(c) Separation of black ink using butan-1-ol, ethanol and 2M ammonia solution
    (3 : 1 : 1 by volume) as solvent
(d) Separation of pigments in spinach (p. 168)

Scratch a line parallel to the base-line about 1 cm from the top of the slide to mark the upper limit to which the solvent front is to travel.

To apply a solution, use a melting-point tube (Section 31.1), allowing the solution to flow into it by capillary action. Then touch the tube onto the slide until the liquid is transferred to the spot. Do not try to hold the tube onto the slide as the spot becomes too big. Instead, touch the spot several times so that the solvent is allowed to evaporate instead of spreading out. The spot should be no larger than 3–4 mm in diameter. A fresh capillary tube must be used for each solution.

DEVELOPING THE CHROMATOGRAM

Place the slide in a beaker or jar so that the surface of the solvent is above the silica gel adsorbent but is below the samples. Place a lid on the beaker, and allow the solvent to rise up the slide until it reaches the line at the top of the slide (Figure 44). Remove the slide and allow the solvent to evaporate.

DETECTION OF SUBSTANCES

Although coloured substances are used in many demonstrations of thin-layer chromatography, colourless compounds can also be separated and analysed. For example, after separation the plate may be sprayed with another compound which will react to form coloured compounds which can be readily seen. Another method is to place the plate under ultra-violet light should any of the compounds to be separated fluoresce. Yet a further method is to use radioactive isotopes so that, after development, the plate is placed on a photographic plate which is in turn developed. The photograph will show how far the radioactive compound has travelled up the plate.

SEPARATION OF PLANT PIGMENTS

(It may be useful to prepare the solution of pigments beforehand and to use the solution for a class experiment on thin-layer chromatography.)

Crush about 20 g of spinach (fresh or frozen) or, if not available, grass, in a mortar with about 20 cm³ of methanol. Decant the solvent and crush the spinach with 50 cm³ of a (2 : 1) mixture of petroleum ether (60–80° C) (or pentane) and methanol. Filter the mixture, collecting the solution in a flask. Repeat the procedure on the spinach with a further 50 cm³ of solvents.

Place the two sets of solvents in a separating funnel and run off the alcohol layer which will contain the water.

Pass the petroleum ether (or pentane) layer into a clean flask and add about 2 g anhydrous sodium sulphate. Shake the mixture for about 5 minutes and decant the solution into a distillation flask. Evaporate off the solvent using a hot water-bath (cf. Figure 23) until only about 5–10 cm³ of solution are left.

Place two spots of the solution on a thin-layer plate. Allow the petroleum ether (or pentane) to evaporate and develop the slide with trichloromethane as the solvent.

Note the number of spots developed, describe their colours and measure their R_F values.

Then place the slide in a covered beaker or jar in which there are some crystals of iodine at the bottom. Note whether any additional spots are developed.

SEPARATION OF FOODSTUFF DYES

Make up a test sample of three foodstuff dyes which are used as artificial colouring (for jam, custards, vegetables, drinks, etc.). The dyes can be bought from grocer shops, supermarkets, etc.

In order to test which solvent will be most satisfactory for elution, place six spots along a thin-layer plate, using a clean capillary tube. To the first spot, add benzene dropwise from a dropping tube, to see whether three sharply defined circles are obtained:

1. Benzene
2. Propanone
3. Ethanol
4. Water
5. Ethanoic acid
6. Butan-1-ol/ethanol/2M ammonia solution (3 : 1 : 1 by volume)

Record which solvents give the most satisfactory separation, that is the solvent, if any, which produces three sharply defined circles of the constituent dyes.

Then, using the test mixture, samples of three constituent dyes, and, if time, *concentrated* solutions of dyes obtained from foods (jams, fruit drinks, etc.), prepare a thin-layer plate and elute with the most suitable solvent.

32.4. Ion-exchange Chromatography

Ion-exchange resins are usually co-polymers of phenylethene (styrene) and diethenylbenzene. Cation exchange resins often have sulphonic acid groups, $-SO_3H$, attached to the polymer, while anion exchange resins have quaternary ammonium groups, $-[R_3N]^+OH^-$

USES OF ION-EXCHANGE RESINS IN ORGANIC CHEMISTRY

1. Removal of inorganic impurities from organic substances.
2. Removal of bases from mixtures of bases with neutral compounds and acids.
3. Removal of acids from mixtures of acids with neutral compounds and bases.
4. Conversion of the salt of a weak acid into the free acid.
5. Conversion of the salt of a weak base into the free base.
6. A strong acid cation resin can be used as the catalyst for the esterification of an alcohol, particularly when either of the reactants is sensitive to mineral acids.

Practical details for 4 and 5 are given below.

PREPARATION OF A COLUMN

Satisfactory strong acid cation resins are either Amberlite I.R.–120 (H) or Zerolit 225. Satisfactory strong base anion resins are either Amberlite I.R.A. –400 (OH) or Zerolit N(ip). For each resin, instructions are given on how to wash the column and regenerate the resin.

Prepare a slurry of ion-exchange resin in water and pour it into a burette, which has a small amount of glass wool at the bottom (cf. Figure 41).

Allow the excess water to run out, but always keep the resin well covered with water. Fill the burette about two-thirds full of resin.

The solutions should pass through the column at about 3–5 cm^3 per minute.

CONVERSION OF A SALT OF A WEAK BASE TO THE FREE BASE

Prepare a column of a strong base anion resin. When it is ready for use, pass 100 cm^3 of a 1% aqueous solution of phenylammonium chloride through the column. Wash the column with distilled water. The effluent contains free phenrylamine. Test the effluent with Universal Indicator paper (or blue litmus paper) to see whether any of the salt is still present. If so, the paper will be turned red.

The column is regenerated with dilute alkali and then washed with water. Instructions for regeneration are given with the resin.

CONVERSION OF A SODIUM SALT OF A CARBOXYLIC ACID INTO A FREE ACID

Prepare a column of a strong cation resin. Pipette 20 cm^3 of a 0.2M solution of sodium ethanoate down the column and then about 50 cm^3 of water should be run down to wash the column. To show that the conversion is quantitative, the runnings, which contain the free acid, can be titrated against 0.2M sodium hydroxide, using phenolphthalein as indicator.

The column is regenerated with dilute acid and then washed with water. Instructions for regeneration are given with the resin.

32.5. Paper Chromatography

A mixture of solids in solution can be separated into its pure components by paper chromatography. The underlying principle concerning paper chromatography is partition of a solute between two solvents. However, there is no doubt that adsorption also plays its part.

Filter paper contains cellulose molecules which have free hydroxyl groups. These groups are able to adsorb water molecules strongly, and thus water acts as one solvent.

If a drop of the solution to be separated is placed on the paper and a second solvent is allowed to run up or down the paper (ascending and descending solvent fronts), the mixture of solutes will be partitioned between the two solvents. The solutes that are more soluble in water will travel more slowly than the solutes that are more soluble in the second solvent.

Paper chromatography is one method of partition chromatography. Other methods which are concerned with partition are gas-liquid chromatography (Section 32.6) and high performance liquid chromatography. The partition of a solute between two solvents is repeated a large number of times and can be compared to fractional distillation, in which liquids are distilled many times in a fractionating column.

APPARATUS FOR PAPER CHROMATOGRAPHY (FOR ASCENDING SOLVENT FRONT)

A glass measuring cylinder or gas jar (of about 500 cm^3 capacity, i.e. 6 cm diameter and 20 cm high) can be used as a tank (Figure 45). The piece of filter paper can be suspended in the tank by a piece of glass rod held in position by a bung. The paper itself is held in position by plastic clips. (Clips used to pack men's shirts can be useful.)

The paper strips (about 4 cm wide and 35 cm long) may be cut from Whatman No. 1 filter paper. A pencil line should be drawn across the paper near the bottom, and the solution should be dropped on to the paper by means of a fine glass pipette. To prevent the zone spreading, it should be dried as quickly as possible. A hair dryer is excellent for this purpose. The zone should not be larger than 0.5 cm in diameter.

Place about 30–40 cm^3 of the solvent into the cylinder and place the end of the paper just below the level of the solvent.

When the solvent has moved up about three-quarters of the height of the paper, the paper should be removed from the tank and dried in a stream of cold air (or, if possible, in an oven at 100° C). If the components are colourless, their presence may be detected by ultra-violet light if they fluoresce, or by a chemical reagent to form a coloured compound (for example, ninhydrin reacts with colourless amino acids to form coloured compounds). The chemical reagent can be sprayed on, using a cheap scent spray, or the paper can be drawn through a shallow bath containing the reagent. Ninhydrin solutions can also be obtained in aerosol bottles, which are convenient but expensive.

R_F VALUES

As with thin-layer chromatography, R_F values characterise the substances (Section 32.3). Again, the values depend on the conditions of the experiment and must be measured under controlled conditions and only compared with other values obtained under exactly similar conditions.

SEPARATION OF AMINO ACIDS

The solvent used is a mixture of 20 parts of butan-1-ol, 25 parts of distilled

water, and 5 parts of ethanoic acid. Butan-1-ol and water must be shaken together in a separating funnel for 10–15 minutes, and ethanoic acid is then added.
The mixture is shaken again.

Allow the mixture to stand, and after it has separated into 2 layers, run off
and discard the lower layer. Use the top layer as the solvent.

Separate solutions of 0.1 g of glycine, 0.1 g proline, and 0.1 g phenylalanine
in 10 cm³ of water should be made up. Phenylalanine is dissolved with difficulty,
and the solution may be filtered to remove undissolved acid.

A mixture of amino acids in solution is then made by dissolving 0.1 g glycine,
0.1 g proline, and 0.1 g phenylalanine in 10 cm³ of water.

Four spots should be placed on the paper: (i) a solution containing the mixture of amino acids, (ii) a solution of glycine, (iii) a solution of proline, (iv) a
solution of phenylalanine.

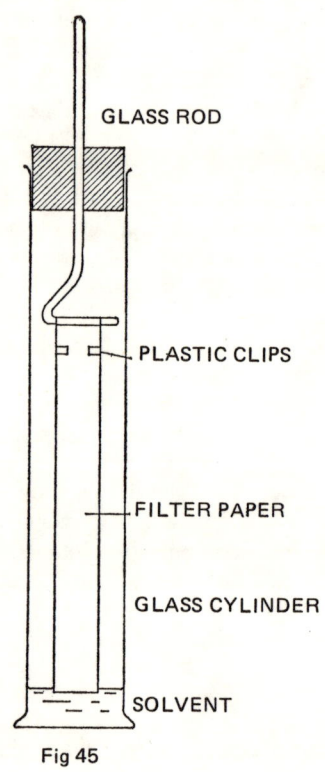

Fig 45

After drying the paper (preferably in a steam oven), the strip should be
sprayed with a solution of 0.2 g of ninhydrin dissolved in 99 cm³ of butan-1-ol
and 1 cm³ of ethanoic acid. If there is no spray, the paper may be drawn through
a shallow bath of ninhydrin solution. The paper must then be dried for about 2
minutes at 100–105° C.

Glycine and phenylalanine react with ninhydrin to form blue compounds, but proline forms a yellow compound.

The spots formed in the controls should be compared with those formed in the mixture by measuring their R_F values under similar conditions.

SEPARATION AND IDENTIFICATION OF AMINO ACIDS IN FRUIT JUICES

(a) Preparation of the fruit juice

Squeeze a tomato, lemon, or orange, filtering or centrifuging the juice to remove solids. To about 1 cm^3 of juice, add 1-2 cm^3 of ethanol, which will precipitate proteins and salts. Filter or centrifuge again. Retain the filtrate.

(b) Preparation of standard amino acid solutions

Dissolve 0.1 g of the following amino acids in 10 cm^3 of water (if the acids are readily available): aspartic acid; leucine; lysine; phenylalanine (which is not easily dissolved).

(c) Separation and identification of the amino acids

Place a spot of each of the prepared amino acid solutions on a piece of filter paper, by the method described above. Place alongside these a spot containing a mixture of these amino acids, and also place a spot of the filtrate of the fruit juice. The solvent is prepared by mixing ethanol, concentrated ammonia solution and water, in the proportions of 80: 10: 10. The locating agent is ninhydrin solution (see above).

32.6. Gas Chromatography

Gas-Liquid Chromatography

INTRODUCTION

Mixtures of gases and volatile liquids can be separated by gas-liquid chromatography. As in paper chromatography, there is partition of the solutes between two solvents. One solvent is fixed in position and is known as the stationary phase (cf. water in paper chromatography). The stationary phase is a non-volatile liquid (e.g. a long-chain alkane or a long-chain ester) which is coated on an inert solid. The moving phase, which can be compared with the second solvent moving on the paper in paper chromatography, is a gas which does not react with either the mixture to be separated or with the stationary phase.

The principles behind the separation are complex, although separation may be generally due to partition of the solutes between the moving gas phase and the stationary liquid phase.

174

DETECTORS

The mixture of gases and vapours is separated, and can be detected and estimated by a number of devices as the gases emerge from the column. These detectors utilise many physical and chemical properties. Two detectors are described in detail. These are

(i) **a katharometer**, which measures changes in thermal conductivity of the the gas as it passes over a hot wire, and

(ii) **a flame ionisation detector**, which measures changes in the concentration of ions formed as a substance burns.

QUALITATIVE AND QUANTITATIVE ANALYSIS

When separating a mixture of three solutes, a graph should be obtained similar to that shown in Figure 46.

The time taken for the solutes to pass through the column (e.g. the retention times (B—A), (C-A), and (D-A)) are characteristic of the compounds. The **retention time** varies, depending on the nature and the rate of flow of gas, the nature and concentration of the stationary phase, and the temperature. Thus, each column has its own characteristics and the time of elution for each substance under investigation must be known before mixtures can be analysed.

The area under the peaks will give the amount of substance present. Generally the area is measured by triangulation, the area being taken as $\frac{1}{2}$(height × width).

If there is poor separation (the peaks on graph incompletely separated) it may be due to bad packing of the column, the employment of too short a column, an incorrect concentration of stationary phase on the solid, the wrong choice of stationary phase or the use of too high a temperature.

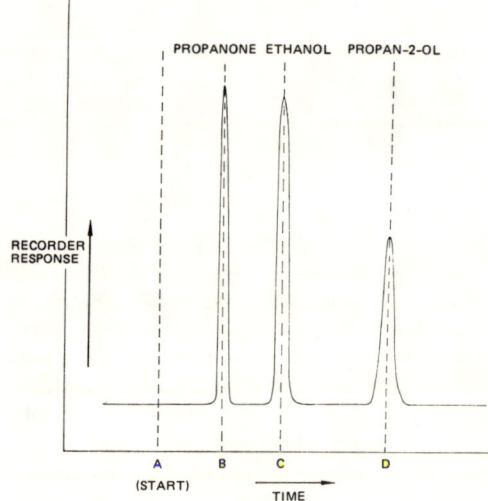

Fig 46

STATIONARY PHASE

Although it is possible to calculate which stationary phase is most suitable for the separation of a mixture of compounds, more often it is selcted by trial and error. Often the stationary phase has a polarity similar to the mixture. Thus, in order to separate a mixture of alcohols, a polyethane diol can be used:

$$HO-(CH_2CH_2O)_n-CH_2CH_2-OH$$

For separating a mixture of hydrocarbons, a hydrocarbon grease (e.g. Apiezon L) is used.

Besides choosing a column which uses polarity to separate the mixture, it is possible to use a non-polar stationary phase, such as Apiezon L, if the compounds in the mixture have widely different boiling-points.

Preparation of the packing material

The packing of the column with the liquid on an inert support is all-important.

A weighed sample of the stationary phase (about 2 g) is dissolved in about 100 cm^3 of a volatile solvent (for example, diethyl ether or dichloromethane). The weighed amount of solid, e.g. Celite (about 20 g), is added. The solvent is removed on a warm water-bath while the flask is rotated gently to ensure as even a distribution of stationary phase as possible. Vigorous shaking must be avoided, for the inert solid must not become too fine. After removal of the solvent, the remaining material should be heated for an hour at 100° C.

The stationary phase prepared in this way is easy to pack, homogeneous, and efficient in separating the solutes.

Packing of the column

Hold the column in a vertical position, and attach paper funnels to each end of the U-tube. Place a small amount of packing material in each funnel and gently tap the sides of the column with a piece of glass tubing surrounded by thick rubber tubing. Continue adding small amounts of material until the tubing is full to within about 15 mm on either side.

The unpacked space at the end of the column can be filled with either glass wool or, better still, with glass yarn.

(a) **Inert solid support**

Celite 80–120 mesh.

(b) **Liquid stationary phase**

Liquid stationary phase	Solvent used to prepare column	Used to separate
Silicone oil	Dichloromethane	General purpose
Dinonyl benzene-1,2-dicarboxylate	Propanone	Alcohols, ethers, aldehydes, ketones
Squalane	Dichloromethane	Hydrocarbons, halogen-substituted hydrocarbons
Apiezon L	Diethyl ether	General purpose. Useful for aromatic hydrocarbons and halogen compounds
Carbowax 400 (polyethane diol 400)	Dichloromethane	Alcohols, ethers, aldehydes, ketones, esters

Gas-Solid Chromatography

Mixtures of gases and volatile liquids can also be separated by gas-solid chromatography. The gases or vapours are separated on a column packed with a solid. The solids generally used are silica gel or alumina (which separate gases by preferential adsorption) and molecular sieves (which separate gases by virtue of the size of their molecules).

As the retention times are much greater for gas-solid systems than for gas-liquid, higher temperatures are used, and generally only comparatively low-boiling components are separated on these columns, gas-liquid columns being used for higher homologues. Thus gas-solid columns are used, for example for permanent gases and C_1–C_6 hydrocarbons.

Apparatus similar to that which is described under gas-liquid chromatography is used. For silica gel, a high column temperature is needed. This is best done by electrical heating, wrapping the column with nichrome wire.

Examples:

Column packing	Treatment before use	Column temperature $^\circ C$	Use to separate
Silica gel (60–80 mesh)	Heat at 250° C for 4 hours	100–200	C_1–C_6 hydrocarbons
Molecular sieve 5A	Crush and sieve. Collect 60–80 mesh. Heat at 250° C for 4 hours	50	$CO, CH_4, C_2H_6, H_2, N_2$

CONSTRUCTION OF APPARATUS TO ILLUSTRATE
PRINCIPLES OF GAS CHROMATOGRAPHY

A column is made of 1 m of polythene tubing (0.5 cm bore) which is packed with a solid coated with a stationary phase. Mains gas is used as the carrier gas (Figure 47).

A still-head, using B10 joints (Figure 47), can be used as an injection port, the gas supply being switched off before removing the stopper and injecting the liquid on to the column. The mixture should be injected straight on to the packing material. Instead of disconnecting the gas supply, a T-piece may be used connecting the polythene tubing, the gas supply and a rubber serum cap (e.g. a 'Subaseal') (Figure 48). The gas eluting from the column is burnt at a jet of a bunsen burner (i.e. with the barrel removed). The flame should be about 1 cm high.

Simple mixtures can be analysed. Examples:

(a) On Apiezon L: an aliphatic and an aromatic hydrocarbon

(b) On Carbowax 400: an alcohol and an ester.

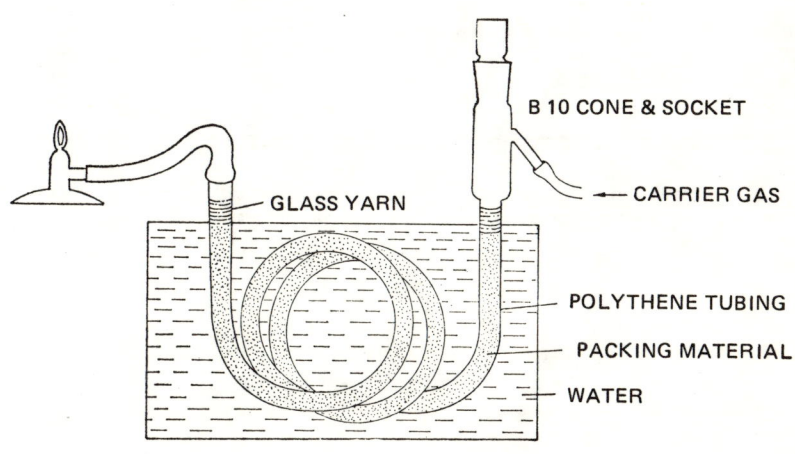

Fig 47

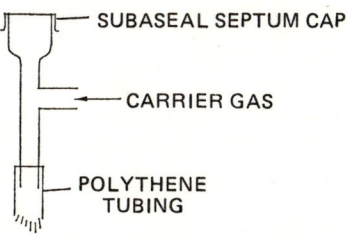

Fig 48

A SIMPLE GAS CHROMATOGRAPH USING A KATHAROMETER DETECTOR

The apparatus consists of:

(i) A supply of carrier gas at constant pressure
(ii) A manometer
(iii) A chromatographic column and an injection system for samples to be analysed
(iv) A flowmeter
(v) The detector—a katharometer

(i) Carrier gas

The carrier gas must be at constant pressure. There are several types of manufactured valves. For example, a gas regulator or a simple needle valve provides an effective means. Although many carrier gases are used nitrogen is chosen here.

(ii) Manometer

A mercury manometer can be placed between the pressure controller and the katharometer. If there is also a flowmeter, the manometer may be unnecessary.

The manometer should be constructed of 4 mm i.d. glass tubing, of about 80 cm length (see Figure 54).

(iii) Construction of the glass column and injection system

The column is constructed of glass tubing of 4-6 mm i.d. It should be about 1m long (or longer, if possible) and bent into the shape of a U to save space.

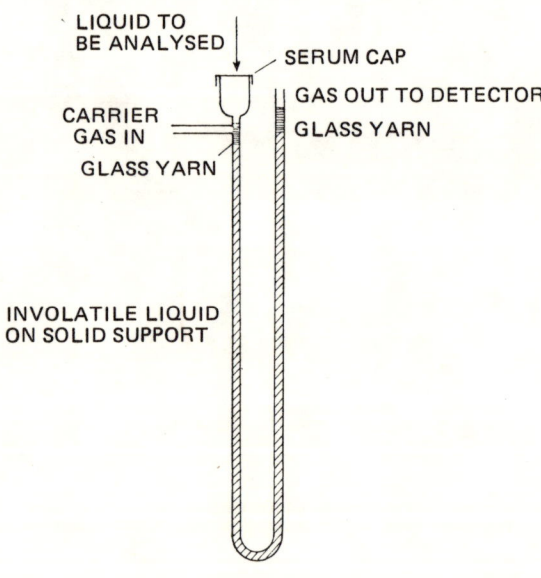

Fig 49

A short length (2-3 cm) of wider glass tubing, of 8-10 mm i.d., is fused on to the inlet arm of the U-tube (Figure 49), and a short length (2-3 cm) of 4-6 mm i.d. tubing is connected into the inlet column, just below the wider glass tubing.

The inlet tube is fitted with a rubber serum cap (for example, 'Subaseal'). The cap is held in position by a few turns of copper wire.

The samples should be injected by means of a hypodermic syringe, through the centre of the serum cap. Long hypodermic needles (up to 15 cm in length) attached to a syringe should be used, so that the liquid to be analysed can be placed directly into the packing material.

For efficient separation the column should be at constant temperature. Moreover, if separation is slow, the column should be heated. A satisfactory thermostat for temperatures up 100° C is shown in Figure 50. The heating element is a

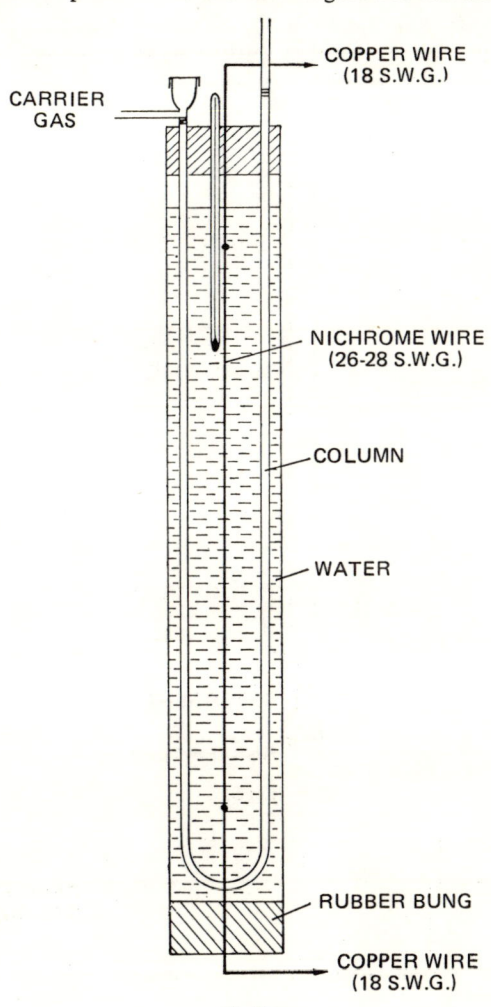

Fig 50

length of nichrome wire (24–26 s.w.g.) heated from an 8-amp Variac. By adjusting the voltage, it is possible to thermostat the column to ±2° C up to 100° C.

(iv) A flowmeter

A simple flowmeter can be constructed from Pyrex glass tubing (Figure 51). Small scratches on the tube should be made to indicate volumes of 5 and 10 cm^3.

If the rubber teat is filled with a liquid detergent, the teat can be squeezed to allow a bubble to form in the tube. The gas will force the bubble up the tube, and the time taken for the bubble to rise up the tube can be measured.

The normal flow-rate is about 40–60 cm^3 per minute. Thus the time taken for the bubble to rise from 0 to 10 cm^3 in the tube should be 10–15 seconds. The exact rate chosen will depend on the other characteristics of the column.

A series of experiments should be performed to see how the flow-rate affects the time for elution of the solutes.

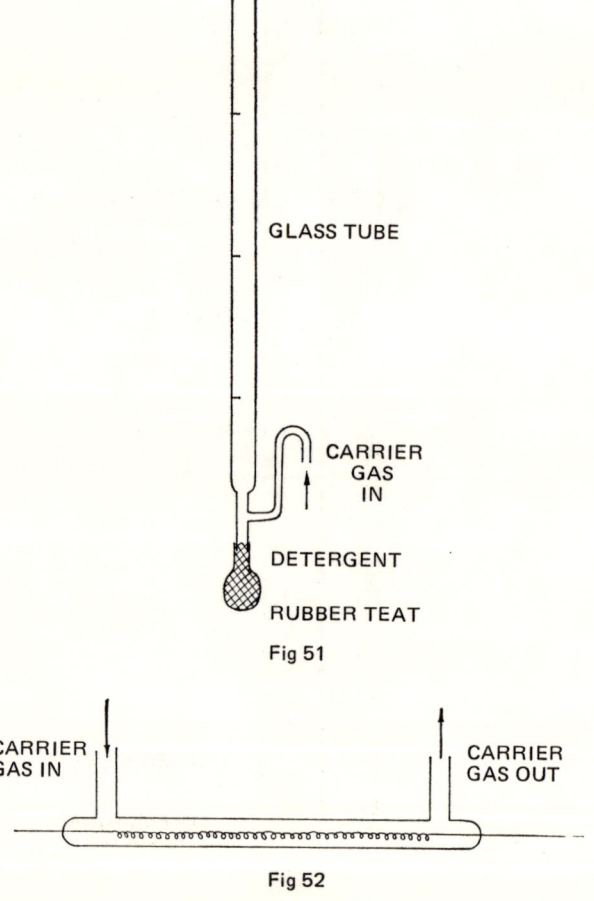

GLASS TUBE

CARRIER GAS IN

DETERGENT

RUBBER TEAT

Fig 51

CARRIER GAS IN

CARRIER GAS OUT

Fig 52

(v) The katharometer

A katharometer consists of two thermal conductivity units (Figure 52). Each unit can be made from approximately 6 mm i.d. Pyrex glass tubing through which a stretched filament from a 150-watt electric light bulb is threaded. The wire is held in position by holding the tube in a flame and allowing the tube to be rounded off. The glass-metal seal is made gas-tight by running either an Araldite resin or Picein into the seal, while it is still hot.

The two thermal conductivity units A and B (which can be placed in a box so that they are draught-free) are then placed in a Wheatstone bridge circuit (Figure 53).

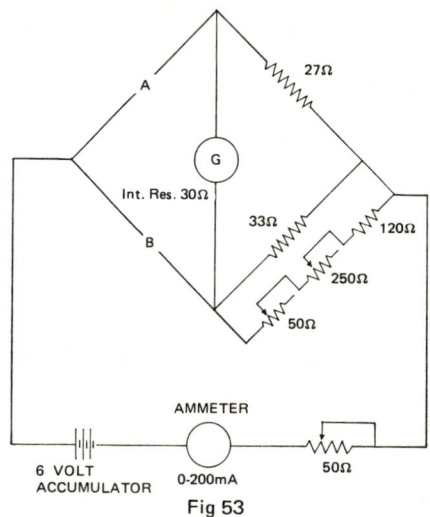

Fig 53

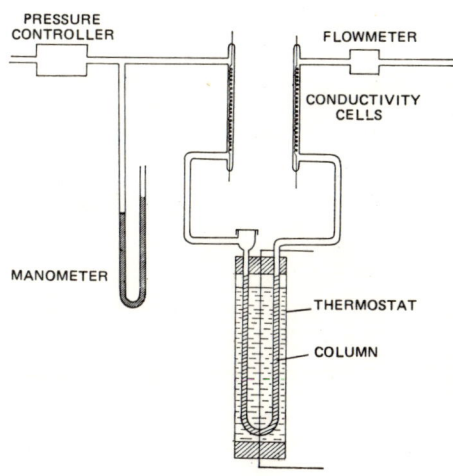

Fig 54

The apparatus is assembled as in Figure 54. The nitrogen flows through the pressure controller, though one arm of the katharometer, to the column. The gas, on leaving the column, passes through the second arm of the katharometer. The connections between the katharometer and the column should be 4-6 mm i.d. glass tubing and should be as short as possible.

A SIMPLE GAS CHROMATOGRAPH USING A FLAME IONISATION DETECTOR

The flame ionisation detector described was designed by D. E. P. Hughes (Shrewsbury School).

Hydrogen is used as the carrier gas and must be at constant pressure. A gas regulator on the cylinder provides this. The gas then passes into the column which should be in a thermostat (Figure 50).

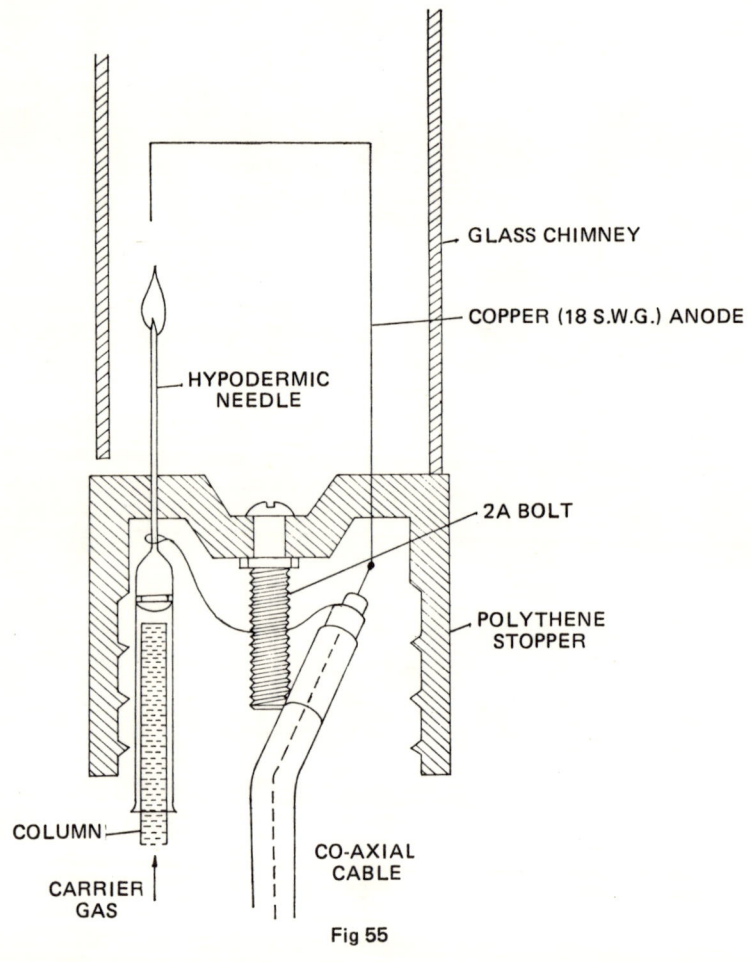

Fig 55

A No. 23 hypodermic needle (2.5 cm long), cut square at the end, is attached to the end of the column (Figure 55). The needle is supported on an insulated base plate and a polythene stopper is useful for this. The needle acts as the cathode and copper wire (about 18 s.w.g.) acts as an anode.

The f.i.d. needs a polarising voltage of about 6 V (Figure 56), and as the current flow is about 10^{-9} A, a high-impedance amplifier is necessary.

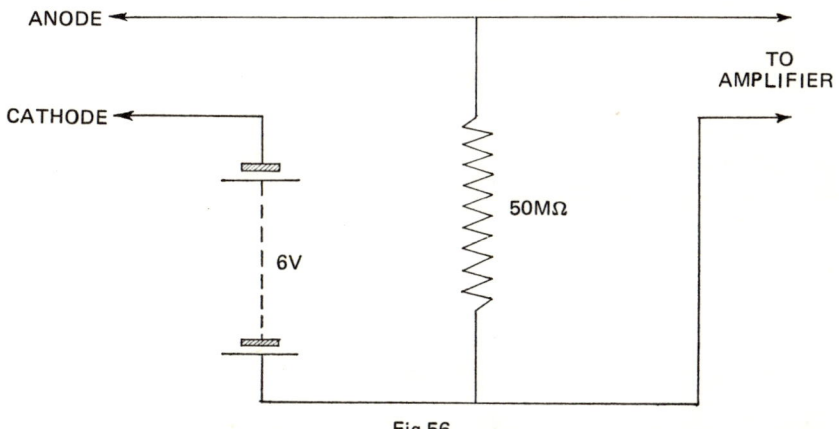

Fig 56

The amplifier can be made from a simple battery triode (Figure 57) with a reduced anode voltage. The impedance of the valve can be as high as 10 Ω. A large condenser (100 μF) is placed across the meter, and this gives a steady baseline, smoothing out any pulses due to dust particles ionising in the flame.

Alternatively, a simple electrometer valve amplifier (Figure 58) can be used, which is attached to a dead beat meter.

Hydrogen flows through the pressure controller and into the column. The gas, on leaving the column, is passed through the flow meter until a satisfactory flow-rate is obtained by adjusting the pressure controller. The flow should be such that the flame is about 0.5 cm high, and it should not make the tip of the needle red hot.

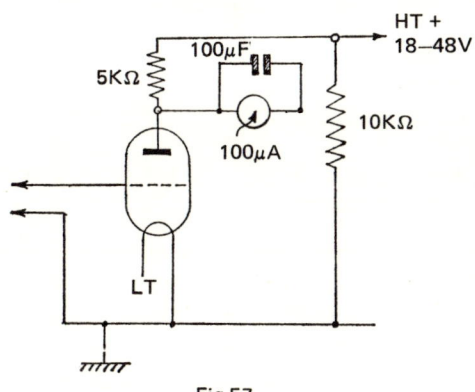

Fig 57

The apparatus must be allowed to settle down in order to give a steady reading on the galvanometer.

This detector is considerably more sensitive than the katharometer and very small injections should be used.

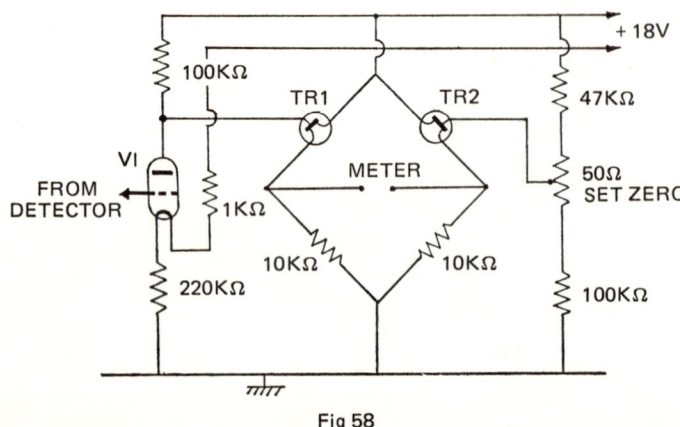

Fig 58

A low voltage electrometer. TR1 and TR2 are Mullard BFY 52 transistors and VI is a Mullard ME1404 electrometer valve. The meter is a 100 μA instrument to which a resistance must be added in series so that the output of the electrometer bridge is at least 1000 ohms.

FURTHER READING

Chromatography and Electrophoresis on Paper. J. G. Feinberg and I. Smith, Shandon Scientific Company. Paperback, Longman, 1972

Dry-column chromatography. G. J. Green, *School Science Review*, Vol. 50, p. 598 (1969) and J. M. Bohen, M. M. Jouille, F. A. Kaplan and B. Loer. *Journal of Chemical Education*, Vol. 50, p. 367 (1973)

Thin-layer chromatography. D. A. Stephens, *School Science Review*, Vol. 48, p. 376 (1967)

Simple chromatographic demonstrations. M. Taylor, *School Science Review*, Vol. 45, p. 75 (1963)

Experimental gas chromatography. D. E. P. Hughes, *School Science Review*, Vol. 47, p. 125 (1967)

Demonstration chromatograph with a flame ionization detector. G. D. Brabson, *Journal of Chemical Education*, Vol. 49, p. 71 (1972)

FILM (on free loan)

Chromatography, I.C.I. Films Unit (1977). Imperial Chemical Industries Limited, Millbank, London, S.W.1.

33

OBSERVATION AND DEDUCTION EXPERIMENTS

1. SUBSTANCE HY

Record what happens when you carry out the following experiments with the substance HY, and say what you think HY is and give explanations of the reactions you have observed.

(i) Heat it.
(ii) Heat it with solid sodium ethanoate.
(iii) To its solution in dilute sulphuric acid, add a few drops of potassium permanganate solution and warm.
(iv) To its solution in water, add silver nitrate solution.
(v) To its solution in water, add ammonia solution gradually until no further action is seen. To the resulting solution, add a few drops of silver nitrate solution and warm.

2. SUBSTANCE D

Carry out the following experiments with D and draw what conclusions you can as to its nature, and the course of reactions you observe.

(i) Heat it.in a hard glass test-tube.
(ii) Allow the residue from (i) to cool and then treat it with dilute hydrochloric acid.
(iii) Treat D with dilute hydrochloric acid.
(iv) To a concentrated solution of D, add silver nitrate solution and then dilute nitric acid.
(v) To its solution, add barium chloride solution.
(vi) To its solution, add iron(III) chloride solution. Boil the mixture gently.
(vii) To its solution, add sodium carbonate solution.

3. SUBSTANCE Q

Carry out the following experiments with Q. Describe and, as far as you can, account for what you observe, and indicate the nature but not the identity of the substance.

(i) Heat a small portion of Q. To the residue when cool, add a few cm^3 of sodium hydroxide solution followed by one drop of dilute copper(II) sulphate solution.

(ii) Add sodium hydroxide solution to a portion of Q and heat the solution.
(iii) Decolorise a few cm^3 of bromine water by the addition of sodium hydroxide solution. To this add a portion of Q.

4. SUBSTANCES L AND M

L is the sulphate of a nitrogen-containing compound; M is a monophenyl derivative of L in the form of a hydrochloride. Carry out the following reactions and suggest what L and M are.
(i) To a solution of M in dilute sodium hydroxide, add a few drops of potassium hexacyanoferrate(III) solution. Identify gases evolved.
(ii) Neutralise the solution from (i) with a few drops of concentrated hydrochloric acid and add iron(III) chloride solution.
(iii) Add L to a solution of copper(II) sulphate and warm.
(iv) Repeat test (iii) using Fehling's solution.
(v) Repeat (iii) with an ammoniacal solution of silver nitrate.
(vi) Add M to a solution of sodium hydroxide and boil. Identify any gas evolved.
(vii) Add M to a solution of glucose containing some sodium ethanoate. Boil for 3–4 minutes and then leave for a little time.

5. SUBSTANCE B

Draw what conclusions you can from the following experiments about the identity of B.
(i) Warm B with concentrated sulphuric acid.
(ii) To a solution of silver nitrate, add 1 drop of sodium hydroxide solution, and redissolve the precipitate in ammonia solution. Then add B and warm the mixture.
(iii) Warm B with Fehling's solution.
(iv) To B, add sodium hydroxide solution, and warm the mixture.
(v) Mix B with a crystal of naphthalen-1-ol, and add concentrated sulphuric acid.
(vi) Repeat (v) but warm with concentrated hydrochloric acid instead of sulphuric acid.
(vii) Boil B with phenylhydrazine hydrochloride and water containing sodium ethanoate.

6. SUBSTANCE LB

Draw what conclusions you can, from the following experiments, about the identity of LB.
(i) Warm LB with concentrated sulphuric acid. Test the gases evolved.
(ii) To an aqueous solution (cold) of LB, add 2 drops of potassium permanganate solution.
(iii) Warm the solution from (ii).
(iv) Treat a concentrated solution of LB in water with a concentrated solu-

tion of calcium chloride. Test the solubility of the precipitate in dilute ethanoic acid.
(v) Heat LB with soda-lime and test the gases evolved.
(vi) Treat LB with iron(III) chloride solution.

7. SUBSTANCE A

Record what happens when you carry out the following experiments with the substance A, say what you think A is and give explanations of the reactions you have observed.
(i) Dissolve a few crystals of A in water. Divide into 2 portions.
   (a) To one portion add Universal Indicator solution.
   (b) To the second portion, add ammonia solution until just alkaline. Boil off excess ammonia then add neutral iron(III) chloride solution.
(ii) Heat a small amount of A in a hard glass test-tube. Smell the vapour evolved.
(iii) Heat a small amount of A on a crucible lid.
(iv) Moisten equal quantities (about 0.1 g) of A and of 1,3-dihydroxybenzene with 2 drops of concentrated sulphuric acid in a hard glass test-tube. Fuse the mixture and allow it to cool. Add excess dilute sodium hydroxide solution.

8. SUBSTANCE C

Carry out the following experiments with C and draw what conclusions you can as to its nature. Wherever possible, explain the reactions you have observed.
(i) Add concentrated sulphuric acid to a little of C in a test-tube. Warm gently.
(ii) Heat a small amount of C in a hard glass test-tube.
(iii) Dissolve a little of C in water. Divide the solution into 4 portions:
   (a) To the first portion add a saturated solution of sodium hexanitrocobaltate(III) in acid. Shake the mixture.
   (b) Pass hydrogen sulphide through the second portion of solution.
   (c) To 1 cm^3 of solution, add 1 drop of iron(II) sulphate solution, 2 drops of hydrogen peroxide solution, and excess of dilute sodium hydroxide solution.
   (d) To the fourth portion, add an ammoniacal solution of silver nitrate. Warm the mixture.

9. SUBSTANCE E

Carry out the following experiments with E, and draw what conclusions you can as to its nature. Wherever possible, explain the reactions you have observed.
(i) Warm a little of E with concentrated sulphuric acid in a test-tube.
(ii) Heat a mixture of E and soda-lime in a hard glass test-tube.
(iii) To about 0.1 g of E, add 5 drops of methanol and 3 drops of concentrated sulphuric acid. Warm the mixture.

(iv) Dissolve a little of E in water and divide the solution into 3 parts:
    (a) To the first part, add Universal Indicator solution.
    (b) To the second part, add dilute sulphuric acid.
    (c) To the third part, add 3 drops of a neutral solution of iron(III) solution.

10. SUBSTANCE F

Carry out the following experiments with F. Say what you think F is, and give explanations of the reactions you have observed.
    (i) Dissolve a few crystals of F in water. Divide the solution into 2 portions:
        (a) To the first portion, add Universal Indicator solution.
        (b) To the second portion, add about 0.1 g of copper(II) carbonate. Warm the mixture.
    (ii) Test the solubility of F in (a) ethanol, (b) diethyl ether.
    (iii) To 1 cm^3 of an ice-cold solution of sodium nitrite in a test-tube, add 1 cm^3 of ice-cold dilute hydrochloric acid. When the effervescence has subsided, add a few crystals of F.
    (iv) Heat a mixture of F and soda-lime in a hard glass test-tube.

11. SUBSTANCE G

Carry out the following experiments with G. Describe what you observe, and give what explanation you can of your observations.
    (i) To about 0.1 g of G, in a test-tube, add dilute sodium hydroxide solution. Heat the mixture until G has completely dissolved. Test for any gas evolved. Boil until the reaction appears to have reached completion.
    (ii) Cool the solution from experiment (i), and acidify with dilute sulphuric acid.
    (iii) Heat a little G on a spatula or on a crucible lid.
    (iv) To 1 cm^3 of an ice-cold solution of sodium nitrite, in a test-tube, add 1 cm^3 of ice-cold dilute sulphuric acid. When the effervescence has subsided, add a few crystals of G.
    (v) To 0.1 g of G in a test-tube, add 3 drops of bromine. Add 2 cm^3 of sodium hydroxide solution. Cork the test-tube and shake for about 2 minutes. Remove the cork, and transfer the mixture to a dilute aqueous suspension of bleaching powder in a test-tube.

12. SUBSTANCE H

Carry out the following experiments with H and draw what conclusions you can as to its nature, and the course of reactions you observe. Dissolve about 0.5 g of H in 5 cm^3 of water. Divide the solution into 5 parts.
    (i) Add Universal Indicator solution to the first portion of the solution of H.
    (ii) Acidify the second portion with dilute nitric acid, and add silver nitrate solution.
    (iii) To a small amount of sodium hydrogencarbonate, in a test-tube, add the

third portion of the solution dropwise.
- (iv) Add dilute sodium hydroxide solution to the fourth part until the solution is just alkaline. Pour the solution into a second test-tube in which there is a dilute aqueous suspension of bleaching powder.
- (v) Dissolve a few crystals of naphthalen-2-ol in 5 cm³ of dilute sodium hydroxide solution, in a test-tube. Cool the solution in ice.

  To the fifth part of the solution of H, in a second test-tube, add 2 cm³ of dilute hydrochloric acid. Cool in ice, and add a solution of sodium nitrite in water dropwise to slight excess, using a starch-iodide paper as indicator. Mix the 2 solutions.

13. SUBSTANCE J

Carry out the following experiments with J and draw what conclusions you can as to its nature, and the course of reactions you observe.
- (i) To a small amount of J in a test-tube, add about 5 cm³ of dilute sodium hydroxide solution. Warm gently.
- (ii) Boil the solution from (i) for about half a minute. Cool the solution, acidify with dilute nitric acid, and add silver nitrate solution.
- (iii) To about 0.1 g of J, in a test-tube, add 1 cm³ of Schiff's reagent.
- (iv) Add Fehling's solution II (or B) to 1 cm³ of solution I (or A) until a deep-blue solution is just obtained. Add a small amount of J, and warm the mixture.
- (v) To about 0.1 g of J in a test-tube, add 1 cm³ of concentrated sulphuric acid.

14. SUBSTANCE K

Record what happens when you carry out the following experiments with the substance K, say what you think K is, and give explanations of the reactions you have observed.
- (i) Ignite 2 or 3 drops of K on a crucible lid.
- (ii) Place 1 drop of K on a moist Universal Indicator paper.
- (iii) To 3 drops of K in a test-tube, add 1 cm³ of dilute sulphuric acid followed by 5 drops of dilute potassium permanganate solution. Shake and warm.
- (iv) To 3 drops of K in a test-tube, add 1 cm³ of Schiff's reagent.
- (v) Add Fehling's solution II (or B) to 1 cm³ of solution I (or A) until a deep-blue solution is just obtained. Add 3 drops of K, and warm the mixture.
- (vi) To 5 drops of a solution of 2,4-dinitrophenylhydrazine in ethanoic acid, in a test-tube, add 3 drops of K. Warm the mixture, and then leave to stand for a few minutes.
- (vii) To 3 drops of K in a test-tube, add 3 drops of iodine solution and then dilute sodium hydroxide solution dropwise until the colour of iodine is discharged. Allow the mixture to stand for a few minutes.

15. SUBSTANCE N

Carry out the following experiments with N and draw what conclusions you can as to its nature, and the course of reactions you observe.

(i) Ignite 3 drops of N on a crucible lid.

(ii) To 2 drops of N in a test-tube, add 2 cm^3 of water. Test the solution with Universal Indicator solution.

(iii) To 5 drops of N in a test-tube, add a small pellet of sodium, *with great care.*

(iv) To 5 drops of N in a test-tube, add about 0.1 g of phosphorus penta-chloride *with care*.

(v) To 5 drops of N in a test-tube, add 2 cm^3 of dilute sulphuric acid. Divide the mixture into 2 parts:

   (a) Add 3 drops of dilute potassium permanganate solution. Note the smell of any vapours evolved.

   (b) Add 3 drops of dilute potassium dichromate solution. Note the smell of any vapours evolved.

16. SUBSTANCE R

Record what happens when you carry out the following experiments with the substance R, say what you think R is, and give explanations of the reactions you have observed.

(i) Heat a little of R on a crucible-lid.

(ii) To a small amount of R in a test-tube, add 1 cm^3 of iodine solution and then dilute sodium hydroxide solution until the colour of iodine is discharged. Allow the mixture to stand for a few minutes.

(iii) Add Fehling's solution II (or B) to 1 cm^3 of solution I (or A) until a deep-blue solution is obtained. Add a small amount of R, and warm the mixture.

(iv) To 5 drops of a solution of 2,4-dinitrophenylhydrazine in ethanoic acid, in a test-tube, add a small amount of R. Warm the mixture, and then leave to stand for a few minutes.

(v) To a small amount of R in a test-tube, add 3 cm^3 of potassium permanganate and 0.1 g of sodium carbonate. Boil the mixture and filter (or centrifuge). Add dilute sulphuric acid dropwise to the filtrate.

17. SUBSTANCE S

Record what happens when you carry out the following experiments with the substance S, say what you think S is, and give explanations of the reactions you have observed.

(i) Heat a little of S on a spatula or on a crucible lid.

(ii) To a small amount (0.1 g) of S in a test-tube, add 1 cm^3 of water. Test the solubility of S (a) in the cold, (b) when the mixture is warmed. Divide the solution into two portions:

   (a) To the first portion, add a little sodium hydrogencarbonate.

(b) To the second portion, add bromine water.

(iii) Mix a small amount of S with soda-lime in a Pyrex text-tube fitted with a delivery tube. Heat the mixture and pass the vapour evolved through 5 cm^3 of an aqueous suspension of bleaching powder (Figure 27). Remove the test-tube containing the bleaching powder to avoid 'sucking back' and allow the heated test-tube to cool. Dissolve the solid residue, in the test-tube, in water and acidify with dilute hydrochloric acid. Add barium chloride solution.

(iv) Dissolve about 0.5 g of S and 0.2 g of sodium carbonate in 5 cm^3 of water in a test-tube. Cool the solution in ice, and add 0.2 g of sodium nitrite dissolved in 1 cm^3 of water. Add 0.5 cm^3 of concentrated hydrochloric acid dropwise, keeping the temperature of the solution below 5° C. To this solution, add a second solution prepared by dissolving a few crystals of naphthalen-2-ol in 2 cm^3 of dilute sodium hydroxide solution.

18. SUBSTANCE T

Carry out the following experiments with substance T and draw what conclusions you can as to its nature. Wherever possible, explain the reactions you have observed.

(i) Ignite 4–5 drops of the liquid in an evaporating basin or crucible.

(ii) Test the solubility of T in (a) water, (b) ether (CARE—Fire).

(iii) Dissolve 5 drops of T in 1 cm^3 of tetrachloromethane in a test-tube. Add, dropwise, a solution of bromine in tetrachloromethane and shake the tube.

(iv) Place 5 cm^3 of concentrated nitric acid in a flask and add 1 cm^3 of T dropwise. Heat the mixture under reflux at 100° C, immersing the flask in a beaker of boiling water for about 15 minutes. Remove the flask from the bath and cool in a beaker of ice. Separate the precipitate and recrystallise from a small volume of water. Dry the crystals at 100° C and find the melting point.

34

DETECTION OF ELEMENTS IN AN ORGANIC COMPOUND

34.1. Carbon and Hydrogen

Make up a mixture of the compound and excess dry copper(II) oxide in a small Pyrex text-tube. Place a delivery tube and cork into the test-tube and heat the mixture. Pass the gases through lime water. If the lime water turns milky, the gases contain carbon dioxide and the compound must contain **carbon**.

If a liquid forms on the side of the small Pyrex test-tube, test it with anhydrous copper(II) sulphate. If it turns blue, the liquid is probably water and the original compound contains **hydrogen**.

34.2. Lassaigne sodium test
Great care must be taken during this experiment.

Place about 0.2 g of the compound in an ignition tube. Incline the tube almost to the horizontal and introduce a small pellet of sodium. Warm the sodium and allow the molten metal to run on to the organic compound. Then hold the tube vertically and bring to a red heat, maintaining the tube at this temperature for about a minute.

Plunge the tube into a small beaker containing about 3 cm^3 of water, laying a wire gauze across the mouth of the tube for protection against spurting. Grind the tube in the beaker and boil the mixture for about 3 minutes. Filter (or centrifuge) the mixture and collect the filtrate. Divide into three parts.

The organic compound on heating with sodium is converted into ionic sodium salts. These can then be tested by inorganic reagents.

Test for sulphur   (If sulphur is present, it has been converted into sodium sulphide).

To one portion of the filtrate from the sodium fusion, add one drop of an aqueous solution of sodium pentacyanonitrosylferrate(II) ('nitroprusside'). A purple colour indicates **sulphur**. Alternatively, one drop of lead(II) ethanoate solution will yield a black precipitate of lead(II) sulphide.

$$Pb^{2+} + S^{2-} \longrightarrow PbS\downarrow$$

Test for nitrogen (If nitrogen is present, it has been converted to sodium cyanide).

To a second portion of the filtrate, add an equal volume of a *fresh* solution of iron(II) sulphate. Boil the mixture, which contains a green precipitate of iron(II) hydroxide, and add 3 drops of iron(III) chloride solution. Acidify the mixture with dilute hydrochloric acid. Filter (or centrifuge) the mixture. A residue of Prussian Blue indicates that **nitrogen** is present in the compound.

$$Fe^{2+} + 2CN^- \longrightarrow Fe(CN)_2$$

$$Fe(CN)_2 + 4CN^- \longrightarrow Fe(CN)_6^{4-}$$

$$Na^+ + Fe^{3+} + Fe(CN)_6^{4-} \longrightarrow NaFe[Fe(CN)_6]$$

Test for halogens (If halogens are present, they are converted into sodium halides).

(a) *If nitrogen is present.* Acidify the third portion with dilute nitric acid and evaporate the solution to a quarter of its former bulk. Hydrogen cyanide boils off.

Test the solution to see that excess nitric acid is present. Add silver nitrate solution.

A white, curdy precipitate, soluble in excess of dilute ammonia solution, indicates chloride. Thus **chlorine** is present in the organic compound.

$$Ag^+ + Cl^- \longrightarrow Ag^+Cl^- \downarrow$$

$$Ag^+Cl^- \downarrow + 2NH_3 \longrightarrow [Ag(NH_3)_2]^+ + Cl^-$$

A pale-yellow precipitate, soluble in a considerable excess of concentrated ammonia solution, indicates bromide. Thus **bromine** is present in the organic compound.

A yellow precipitate, insoluble in excess ammonia solution, indicates iodide. Thus **iodine** is present in the organic compound.

(b) *If nitrogen is not present.* There is no need to evaporate the solution. Add excess dilute nitric acid, followed by silver nitrate solution.

Tetrachloromethane and other highly chlorinated hydrocarbons must not be subjected to the sodium fusion test, nor should any recognized unstable substance.

APPENDIX I

ORGANIC REAGENTS

Alkyl benzene (Appendix III)

Amberlite I.R. – 120 (H) (or Zeolit 225) (Appendix III)

Amberlite I.R.A. – 400 (OH) (or Deacidite Zeolit N(ip) (Appendix III)

4-Aminobenzenesulphonic acid (Sulphanilic acid)

bis-(2-Aminoethyl)amine (Diethylenetriamine) (Appendix III)

Anthracene

Anti-freeze fluid

Apiezon grease (Appendix III)

Aspartic acid

Benzaldehyde

Benzene

Benzene-1,2-dicarboxylic anhydride

Benzoic acid

Benzoyl chloride

Bromobenzene

1-Bromobutane

2-Bromobutane

Bromoethane

2-Bromo-2-methylpropane

Butanedioic acid

Butan-1-ol

cis-Butenedioic anhydride

Caradate 30 (Appendix III)

Caradol GXR 13 (Appendix III)

Carbamide (Urea)

Carbowax 400 (Appendix III)

Charcoal Wood

Chlorobenzene

2-Chlorobenzoic acid

(Chloromethyl)benzene

Coal Powdered

Copper(II) ethanoate

Cyclohexanol

Cyclohexene (Appendix III)

Deacidite Zeolit N(ip) (or Amberlite I.R.A. –400) (OH) (Appendix III)

1,6-Diaminohexane (Appendix III)

1,2-Dibromoethane

Dichlorodimethylsilane (Appendix III)

1,1-Dichloroethane

1,2-Dichloroethane

Dichloromethane

2,4-Dichlorophenol

Di(dodecanoyl) peroxide (Lauroyl peroxide) (Appendix III)

Diethylamine

Diethylammonium chloride

Diethyl ether

Diisopropyl ether

N,N-Dimethylphenylamine

2,4-Dinitrophenylhydrazine To prepare a solution shake 1 g of solid in 50 cm^3 of methanol and add slowly 2 cm^3 of concentrated sulphuric acid. Shake and filter if necessary.

Dinonyl benzene-1,2-dicarboxylate (Appendix III)

Diphenylamine

Dobane JN (Appendix III)

Dodecanol (Appendix III)

Epikote 815 (Appendix III)

Ethanal

Ethanamide

Ethanedioic acid

Ethane-1,2-diol

Ethanoic acid (a) Glacial, (b) Dilute solution – 2M

Ethanoic anhydride

Ethanol

Ethanonitrile

Ethanoyl chloride

Ethylamine solution (or Methylamine solution) 33% (w/w) in water

Ethylammonium chloride (or Methylammonium chloride)

Ethyl ethanoate

Formalin 40% solution of methanal in water

Fructose

Fuchsine

Glucose

Glycine

Hexane (or Petroleum ether (80–100°C))

Hexanedioyl chloride (or Decanedioyl chloride) (Appendix III)

2-Hydroxybenzoic acid

Iodoethane
Iodomethane
Iron(II) ethanedioate

Leucine
Lycine

Malachite green
Melamine (Appendix III)
Methanal (Formalin)
Methanoic acid
Methanol
Methylene blue
2-Methylbutan-2-ol
Methylamine solution (or Ethylamine solution) 33% (w/w) in water
Methylammonium chloride (or Ethylammonium chloride)
Methylbenzene
Monochloroethanoic acid

Naphthalen-1-ol
Naphthalen-2-ol
Ninhydrin
Nitrobenzene
Nitroethane (Appendix III)
Nylon 6   Pellets (Appendix III)

Paraffin oil
Pentane (or Petroleum ether (60–80°C))
Perspex (Appendix III)
Petroleum ether (60–80°C) (or Pentane)
Petroleum ether (80–100°C) (or Hexane)
Phenol
Phenolphthalein
Phenylalanine
Phenylamine
Phenylammonium chloride
Phenylethanone
Phenylethene (Appendix III)
Phenylhydrazine
Phenylmethanol

Phenylethyne (Appendix III)
(Phenylmethyl)amine
Poly(ethane-1,2-diol) (Polyethylene glycol 400, Carbowax 400) (Appendix III)
Polyether resin (Appendix III)
Polyisocyanate (Appendix III)
Proline
Propanedioic acid
Propane-1,2,3-triol
Propan-1-ol
Propan-2-ol
Propanone
Pyridine

Schiff's reagent (0.1% solution of fuchsine through which sulphur dioxide is passed until the solution is colourless)
Silicone oil (Appendix III)
Sodium benzenesulphonate
Sodium ethanedioate
Sodium ethanoate
Sodium methanoate
Sodium potassium 2,3-dihydroxybutanedioate
Squalane (Appendix III)
Starch   Soluble
Sucrose

Tetrachloromethane
Trichloroethanal hydrate (Chloral hydrate)
Trichloromethane
Triethanolamine
Triethylamine
Triethylammonium choride
Triphenylamine
Triphenylchloromethane (Appendix III)

Urease

Yeast

Zeolit 225 (or Amberlite I.R. – 120 (H)) (Appendix III)

APPENDIX II

INORGANIC REAGENTS

Aluminium Powder (or Devarda's Alloy)
Aluminium chloride Anhydrous
Aluminium oxide For column chromatography (Appendix III)
Aluminium sulphate Hydrated
Ammonia solution (a) Density 0.880 g cm^{-3}, (b) Dilute solution −2M

Bleaching powder
Bromine
Bromine water

Calcium carbonate Powdered
Calcium chloride Anhydrous
Calcium dicarbide
Celite 80–120 mesh (Appendix III)
Copper Turnings
Copper(I) chloride
Copper(II) carbonate
Copper(II) oxide
Copper(II) sulphate (a) Anhydrous powder, (b) Crystalline solid, (c) 7% solution of crystals in water

Devarda's Alloy (or powdered aluminium)
Disodium tetraborate(III)-10-water (borax)

Fehling's solution I (or A) 7% solution of copper(II) sulphate crystals in water
Fehling's solution II (or B) 12 g of sodium hydroxide and 5 g of sodium potassium 2,3-dihydroxybutanedioate in 1 dm³ water

Hydrochloric acid (a) Concentrated, (b) Dilute solution − 2M
Hydrogen peroxide
Hydroxylamine hydrochloride

Iodine (a) Solid, (b) 1% solution in 20% solution of potassium iodide
Iron Filings or wire
Iron(II) sulphate Crystals
Iron(III) chloride 1% solution in water
Iron(III) sulphate Crystals

Lead ethanoate 1% solution in water

Lime water Saturated solution
Lithium aluminium hydride

Magnesium Turnings (Grignard)
Mercury(II) chloride 5% solution in water
Mercury(II) oxide
Mercury(II) sulphate
Molecular sieve 5A (Appendix III)

Nickel Foil
Nitric acid (a) Concentrated, (b) Dilute solution − 2M

Phosphoric acid
Phosphorus Red solid
Phosphorus(V) oxide
Phosphorus pentachloride
Phosphorus trichloride
Platinum Wire, about 28 s.w.g.
Porous pot Chippings
Potassium bromide
Potassium carbonate Anhydrous
Potassium dichromate (a) Solid, (b) 5% solution in water
Potassium hydrogensulphate
Potassium hydroxide Pellets
Potassium iodide (a) Solid, (b) 20% solution in water
Potassium permanganate (a) Solid, (b) 1% solution in water

Rocksil wool

Semicarbazide hydrochloride
Silica gel (a) 60–80 mesh, (b) For thin-layer chromatography (Appendix III)
Silver nitrate 2% solution in water
Soda-lime
Sodium
Sodium carbonate Anhydrous
Sodium chloride
Sodium dichromate Solid
Sodium ethanedioate
Sodium ethanoate Anhydrous
Sodium hydrogencarbonate
Sodium hydrogensulphite
Sodium hydroxide (a) Pellets, (b) 20% solu-

tion in water
Sodium hypochlorite Solution in water
Sodium methanoate
Sodium nitrate
Sodium nitrite
Sodium sulphate Anhydrous
Sulphur Flowers

Sulphur dioxide Syphon
Sulphuric acid (a) Concentrated, (b) Dilute
solution – M

Tin Granulated

Zinc Dust

APPENDIX III

SUPPLIERS OF CHEMICALS AND APPARATUS

Although most of the chemicals and apparatus in this book can be obtained from all laboratory suppliers, the following are less usual and may be obtained from the suppliers shown:

Section	Page	Chemical or Apparatus	Supplier
Introduction	xii	Cylindrical rubber teats	5
1.1 and	1	Rocksil wool	3,4,5
other sections			
2.5	8	Cyclohexene	1,3,4,5,7
3.3	14	Phenylethyne (Phenylacetylene)	1,3,7
12.1	75	Nitroethane	1,4,7
18.3	101	Triphenylchloromethane	1,7
23.2⎫	127	Alkylbenzene (Dobane JN)	7,8,11
28.4⎭	147		
28.3	147	Dodecan-1-ol	1,3,4,5,7
30.1	151	Di(dodecanoyl) peroxide (Lauroyl peroxide)	1,4,5,7
	151	Phenylethene (Styrene)	1,3,4,5,7
	151	Perspex, chips	3,4,5
	152	1,6-Diaminohexane	1,3,5,7
	152	Hexanedioyl chloride (Adipoyl chloride)	1,3,4,5,7
		Hexanedioyl chloride (Adipoyl chloride in ampoules, 5% in tetrachloromethane)	4,5
	152	Decanedioyl chloride (Sebacoyl chloride)	1,3,5,7
		Decanedioyl chloride (Sebacoyl chloride, 5% in tetrachloromethane)	5
	153	Nylon 6, pellets	1,3,4,5
30.2	154	Melamine	1,3,4,7
	155	Epikote 815	6
		Bis-(2-aminoethyl)amine (Diethylenetriamine)	1,3,7
30.3	155-6	Caradol GXR13	9
		or Polyurethane foam, polymer A	4
	155-6	Caradate 30	9
		or Polyurethane foam, polymer B	4
30.5	156	Dichlorodimethylsilane	1,3,4,7
32.2	163-4	Alumina for column chromatography	
		Aluminium oxide, active basic (activity 1)	1,3
		Aluminium oxide H	3,7
32.3	165-6	Silica gel G for thin-layer chromatography	1,3,4,5,7
32.4	169-70	Ion-exchange resin (Strong acid cation)	
		Zeolit 225	1,3,4
		or Amberlite IR-120(H)	1,3
		Ion-exchange resin (Strong base anion)	
		De-Acidite Zeolit N(ip)	1,3,4
		or Amberlite IRA-400(OH)	1,3
32.6	175	Celite (80–120 mesh)	1,3,7

Section	Page	Chemical or Apparatus	Supplier
	176	Silicone oil MS550	1,3,4,5,7
	176	Dinonyl benzene − 1,2-dicarboxylate (Dinonyl phthalate)	1,3,7
	176	2,6,10,15,19,23-Hexamethyltetracosane (Squalane)	1,3,7
	176	Apiezon L grease	1,3,7
	176	Poly(ethane-1,2,-diol) 400 (Polyethylene glycol 400 or Carbowax 400)	1,3,7
	177-8	Glass yarn	9
	176	Silica gel (60–80 mesh)	3,4,7
	176	Molecular sieve 5A, pellets	1,3,5,7
	177	Subaseal septum caps	5
	178	Gas regulator M 30–NG (Nitrogen)	2,3,5,7
	178	Gas regulator M 30–HG (Hydrogen)	2,3,5,7
	179	Agla Hypodermic Syringe	10

SUPPLIERS

1. B.D.H. Chemicals Ltd., Poole, Dorset, BH12 4NN
2. British Oxygen Co. Ltd., Deer Park Road, London, SW19 3UF
3. Educhem., P.O. Box 1, Romford, RM1 1HA
4. A. Gallenkamp & Co. Ltd., Frederick Street, Birmingham B1 3HT
   or Braeview Place, Nerston, East Kilbride, Glasgow G74 3XJ
   or Portrack Lane, Stockton-on-Tees, Cleveland, TS18 2PT
   or P.O. Box 19, Croft Street, Widnes, Cheshire WA8 0NL
5. Philip Harris Ltd., Lynn Lane, Shenstone, Staffordshire, WS14 0EE
6. Hermatite Products Ltd., Tavistock Road, West Drayton, Middlesex VB7 7RA
7. Phase Separations Ltd., Deeside Industrial Estate, Queensferry, Flintshire CH5 2LR
8. Shell Chemicals U.K. Ltd., Public Relations Department, Downstream Building, Shell Centre, York Road, London SE1 7PG
9. Strand Glassfibre Ltd., Brentway Trading Estate, Brentford, Middlesex TW8 8ER
10. Wellcome Foundation Ltd., 183 Euston Road, London NW1 2BD
11. Education Section, Unilever Ltd., P.O. Box 68, Unilever House, London EC4P 4BQ

INDEX

Page numbers given in **bold type** (for example, **46-9**) refer to particularly important properties of a series of compounds or of an individual compound. Preparations of compounds are shown with an asterisk *, indicating that small-scale ground-glass apparatus is used and with † if the substance is prepared using simple 'test-tube equipment.'